David Brazier is spiritual teacher to the Order of Amida Buddha, a religious community dedicated to socially engaged Buddhism with an international membership and projects in Africa, Asia and East Europe. He is also a registered psychotherapist and holds a doctorate in Buddhist psychology. He is author of five books. Further information about his work can be found at www.amidatrust.com or by contacting the Amida Trust at Sukhavati, 21 Finsbury Park, London N7 6RT.

By the same author

A GUIDE TO PSYCHODRAMA
BEYOND CARL ROGERS
THE FEELING BUDDHA
THE NEW BUDDHISM

ZEN THERAPY

David Brazier

ROBINSON
London

Constable Publishers
3 The Lanchesters
162 Fulham Palace Road
London w6 9ER
www.constablerobinson.com

First published by in the UK by Constable,
an imprint of Constable & Robinson 1995

This paperback issue published by Robinson,
an imprint of Constable & Robinson 2001

A copy of the British Library Cataloguing in Publication Data is
available from the British Library

ISBN 1-84119-352-6

Printed and bound in the EU

Contents

Part 3 · Therapy as a Zen Way

Acknowledgements

I would like to acknowledge the debt of gratitude I owe to my family and especially my mother whose unfailing support and unconditional love have taught me most.

I wish to acknowledge the spiritual teachers who have given me so much: Nai Boonman, Chogyam Trungpa Rimpoche, Roshi Jiyu Kennett, Katsuki Sekida, Achaan Viradhammo, Geshe Kelsang Gyatso, Dhyana Master Thich Nhat Hanh and many others, and all those who have contributed to teaching me the psychotherapeutic art, including Anne Trembath, Elaine Sachnoff, Marcia Karp, Jenny Biancardi, John McLeod, Valerie Davies and others too numerous to mention.

I also wish to acknowledge a number of scholars and practitioners who have contributed stimulating discussions and vitally important material which have added substantially to the argument and final form of this work: Mieko Osawa from Japan, Chang Yong Chung from Korea, and Caroline Beech, Campbell Purton and Mike Berners-Lee from the UK.

Technical Terms

In this book, Buddhist technical terms are introduced as appropriate as we go along. In their first occurrence such words are italicized and their basic meaning indicated. Many such words have no precise equivalent in English and a process is well under way by which many of them are becoming accepted as part of the English language, at least amongst people with Buddhist interests. Some, like buddha, karma and nirvana, are long established. The terms used in this book derive from Sanskrit, Pali and Japanese. Often a choice of terms or spellings is available for a single meaning. In each such case I have selected for use in this book the one which appears most likely to myself to be on the way to becoming the standard Anglicized form. This leads to some inconsistency in terms of scholarship but seems the best policy as a contribution to the integration of Buddhist thought into the culture of the English-speaking world. Consistent with this policy, no diacritical marks are added and, except in explanatory passages, the terms are not italicized. There is a glossary at the back of the book, for the reader's convenience.

Part 1

Foundations

· 1 ·

First Steps

ONE COLD SPRING DAY

My first encounter with the therapeutic power of Zen occurred in my first interview with my first Zen teacher on the first Zen retreat I ever attended. This was some twenty-five years or so ago. It became a turning point in my life. For some years Buddhism had interested me, but this was the real test. Now I was exposing myself to the experience and a large part of me was prepared to be disappointed.

We had been in silent meditation for most of the day. Outside the weather was sharply cold. The snow which had fallen the day before had frozen, overnight, and crunched under our feet when we went outside for short breaks between periods of sitting.

When my turn came, I went upstairs to the little room above the meditation hall, knocked, was invited in, entered, and sat down. A few moments of silence passed. I imagine that she was giving me the opportunity to begin. I stayed silent. She must have sensed my embarrassment. I was shy.

She looked at me in a very direct way. It was impossible to divine her mood, but I sensed a kindness in her eyes. After what seemed like an age, but could only have been a minute or so, she helped me out:

'Is there anything to report?' she asked.

In the context, this was a very open question. I could have used it almost any way. It could have been a basis for talking about technicalities of meditation practice. I could have used it as a springboard for a report upon my life. However, I was now even more paralysed than before.

There was something about her whole way of being which prevented me from saying anything trivial, and in that moment everything seemed to fall into that category. All the things which had seemed so important about my life before I entered the room now no longer seemed consequential at all. This seemingly simple question, 'Is there anything to report?' somehow demanded more than a commonplace response. It seemed to demand: 'Can you say something which is ultimately true? Can you say it now?' Although a thousand things flashed through my mind, nothing in my life seemed to pass the test.

Then, it was as though the universe rescued me. My life dropping away, all that remained was the two of us sitting face to face, in a room on a cold day with the window open on to the frozen garden.

'The birds are singing,' I said.

She smiled.

It was an exchange of nine words in all, yet it contributed substantially to changing the direction of my life.

SAY A WORD OF TRUTH

The challenge which Zen poses us is to reach deeply into the experience of being alive to find something authentic, some real light. Even if, as in my own encounter recorded above, it is only the light of a small glow-worm, the effect can be profound. Light is light after all.

Zen is simply to be completely alive. Of course, Zen is also a form of Buddhism, but this is really just another way of saying the same thing. Buddhism is the way of spiritual liberation which finds its origins in the experience of enlightenment. It traces its history back to Shakyamuni Buddha, who lived in India twenty-five centuries ago and realized the truth of his life after a long and arduous quest. Zen is thus rooted in experience, rather than ideas. It applies the same spirit and method as Shakyamuni, but does so in the context of contemporary life.

It is, in the famous words of Bodhidharma:

A special transmission outside the teachings,
Not relying upon the written word,
Directly pointing to the heart,
Seeing its nature and becoming Buddha.

Zen is simply the awakening of one heart by another, of sincerity by sincerity. Although words can express it, and can point to it, they cannot substitute for it. It is the authentic experience which occurs when concern with all that is inessential drops away.

Shakyamuni Buddha was born an ordinary human being, like you and I. He was not a god. He found within himself a burning question. He wanted an answer. He was willing to give up everything in order to get it. His question was: What is the way to liberation from suffering?

To grow pearls there has to be some grit in the oyster. Each of us also has our gritty question. All too often, however, we devote our lives to ignoring rather than working on it. According to Zen, it is this ignoring (*avidya*) which keeps us in the realm of suffering (*samsara*), but it is the grit (*dukkha*) which gives us the opportunity to liberate ourselves.

The grit, dukkha, can be translated as 'suffering', or 'bitterness' or 'bad states of mind'. Everywhere he looked, Shakyamuni saw people in bad states. We are born weeping and we die protesting. In between we hate getting older, getting sick, becoming tied up with circumstances we dislike, and being separated from the things we do like. We may even hate getting up in the morning. There is never a time when we are totally at ease. The body never feels completely comfortable from one minute to the next. Even more so the mind. Not only that but these bad states can have terrible consequences in the form of wars, persecutions, strife, competition, oppression and cruelty.

According to Zen, it is this very dukkha which is our best friend. Dukkha tells us that we need to do something about ourselves and shows us where, when and how to do it. By working with our own grit, we become a 'true being', a true pearl. We can be greatly helped in this process by 'good friends' (*kalyanamitra*).

Shakyamuni wanted to know why there was so much trouble

in the world, and he gave up a kingdom to find out. We also inwardly long for an answer, but, in most cases, we are unwilling to give up our kingdom. We have mastered many techniques for keeping our question bound and gagged. We coat our grit in plastic so as not to feel its sharp edges. Plastic does not work for long, however. The grit demands real pearl. The advance of life, again and again, inevitably, exposes the inadequacy of our efforts to cover up the trouble inside.

These days, at such times, we are apt to seek out a therapist to, if I may change the metaphor, help us get the dragon back into its cave. Therapists of many schools will oblige in this, and we will thus be returned to what Freud called 'ordinary unhappiness' and, temporarily, heave a sigh of relief, our repressions working smoothly once again. Zen, by contrast, offers dragon-riding lessons, for the few who are sufficiently intrepid.

I have always been aware, therefore, that Zen is a therapy, if a rather unusual one, and in this book I present it as such. It tells what Zen in particular, and Buddhism in general, has to teach us about transcending the sorrows of the human mind. Shakyamuni discovered how human ill-being works and how such understanding offers a path to liberation. The path is Zen. Zen is simply the heart of all Buddhist practice. I will draw on sources from many branches of Buddhism, and, indeed, some from outside Buddhism. No one has a monopoly on truth. Who can say a word of truth? Can you say it now?

Why not? Because we live lives conditioned by the past and future. This is examined in Buddhist psychology and I will therefore include a substantial section on that subject. I will also describe the essential characteristics of the path of the *bodhisattva*, the person who lives on the way to enlightenment, for the sake of all sentient beings. This is the Buddhist model of the ideal therapist. At the end of the book, I will look more at the application of this path to the sufferings of individuals and the world. I hope to convey the essential Zen message that everything that happens is a doorway to liberation. Spiritual enlightenment is always available, irrespective of what the past or future may hold. Zen is to be free of all that. Even in the midst of the ordinary world we can establish our lives on new ground.

A RATHER FORMAL BREAKFAST

At the Amida Centre, every Tuesday morning, we have a special time for practising mindfulness. Anybody can join in. We start with meditation. Meditation is the foundation stone of Zen. Meditation begins with the sound of a bell. Its clear note brings our minds back into the present moment. There is a verse, composed by Zen Master Thich Nhat Hanh, based on traditional sources:

> Listen, listen, that wonderful sound
> Brings me back to my true home.

We can say this verse silently to ourselves when we hear the bell, or we can simply allow it to work its magic upon us unaided.

Then we sit still, just as the Buddha himself sat under the Bodhi Tree in India many centuries ago. We just sit, allowing everything to fall away, yet remaining sharply alert. By this simple exercise we may even touch the profound peace called *samadhi*. Sometimes we use attention to the breath to settle the mind and sometimes we focus upon particular imagery designed to evoke wholesome states of mind. Sometimes we just sit.

Meditation is ended again by the bell. We try to carry the same spirit of simplicity and direct attention over from formal meditation into the events of daily life. This is aided by a degree of ceremony.

The group leader, together with whoever wishes to join in, chants some more traditional lines. These may include the 'Bodhisattva Vow':

Innumerable are sentient beings: we vow to save them all.
Inexhaustible are deluded passions: we vow to extinguish them all.
Immeasurable are the Dharma teachings: we vow to master them all.
Infinite is the Buddha's way: we vow to fulfil it completely.

Breakfast is brought in. Everything is done slowly and mindfully. Cereals, fresh and dried fruits, nuts, milk, hot beverages;

ordinary foods treated and arranged with great care. When everything is in place, we recite some more words which remind us that we are not separate from this food, nor it from the world and all other sentient beings. These are not resources and commodities. We, the food and the universe are all momentary manifestations of one flowing, living process. We sense the specialness and richness of the moment.

Food is served formally. The server approaches group members one by one, arranges bowls and cutlery for them and then begins to offer the food. The person served sits calmly and uses traditional gestures to indicate yes, no, please and thank you. The whole serving is done in silence. The server feels an onus to be gentle and attentive, doing their very best to ensure that the person served is looked after as well as can be. Zen comes to life in simple acts of kindness.

When everyone has received their food, we eat in silence for the first quarter-hour of the breakfast. We eat slowly, enjoying the tastes and noticing the process whereby food becomes body: the everyday transmutation. We live in the world and it in us.

After a quarter-hour, the bell master raises the bell again. Three sounds of the bell bring us back to mindfulness and tell us that now we can talk. Often there are people present who have never experienced a meal like this before. Commonly the talk is of the impression it has made upon them. One says how difficult they found it to be served by another person, how it brought up all kinds of programming about looking after oneself and not depending upon others. Another talks of how magical it felt to treat the whole eating process with such respect and contrasts it with TV dinners and their normal casualness. People speak of greed and self-consciousness, of love and caring.

Almost everybody in modern society suffers from 'eating issues' of one sort or another. Our neurosis is manifest in our relation to the most basic of daily necessities: food. Our relation to food highlights our mortality, our dependency, our attachments, aversions and ambivalence about life. The Zen meal-time formality brings all of these things into high relief. As we use this form, we are not going through a meaningless ritual, we are using a powerful method for self-diagnosis and providing a rich medium for self-treatment. This is called Zen training.

In our rather formal breakfast, participants have a practice ground. They can investigate their experience of being a material body, of caring and being cared for, of relating to the universe which nourishes and destroys, and, through all of this, of having space to feel more vividly and simply to be. These four dimensions, self, others, the universe and space, are the fundamental considerations of therapy.

... AND TIME TO BE CREATIVE

Breakfast eaten and immediate impressions shared, we clear away and wash up, all in the same mindful spirit. The meditation room, where breakfast was eaten, remains available as a quiet space. Along the corridor is another room with a large table and a variety of art materials. The next hour and a half is taken working, mostly singly, on painting, sculpting, collage, weaving or whatever work the individual may choose. Some will write. Some will return to meditation. Most will create something. The emphasis here is not upon the product, but on the process. This is a time for spontaneity, and for listening to the promptings of intuition. Sometimes things of great beauty result, but this, in itself, is not the aim.

About eleven o'clock, the bell is rung again and we assemble to share thoughts, feelings and impressions. One person displays a series of three pictures, all abstract. The mood of the first is active, going somewhere. The second less so. The third has a harmony and peacefulness which was lacking from the earlier two. There is a definite impression of a personal process having been worked through to some new balance. Explanations are not required. We do not have to put things into words, necessarily, to know that something important has occurred.

Another person has been weaving: not on a loom, but by hand. On the door of the quiet room, a year or so ago, Caroline set up a warp of threads and string running vertically. Ever since, different people have added to the gradually emerging unplanned design, using wool, paper and pieces of cloth, woven in and out of the string and thread. An hour or so of work advances the whole only a small amount. The weaver shares with the group their feelings about this slow careful work and many members contribute their comments about what different parts of the weaving mean to them.

In these sharing sessions, there is generally a rather wonderful atmosphere. Each person seems to be able to give something special and we are all aware that we are receiving gifts. This atmosphere of mutual care, and of a rare presence, arises quite naturally in most of these sessions. Even if we can experience this only once in a while, it is marvellously restorative and allows us to continue about our daily business for the rest of the week with a renewed confidence and calm.

This type of unstructured artwork contrasts with and balances the formality of breakfast time. In the formal meal, the time-honoured form serves to help highlight our spontaneous and habitual responses. In the artwork, we see how harmonious forms emerge out of spontaneity. Both processes reveal our mind-heart in relation to its world, but do so in opposite complementary ways. Yang and yin, masculine and feminine. Zen helps us restore balance. Spontaneity from form, form from spontaneity. This kind of work is therapeutic without being self-consciously designated as therapy.

BUDDHISM AS A THERAPY

Therapists and spiritual practitioners are all concerned with the human spirit, its dis-ease and its liberation. The Greek roots of the word psychotherapist can be quite satisfactorily translated as one who serves or attends to the soul. In the twenty-five years since my first Zen encounter, I have experienced, learned, made many mistakes, suffered and gained much. I have found ways of reaching out. I have found that the suffering of those who come to me as clients, their anguish about life, is essentially no different from my own.

They tell me about their pain and confusion, their frustrations and fears. I likewise am concerned about my own suffering which arises out of my own desires for security, recognition and comfort, for immunity from disease, pain and loss. In short, my clients and I myself long for a world which does not exist: an ego-centred universe. We are not different in this. We are each unique, but we are also all in the same boat. We all dream of unreal worlds where we will never be embarrassed nor thwarted. We suffer great frustration in consequence. As soon as we stop doing so, we are free. As Hamlet said: 'I could be bounded in a nutshell and count myself a king of infinite space, were it not that I have bad dreams' (Act 2, Scene ii).

The Buddha was moved to begin his spiritual quest by the sight of suffering. He found the root of suffering to be within the mind. He prescribed a remedy whereby the common mentality may be transcended and suffering overcome. In consequence, he was called the great physician and his teaching, the *Dharma*, the supreme medicine that relieves all mental pain (Gyatso 1990, p. 19). The notion of Buddha's teaching as a medicine for the universal human sickness is one of the commonest analogies used to describe the Dharma and it is certainly one which the Buddha himself encouraged as a useful aid to understanding his message.

Fig. 1. The Four Noble Truths: Buddha's diagnosis of human ill	
Disease	*Dukkha:* bad states of mind
Aetiology	Craving, lust, attachment, selfishness
Prognosis	A cure is possible, but not easy
Remedy	*Sila:* ethics *Samadhi:* pure mind *Prajna:* wisdom

Westerners when they first encountered Buddhism, a religion which did not speak of god, were unsure how to classify it. It became popular to consider Buddhism a 'way of life' rather than a faith. Actually, Buddhism is many things. It is a religion, with religious institutions. It is a community. It is the blueprint for a civilization (Ling 1976). It is a path of personal salvation. It is written and oral tradition of venerable antiquity. It is an order of monks and nuns, perhaps the original such in the world, and certainly the most enduring. When the Buddha himself was asked what his teaching was, he said that it was whatever led to the true cessation of suffering. Buddhism, therefore, is also, and perhaps we may say primarily, a therapy.

In 1978, the Buddhist monk Punnaji published an article in which he wrote: 'Of course, the Buddhists of ... Buddhist countries don't look upon Buddhism as a psychotherapy. It is mainly understood as a form of religion. Of course, those scholars who study the teaching of the Buddha ... tend to regard the teaching as a philosophy. Now as I see it, these two ways of thinking ... can be seen as two extremes ... Avoiding these two extremes, I would like to take the Middle Path, which is to treat the teaching of the Buddha as a form of psychotherapy ... I would say that if Buddhism is introduced into the modern world as a psychotherapy, the message of the Buddha will be correctly understood' (Punnaji 1978, p. 44).

Bhikkhu Punnaji believed that the danger in seeing Buddhism as religion was that it then tended toward dogmatism, supernaturalism and the occult. The danger of seeing it as philosophy is that this separates it from our real lives. So he preferred to see it as a therapy since 'the teaching of Buddha is freedom from mental disease' (ibid., p. 45).

I am a practising psychotherapist and a Buddhist. I have, therefore, been interested in this topic a long time. I try to apply the Buddha's timeless teachings to the particular contemporary circumstance of my work in a modern western culture. My clients suffer from a wide range of emotional troubles. I know that I am not alone in trying to work this way, so I have written this book to share what I have learned and to encourage others who are interested. The book is more than simply a manual for therapists. It also offers an interpretation of Buddhism and Buddhist psychology which will be relevant to everyone interested in the Dharma as a way to peace of mind.

Over the past few years I have made some researches into the connection between Buddhism and psychotherapy. This book is one of the results. It reflects the work we now do at the Amida Project in North-East England, Central France and elsewhere. We have been helped a lot in developing a style of work which integrates eastern and western wisdom by the example provided by many other people currently active in this field. The bodhi-sattva spirit seems to be very much alive in the west.

This book, then, presents Zen as psychotherapy. It introduces theory and method which have their roots in Zen practice and Buddhist psychology. Much of it is organized around the idea of helping people to find freedom from conditioning. Freedom, in Zen, however, is a different matter from the freedom of western concern with 'consumer choice'. The freedom referred to in Zen is the freedom which is experienced when one lives from one's deepest inner necessity, or, we could say, from the true reality of our lives. The Zen monk Hogen expressed this as follows: 'There is no space in our lives to be distracted by choice when the awakening flood of our deepest vow overflows from the abyss of Buddha within' (Hogen 1993, p. 32).

It is clear that any attempt to express Zen through the linear flow of words and logic will be inadequate, just as an attempt to describe a tree one leaf at a time will not convey a sense of the whole. This, however, does not mean that we can do nothing useful; just, the reader must bear in mind that we are here walking upon an 'open way' and whatever particular bit of the path we are moving along, should not be taken as the whole story.

Finally, before embarking further upon this book, a warning from the eighteenth-century Zen Master Torei Enji:

Written words can be a source of entanglement as well as of liberation; unless the right person takes it at the right time, the elixir turns to poison. Please be careful. (Okuda 1989, p. 28)

Clean Space

RITUAL

Zen uses ritual therapeutically. Rituals have traditional forms, but real ritual is not stereotyped. It is a living drama with great healing power. In the interview which I described at the beginning of the last chapter, there was ritual. We each went in turn. The teacher wore elaborate robes. The walk from the meditation hall to the upper room provided the experience of going to a special place. Location, timing, props and choreography all conspired to make this no casual conversation.

Therapy too is a ritual. Ritual is sacred action. Modern life tends to destroy the sacred. Zen enhances it. Zen would have us experience the sacredness of breathing, of stepping on the earth, of standing still a moment, of sitting, of lying down. In Zen, getting up and going to bed, eating, drinking, defecating and passing water are all sacred acts. This ritualization of daily life adds sharpness to experience. We come fully to life, just as we were originally meant to be. A perfect life is a life of perfect moments.

Many rituals begin with the delineation of a special space. The magic circle has a history lost in antiquity. Perhaps we create this space by making a beautiful meditation room with flowers and candles and incense and a picture or statue of Buddha or some other person as inspiration. Perhaps we do it by standing in a circle and holding hands. Perhaps by sitting in a circle, on chairs or cushions. Perhaps by going into the therapy room. However we do it, creating a conducive space is important.

The space is empty. We begin in silence. Of course, we do

not really make space. Space is already here. But by demarcation we make emptiness visible. We might think that what heals is whatever we then fill this space up with: actions, speech, interpretations, empathic reflections, a relationship, dramatic or artistic activity. Modern people put trust in the things that fill life up. None of this is useful or even possible, however, without the original space which underpins everything. All these are the adornments of emptiness. To return again and again, inevitably, to the fertile void, to silence, to aloneness – returning to it and finding it rich – will be a thread running through the whole of this book.

Space is a womb: room to grow. The most important skills in learning to be a therapist have to do with giving the client room to grow. According to Buddhism, we are all 'embryo buddhas' (*tathagata-garbha* – see the *Sri Mala Sutra*). For our original buddha nature to become apparent, we need a womb in which to mature.

Therapy, therefore, creates a safe space within which the client can naturally grow, bringing forth their own particular manifestation of original enlightenment. Safe means wholesome. Unwholesome safety is not really safe. What does this mean? Real safety is not built on enmity. Many people remember the war as a time when they felt particularly close to others, but it was not safe. It is fairly easy to create a safe space of sorts by creating an outside enemy and this temptation is always there in therapy. Clients generally talk about things which are going wrong and it is easy enough to create a temporary safety by agreeing that these are all somebody else's fault. However, if a space is made safe by reinforcing enmity toward a third party, the healing achieved will be superficial. The therapist's acceptance of the client, therefore, has to be profound and vast, encompassing their world, not just their self. In the short run the client seeks to bolster the self against the world. Zen shows us, however, that when we look more deeply, self is a reflection of the world and to reject the one is also to reject the other.

Deeper acceptance begins with the therapist creating space inside themselves: a positively receptive frame of mind. There is a well-known Zen story of an intellectual who goes to see a Zen master to test his theories. The master serves tea. As he pours the tea slowly from the urn, the cup fills to the brim. The master seems not to have noticed, continues pouring, and tea goes everywhere. 'Stop, stop,' cries the guest. 'It's full. No more will go in.' The master stops and says, 'Yes. A cup is like the mind. When it is already full, no more will go in. If we are going to learn anything, we must first empty our minds.' The visitor realized that he had come with his mind already too full to really learn anything new. It is the same in therapy. The client comes to enlighten me by showing me his view of our world (cf. Bettelheim 1992, p. 34). The therapist, therefore, empties themselves so as to have room for the client to fill them. It is our own emptiness which begins the therapeutic process.

I, therefore, find it enormously helpful to have a short period of quiet sitting before my client arrives. Even a few minutes of meditation help me become calm and grounded. I think these moments of stopping (*sati*) make me a better instrument for the work ahead. I am then in touch with the universe, with the common ground: open to the one who is coming to see me. Once I have this stillness, I find it helpful to focus attention on the, perhaps as yet unmet, client and to generate feelings of warmth and appreciation for them, whoever they may be. This small ritual of preparation sharpens the work to follow. If we can, in whatever way works for us, go through this process of achieving first an open peaceful state of mind (*shamatha*) and then a kind, loving one (*maitri*), we will have prepared the ground well.

The first few moments of encounter with the client generally prove to be disproportionately significant. They set the tone. The therapist's manner conveys important messages about openness, reliability, compassion and resilience. The client, for their part, being full of need, may well say crucially significant things in the first few moments which can easily be missed if the therapist is still getting oriented. Manuals not infrequently advise therapists to spend time putting the client at ease. If, however, the therapist is preoccupied with offering tea or commenting upon the client's journey, significant things may be missed and the process be slowed down unnecessarily. The moment is important. Begin at once.

At the beginning, there is, again, a need for space. It is tempting to take the lead, but much can be lost by doing so. If the client begins, all is well. If the client seems not to know how to begin, then I may need to say something which opens dialogue without leading. The client is probably already over-full and needs opportunity to empty themselves. Nothing is generally served by adding further to the client's existing burden. The therapist is empty and willing to be filled by the client's world.

The therapist listens very carefully with the eyes as well as the ears and tries to understand both what is said and what is left out. But I try not to let myself become filled up with understandings. Space is more important than knowledge: imagination than interpretation. As I listen, I imaginatively flow into the world of the client. From our interplay of images creative expressions of the truth emerge. Thus the ritual of therapy begins to unfold.

BRYAN'S VACUUM

Zen is more interested in emptying than filling. Getting is delusion; letting go is enlightenment. Health is a matter of having space. This difference between east and west has become apparent in the process of introducing psychotherapeutic ideas into Japan, a country strongly influenced by Zen thought. Much of the work of the leading humanist psychologist Carl Rogers, for instance, has found favour in Japan, even though Rogers' theory of self has not been readily accepted there. A friend of mine, Mieko Osawa, has brought my attention to the work of Fujio Tomoda. Tomoda was one of the leading translators and interpreters of Rogers. He considered Rogers' views on self to be the weakest point in Rogers' theory. Tomoda thought that the idea of a singular, internally consistent self was unrealistic.

The Japanese liked Rogers' method because it is non-intrusive and gives the client considerable freedom. However, a crucially significant shift was introduced by Tomoda when he analysed Rogers' early major work *Counseling and Psychotherapy* (1942). This book was a landmark in therapy literature. It was the first book to contain an extensive transcript of an actual therapy session and it thus inaugurated a new phase in therapy research focused on what therapists actually do rather than simply what theories they espouse. The case quoted is called the case of 'Herbert Bryan'. The therapist is not named, but could have been Rogers himself.

Tomoda noticed that on a number of occasions, 'Mr Bryan' refers to a need to be in a 'vacuum', a state of solitude. The therapist responds to this, on each occasion, in either a neutral or a negative way. Although the therapist was in theory being non-directive, we may surmise that a western therapist was not overly enthusiastic about the healing virtues of solitary or vacuum conditions, and this bias shows through. To Tomoda, however, these statements by Bryan were of the utmost importance and 'represent the only truth of a person' (Hayashi, Kuno, Morotomi, Osawa, Shimizu & Suetake 1994, p. 5). Tomoda was critical of the counsellor's inability to recognize the importance of Bryan's insight at this point.

In Tomoda's view, 'The true leap or growth of a person occurs when he is utterly alone. It is in human relationships or in the actual world that he makes sure of his own leap or growth. But it is not in the actual human relationship or in the actual world that true growth occurs.' Tomoda goes on to say: 'That also holds true of Zen . . . In regard to counseling, the true meaning of Rogerian techniques is that these techniques help a client be in the state of being utterly alone' (ibid., p. 6).

This reinterpretation of the Rogerian method is highly significant and controversial. Most therapists influenced by Rogers consider the effectiveness of the method to be attributable to the closeness of relationship which it makes possible, but Tomoda says that the crucial factor is something quite different: aloneness. This state of singleness, *ekagata*, will figure significantly in this book.

What does Tomoda mean by 'utterly alone'? When a person is physically alone, they are not necessarily really alone. This is because there will be in the mind 'inner strangers', images of others. A person is nervous of the regard of these others and so does not feel alone. However, when he is with a person who deeply and accurately understands him, he is able to leave that person to take care of the inner strangers so that he himself is relieved, temporarily, from the need to do so. Freed in this way he is then able to pursue his inner search without interference. This is Tomoda's theory, but it reflects traditional Buddhist views.

In this reconceptualization, we see that true aloneness may sometimes require the presence of an empathic listener or spiritual friend. The primary task of the therapist is to create space of a particular quality in order that the client be freed.

In Buddhism, a particular form of 'being alone' is highly valued. This is the kind of aloneness in which one is not troubled by visitations from either seductive or troubling memories from the past, in which one is not hanging on to 'unfinished business', in which one is not living in hope or longing, nor waiting for real life to begin. This particular form of being alone involves letting go of 'internalized objects' and accepting life as it is, as it comes. Tomoda called this 'Bryan's vacuum' and the term 'Bryan's vacuum' has become an accepted term in Japanese psychology.

Tomoda is suggesting that there is a way of being with another person which makes it easier for them to attain this kind of aloneness. In this the kinds of conditions which Rogers speaks of – empathy, unconditional appreciation and genuineness – play an important part, and we will look at why this is so. Creating space clear of the clinging visitors from the past and future must be a central effective ingredient of therapy. Such space begins within the therapist.

KEEP THE SPACE CLEAN

A clean approach is one which does not sacrifice persons to principles – not even to Buddhist ones or those of any other therapeutic ideology. Even the therapist's ideals can become dangerous contaminants of the therapeutic space. In general, people are more likely to sacrifice others in the service of ideals than for most other reasons. And most therapists are idealists.

A therapist may, for instance, believe in liberty, equality, justice, non-violence and so on, but the client might not believe in any of these things. The client might be a soldier who believes in loyalty, obedience and the importance of people knowing their place in life, or she might be a member of a right-wing extremist party, or he might be a murderer or she might be a child abuser. In these situations, the therapist is only going to be able to provide a safe space for the client if they can achieve a deep understanding of the client's viewpoint, their orientation toward their world and how it makes sense (i.e. becomes meaningful) for them. When the therapist has space within themselves, then they can be at one with anybody. This is the path of the *bodhisattva* who cares for all sentient beings, not just the ones they or society approve of. When we cannot accept someone, it is because our space has become contaminated.

The therapy space gives the client room to express shame, guilt, fear, anger, grief and other painful material. The client's inner space has been unsafe for them. It is contaminated. The contaminants are called *kleshas*, and there will be much more to say about them later. Kleshas are sticky. Once they are in, it can be very difficult to get free from them again.

When I create a space for therapy, I know that I am opening myself up to the kleshas of the client. It is important that I know how to embrace them without myself becoming infected. Once the client has opened up, I must ensure that no new poison gets in. Psychotherapy is a bit like surgery. There is an open wound. It is very important that no new germs are allowed into the operating theatre. The space must remain clean.

What are the poisons which can cause us so much trouble and against which we must guard if we are to keep the therapeutic space safe? They are innumerable and we will investigate them in a different way later. One simple classification may help us here, however. Basically, there may be difficulties in the therapist's attitude toward the client, toward themselves and toward life and we may say that each of these tends to have two different kinds of manifestation which are opposite to each other. We thus, speaking very generally, have six categories of poisons, grouped in three pairs.

Fig. 2. Factors which contaminate the therapy space		
Attitude to client	Attachment	Rejection
Attitude to self	Conceit	Dejection
Attitude to life	Envy	Fear

The first pair, attachment and rejection, are likely to show up in therapy as judgemental attitudes. We may find ourselves approving of one client and disapproving of another. We like to have this client and we do not like having that one. We would like just to have clients of a certain type – those who work hard at their therapy, say – and we hate having to deal with some other clients who, perhaps, seem stuck, make us feel inadequate, have a different attitude to life from ourselves or evoke emotions in us which we find hard to handle.

The second pair, things which poison our attitude to ourselves, are aspects of self-consciousness. When we are self-conscious, we are more concerned with whether we look like a good therapist than with the actual process or the needs of the client. We might be carried away by our own ability and by how clever we are, or we might be feeling hopeless and inadequate and thinking that we are incapable of helping anybody, but either way we have become more concerned with our image than with the client. We are inwardly looking for audience approval, either from the client, or our supervisor or our own inner critic rather than getting on with the work in hand.

The third pair is envy and fear. Either we think that everything would be all right if only such and such were to happen, or we are preoccupied with the thought of how terrible it would be if such and such happened. This pair are to do with defences, with what Freud called 'warding life off'. They are likely to show up in therapy as a concern with our own issues rather than those of the client. What the client tells us may well trigger our own aspirations or fears. It is then quite easy for the mind to slip away from the client and become occupied with our own difficulty and what we are or are not going to do about it. Our mind is on other things. There is a more complex version, however, in which we are engaged with the client superficially, but are really working out our own problems vicariously through them. In this latter case we will steer the client on to topics which are related to our issues and interests, rather than going where the client wants to go, and we will try to get the client to adopt our own preferred solutions so that we can find out from the client whether they work or not.

The clean mind arises when we put these six pre-programmed bits of our self on hold by giving our attention fully to the client's world. It is obviously progressively more difficult to do this the more pressing our own issues become. Thus the amount of effort which it takes to keep the space safe is closely related to the character of the therapist. To some extent technique can compensate for personal preoccupations, but this is limited. If the therapist is not beset with pressures from their own hang-ups, it is obviously much easier and in the extreme case, we could say that a person who was completely inwardly liberated would be a natural therapist without special effort.

Insofar as the therapist is content and at peace, they will find it easier to avoid becoming judgemental. Insofar as they overcome self-centred concern, they will find it easier to stay with the client. Insofar as they live in the present and are free from serious preoccupation with their own past and future, they will find it easier to flow with the client. Insofar as we are free from these contaminating influences, there will be space which is safe for us and safe for the client. The therapist needs to create the same kind of inner space which the client is trying to find. Therapist and client are on the same path.

ENLIGHTENMENT, ABSOLUTE AND RELATIVE

The Buddha proclaimed the possibility of complete enlighten-ment: perfect space. Zen can, therefore, sometimes seem an all or nothing affair: to be not about the relief of mundane forms of dis-ease, but only about an ultimate salvation beyond all suffering, beyond all grief. Some people see this as an essential difference between Buddhism and psychotherapy. Buddhism is concerned with liberation, psychotherapy is concerned with psychological adjustment (Kornfield et al 1983) and, it is said, these are not the same.

Immediately after his enlightenment, the Buddha thought there would probably be nobody who was in a position to really appreciate what he had discovered. However, after an initial period of solitary retreat, he had a vision of Brahma and was persuaded to try to share what he had understood. So he went forth to those whom he thought had the best chance of realization.

At first, therefore, the Buddhist message was not offered to those in deepest darkness. It was offered to those who were already spiritually advanced. Later, however, the Buddha encountered all manner of folk and, during the forty-five or so years he spent teaching, he found ways of helping a great range of people from all walks of life.

Was the Buddha doing two different things? I am inclined to think not. We all suffer from the same complaint: the conditioned mind. In Zen, there is no difference in principle between a big enlightenment and a little one. Whether our attachment to our troubles is great or small, we must still try to get beyond it. Who can say who will enter the great gate first? Buddha would do whatever he could to help a person move in the direction of truth.

Does psychotherapy move people in the same direction? Here I think the answer is mixed. Buddhism and the various western psychotherapies are all dedicated to overcoming human suffering, but they do not always agree about the causes nor about the remedies. Those who have sought to distinguish Buddhism from therapy are essentially saying that Buddhism has a different diagnosis: that it is a different therapy, rather than that it is not a therapy.

If Buddha was right, then some western therapies are misguided. They will not, for instance, achieve their aim if they seek to strengthen the individual's sense of entitlement and to reinforce the ego's anger against a world that does not provide instant gratification. It is an interesting paradox of much western therapy that the therapist is expected to put self aside and give complete attention, unconditionally, to the client (Rogers 1951, p. 35), but the client is expected to be more self-indulgent. From a Buddhist perspective, psychotherapy of that kind could be something from which the therapist would make more progress than the client. Depending upon how the therapy proceeds, clients may pick up the therapist's attitude and become less narcissistic, or they may not (Brazier 1993).

There is a danger nowadays that therapy is regarded as a job like any other. One learns some skills and then sells one's services. If, however, a person does not have the necessary space inside themselves, 'competencies' will not help them very much. In such a situation, therapy becomes a dead ritual which can be destructive. Therapy can do harm as well as good. Not all therapies are the same and, even more important, not all therapists are equivalent. To become a therapist requires that a person has gone through some of the tests of life and learned to let go of some of their pride in the process. Therapy begins with cleaning up the space inside ourselves.

· 3 ·

Buddha Nature

WHAT IS OUR DEEPEST WISH?

An early Zen test (*koan*) challenges us with the question, 'When the stone box breaks open, what is the perfect mirror like?' The image of our lives as a stone box, a coffin, within which we may find the mirror mind of perfect realization is a powerful one. We may have a sense that there is something fundamentally sound at the core of human nature, but can we express it in our actual lives here and now?

Zen as therapy, then, requires a strenuous attempt on our part to become open-minded and open hearted – to get out of the dead box of preconditioned feelings. As therapists we need a confidence that the perfect mirror is there, even when we or our client seem closed. We call this trusting the 'buddha-nature' (*buddhata*). Trusting the buddha nature is similar to the humanistic idea that there is a reliable constructive growth process called the 'actualizing tendency'. This idea has been a powerful force in western psychology, too. The idea of self-actualization freed practitioners from the narrow mechanistic ideas of 'scientific' psychology and made room for human potential.

The humanist idea, however, has its blind spots as well as its strengths. There is very little written in the person-centred literature about death, disease, loss, guilt, tragedy and the other basic existential dilemmas we are prey to. The optimistic spirit prevails over all. People, however, are not omnipotent. The confrontation with powers greater than oneself, and with the simple fact of otherness, is the making or breaking of a person. If the universe is in some sense a whole, then we are part of something greater than self.

Buddhata, therefore, is not really something *possessed* by an individual. It is, rather, one way of expressing the idea that we are all part of one another. Our buddha nature is our participation in the cosmos and is the cosmos participating in us. It is the spiritual dimension of existence: the 'other power'. It highlights the necessity of living in harmony with nature rather than putting ourselves at the centre of things. Buddhata is a self-transcending tendency rather than a self-actualizing one: a longing to return to a state which inherently exists prior to intoxication with our own importance, before our separation from the cosmos. According to Buddhism, neurosis derives from self-seeking. Its cure is a quest for original simplicity. One of the central themes of this book is that Zen is the attempt to decondition ourselves.

As we grow, we experience. As we experience, we learn. As we learn, we run the risk of encapsulating ourselves in a shell of set views, the dead bones of experience past. Within our armour of views we start to put our trust in security. We are then affronted by the vicissitudes of life which disturb our illusions. Zen, as therapy, aims to help us hatch out of our shell and experience the world once again fresh and new.

BUDDHATA

If we are all part of one another, then the actualization of our true nature will be something which intrinsically creates harmony. If we are all separate individuals, then the actualization of each self is liable to bring us into conflict with one another. Buddhist psychology affirms the former position and asserts that there is an ethical process at the heart of being human.

Buddhata, the buddha nature, is 'a reality beyond self' (Suzuki 1950). The common ground between the humanistic and Zen concepts is that both approaches believe there is something essentially trustworthy at the core of the person. Where they differ is, firstly, in that Zen emphasizes the transpersonal nature of this 'something' and, secondly, that Zen strongly warns against considering even this 'something' a definite entity.

I will try here to explain what I mean by saying that buddha nature is not a definite entity. We need words and so we provisionally call the core element of a person 'their buddha nature,' but buddha nature is not to be thought of as a thing (like a soul) and certainly not really as anything that could be considered to be 'theirs' or 'our own'. Buddha nature is simply the fact that a person is, in every particular, dimension and element, part and parcel of the cosmos. The Zen vision, therefore, is one of primordial unity, not one of separate existence.

Buddha nature, then, is not individuality, but rather is the fact that no ultimate individuality can ever be real. We can act as if there is something called buddhata operating as the reliable basis for personal life, and in so doing we will find much common ground between western and eastern psychology. Nonetheless, this seeming agreement can be deceptive. The idea of an actualizing tendency and the emergence of humanistic and then of transpersonal forms of psychotherapy in the west has certainly been influenced by the Zen notion of buddhata (Fox 1990, pp. 289 *et seq.*). However, western psychology generally leans toward the idea of a self, soul or psyche which exists as an entity in its own right and which can make demands and claims. This is all in accord with long-standing western tradition where, especially in America, a culture has been created around the idea of individual rights and needs. Buddhist psychology, however, recognizes no such entity. The buddha nature is not a soul which makes any demands upon other souls. The buddha nature is simply the fact that the universe lives in us and we in it. This identity of self and cosmos is the ultimate foundation of Zen ethics.

Buddhist psychology thus challenges the individualistic foundation of conventional psychology and this challenge is very similar to the one which the Buddha himself engaged in in India 2500 years ago. In some ways, the Buddha lived in times not unlike our own. Individualism, ultimately underpinned by the Brahman idea of an *atma* or soul, was becoming a principle of social organization (Ling 1976). The Buddha offered an alternative path which did not have the consequences which we see all around us of humankind's alienation from the environment and, even more pernicious perhaps, our alienation from one another. The Buddha recommended that we take refuge not in our little selves, but in our buddha nature, in the truth (*dharma*), and in community (*sangha*). In the Buddha's way of thinking, these are not really three different things, simply three aspects of a single principle. Our buddha nature is truth and community as they manifest in us.

A quite different feeling for the place of ethics emerges from these two different visions of what a person is. From the western perspective, ethics and morality are generally conceived as limiting factors curbing the excesses of the individual. They are boundaries which prevent a person from straying, just as the fence around a field prevents a bull from wandering and causing damage. This model of ethics as a boundary portrays morals as a source of frustration, necessary but irksome. We hate to live by 'oughts' and 'shoulds'. The growth in popularity of humanistic psychology probably owes something to the desire to rebel against restrictive morality, but it cannot really be said that humanism has solved the problem. Similarly, in psychoanalytic approaches the ideas of repression and defence play a central part: the person has to come to terms with 'the reality principle' and civilization must, therefore, by definition, be full of discontents.

Zen offers a very different picture. Since buddha nature is our inseparable unity with the whole of existence, ethics are not seen as a restriction, but as a liberation. They are the way to realize our core nature and consequently are the path of truth and happiness. Moral codes are simply an approximate description of the life of a fully realized being. A Buddhist will say, 'How can we possibly be happy if we are at war with ourselves, and how can we possibly find peace within ourselves unless we live a pure life, in harmony with others?' This line of reasoning leads us to the conclusion that, in the quest for peace of mind, the way to start is by re-examining our relations with the world around us. Whenever the Buddha was asked to describe the path he taught, he started by talking about ethics (*sila*). Sila means to cultivate our fundamental ethical nature. This is the first step to training the mind as well as the foundation for future happiness.

Fig. 3.

Self psychology (humanistic)	Ethics define a boundary for human action	A conflict model
Non-self psychology (Buddhist)	Ethics point out the core of human nature	A harmony model

We can see, therefore, that although there can be important similarities between western and Buddhist psychology, we have to be careful that we are not being deceived by similarities of language which do not represent similarities of substance, and that we are not simply projecting our favoured ideas on to the eastern material. An integration of east and west will be best served by clarity about what the real differences are.

To try to understand this notion of buddhata is an important first step. The syllable 'buddh' indicates a process of clear perception. A buddha is one who perceives the world just as it is. Consequently, a buddha is also one who acts in a clean and clear manner, doing things just as they are, without fuss, we might say. This characteristic is called *tathata*, a word very difficult to translate, which is variously rendered as 'thusness' or 'just-so-ness'. It suggests one who lives in a totally straightforward way, from a mind which is completely clear of neurotic distortion.

This state of liberated mind may also be equated with complete mental health. Here we can rely upon a rather different comparison with humanistic psychology. Let us turn again to Rogers. In his person-centred approach there is considerable emphasis upon 'non-directiveness' and this speaks directly for the idea of avoiding codes of rules and directions. However, in almost all of Rogers' major books, there is a substantial description of what he called 'the fully functioning person'. So, although the approach is called non-directive, we are told where it is going. In this context we could say that the Buddhist precepts, about which we will say more in the next chapter, are a description of 'a fully functioning buddha'.

The precepts are not, in fact, rules in the normal sense. They are rather a finger which points persistently toward our buddha nature. This is just like a compass needle that always tells us which way is north. When we are going in the wrong direction, if we have such a compass, we know what we are doing.

A good deal of the allergy which many western people have toward rules is due to a history of a culture ruled by an avenging god. If we believe in such a god, we are likely to remain children. In Buddhism, however, no such god is acknowledged. Consequently, we have to take responsibility for ourselves.

The Buddhist precepts are not, in fact, a basis for judgement about other people at all. Commonly, codes of ethics are part of some kind of procedure which exists to justify complaints, and this is why they are resented. In Buddhism, to judge or complain about others would be to break the precepts oneself. The precepts are not for that purpose. They exist purely to enable each of us to find our way back to our own heart. In our hearts we all want to act in the way the precepts describe, because, in the heart of each of us, there is a fully functioning buddha.

Most of the time, however, the buddhata is obscured by conditioning. Since this is a book about Zen psychotherapy, a large section (Part Two) will be devoted to examining this process of conditioning, as described in Buddhist psychology. Everybody who is not enlightened is lost in this obscuring fog.

According to Buddhism, then, there are not many people who are really psychologically healthy. Most of those who do manage to live relatively stable lives do so more because of fortunate circumstance than real stability. Nonetheless, although we are almost all of us subject to neurotic, psychotic and hysterical distortions in our perception of our world, we all do also have an original pristine, clear nature: an unsullied basis for real perception and contact. The buddhata is like the sun behind the clouds.

In the traditional texts, the Buddha, as the exemplar of buddha nature, is described as follows. The Buddha is called *tathagata*, one who goes (*gata*) through life in a completely non-neurotic (*tathata*) way: whose life is clean. He is called *samyak sambuddha*, one who is completely enlightened. He is called *vidya-carana samapana*. This means that he has perfected perception and practice. His way of life is rooted in deep understanding. The kind of understanding referred to here is not an accumulated bank of wisdom, but an ability to directly see just how things are in each moment of life. He is called *lokavid*: one who sees this and other worlds. He is called an *arhat*, one who has defeated the enemy: the enemy is everything which obscures wise and compassionate contact with the world. Then he is called *sugata*, which means blissful. In Buddhism goodness and happiness coincide. This is the ideal picture of the potential we all share.

If we consider again, briefly, the difference between Buddhist and western conceptions of the core self, therefore, for a westerner, liberation is liable to be conceived in terms of eliminating frustrations which stand in the way of getting what they believe their self needs in order to be happy. This inevitably brings a person into conflict with at least some aspects of the natural or social environment. Ethics are external to the self or they are a matter of personal choice, as though an individual could change the laws of the universe by wishing them different. From the Buddhist perspective, however, ethics are not an external limitation, nor something we can shop around for. Rather, they are the voice of our buddha nature crying out from within. Our deepest nature wants us to live in harmony with the universe because we are it and it is us. To act in an unethical way is to act against ourselves. Liberation is thus in no way served by kicking over the traces. Indeed, the liberated mind does not perceive any traces.

Of course, for ordinary people, Buddhist or otherwise, whose minds have for a very long time been conditioned into a distorted state, following preceptual guidelines may be a struggle. The Zen adept adopts this struggle, however, not in the spirit of self-restriction, but of self-discovery. This is a very important distinction central to our understanding of what therapy means. All Buddhist psychotherapy must rest upon the principle that there is that in us which longs to return to the primordial harmony and following moral guidelines may help us find it. This longing is our deepest instinct and something upon which we can rely: something which, in Buddhist terminology, we may call a true refuge. Within it, perceptions of a division between body and mind, or between self and world, evaporate.

RELYING ON TRUTH

Buddhata, then, is that in the client which we can rely upon to be always moving toward transcendence and resolution. It is also that in us which enables us to put self-passion aside in order to be deeply receptive. In this respect there are parallels with other developments in western thought, particularly the growth of phenomenology since Husserl (Solomon 1988). Husserl's own work (Husserl 1925, 1931a,b, 1983) has permeated European thought and influenced the whole development of psychotherapy from Freud onward. Husserl's 'phenomenological method' has had widespread influence upon psychotherapy (e.g. Binswanger 1975; Boss 1982; Cox & Theilgaard 1987; Frankl 1967; Gendlin 1962; Laing 1961; May 1983; Perls 1969; Rogers 1951) and this influence appears to be growing (Spinelli 1989). What Husserl was trying to do was to establish a firm basis for philosophy beyond the distorting influence of personal preconceptions. As a philosopher Husserl aimed to create a totally unbiased philosophical method by a 'reduction' or 'epoché' (ἐποχή), a 'bracketing' of all received ideas. This is very close to the Zen notion of realizing original mind, or, indeed, what is sometimes called 'no-mind' (Suzuki 1969). For Zen, however, this is not a way of thinking but a way of being (Sekida 1975).

In philosophy, Husserl's approach was further developed by the existentialists. Thus Maurice Merleau-Ponty wrote that phenomenology 'is largely an expression of surprise at [the] inherence of the self in the world and in others, a description of this paradox and permeation, and an attempt to make us see the bond between subject and world, between subject and others, rather than to explain it' (Merleau-Ponty 1964, p. 58). How Zen! The self is actually composed of its world, fundamentally without separation. Heidegger pointed out that 'man does not look out upon an external world through windows from the isolation of his ego: he is already out-of-doors. He is in the world because, existing, he is involved in it totally. Existence itself, according to Heidegger, means to stand outside oneself, to be beyond oneself' (Barrett 1961). So we see that there have been a number of parallels with Buddhist thought in the west even though these have generally not led to the development of precise systems of self training like Zen.

If the truth is within us and all around us, we will not find it by hanging on to a partial view. Husserl, like the Buddha, advocated that we try to let go of our preconceptions so as to achieve a wider perspective and openness. Zen stresses that it is we ourselves who are hanging on to our blindfold. The mind will do its job if we trust it. Closed minds are the result of a failure of trust.

Many of the formative steps in the development of modern psychotherapy took place in central Europe in the first half of the twentieth century, during the period when Husserl's influence was at its height. In Vienna, Freud was at the centre of a highly creative circle who were willing to look deeply into the questions of conscious and unconscious life. Freud's concept of the unconscious parallels the earlier Buddhist notion of an *alaya* or store-house consciousness where the influence of past karma remains active. Freud's colleague Jung also allied himself with the phenomenological approach (Brooke 1991), and interested himself in eastern thought (Jung 1978; Spiegelman & Miyuki 1987; Moacanin 1986). Jung's work has helped pave the way for a better understanding of Zen.

Phenomenology and humanism came together for western psychology in the work of Carl Rogers whom we will refer to frequently. Many of Rogers' concepts help bridge the east–west divide. Interestingly too, there is an iconoclastic flavour in Rogers very like that of Zen, which has always been wary of the effects of any settling into orthodoxy.

In Zen, it is common for what could be called shock tactics to be used to jolt the mind out of its ruts. This need for spontaneity was also very clearly in the mind of another contemporary of Freud in Vienna, Jacob Moreno. What Freud was to individual analysis, Moreno was to group psychotherapy (Marineau 1989). Moreno saw a failure of mental health as an inadequacy of spontaneity. Over against spontaneity, there was what Moreno called 'the cultural conserve'. When something is done for the first time, it is spontaneous. When it is repeated, it has become part of the cultural conserve. The cultural conserve should provide the spring-board for spontaneity but, too often, it becomes a strait-jacket within which spontaneity is stifled. For Moreno, spontaneity is the spark of the divine within us, the eruption of the transcendental into our lives. This again clearly parallels Zen and we may say that a fair bit of Zen training has to do with using ritual (the conserve) as a spring-board for spontaneity. Moreno's emphasis upon spontaneity and action echoes important Zen themes (Watts 1957). He provides us with a repertoire of actual practice methods which can be endlessly adapted to illuminate our lives.

THE TRANSPERSONAL TREND

Finally, in this very brief review of east–west parallels, we must mention the recent development of transpersonal psychology. Here the influence of the east is direct and acknowledged. The transpersonal approach is, in some ways, a reaction to humanism. Humanism, linked to the idea of 'self-actualization', proved to be both individually liberating and culturally fragmenting. It was, in a word, narcissistic. 'We pay a high price for our illusion of autonomy – in the form of loneliness, unsatisfying relations with mates and families, longing for a sense of community, a pervading sense of isolation in an indifferent universe, and other modern angsts. To the extent that humanistic psychology theory gives scientific-sounding or religious-sounding credibility and support for this illusion, it may itself become a source of alienation and suffering' (O'Hara 1989, p. 272).

Transpersonal psychology has attempted to examine phenomena which are an intrinsic part of the quest for wholeness in a situation in which 'Boundaries are illusions' (Wilber 1985, p. 31). It is, then, an attempt to once again find a place for ourselves as part of the universe rather than as its exploiters and dominators (Fox 1990), and to bring back into consideration experiences and ideas which are generally regarded as 'spiritual' rather than scientific.

Aiding the emergence of transpersonal psychology within psychotherapy and society generally, is the growing concern about ecological issues. Unless people can come to feel themselves to be part of a world-life, Gaia, they will never be able to really see why they should stop exploiting the world around them. The emergence of the Green Movement thus has implications for psychology. Joanna Macy writes:

> The conventional notion of the self with which we have been raised and to which we have been conditioned by mainstream culture is being undermined. What Alan Watts called 'the skin-encapsulated ego' and Gregory Bateson referred to as 'the epistemological error of Occidental civilization' is being unhinged, peeled off. It is being replaced by wider constructs of identity and self-interest – by what you might call the ecological self or eco-self, co-extensive with other beings and the life of our planet. It is what I will call 'the greening of the self'. (Macy 1991, p. 183.)

In Zen, one might say, the self has always been green. Zen culture is close to nature. Go for a walk. Sit by a waterfall. Hug a tree. Feel the rain on your skin. Direct perception of nature brings us back to our original sanity. The Buddha himself was enlightened sitting under a tree. He strongly and repeatedly recommended that people spend extended periods of time away from towns and cities, in quiet beautiful places where artificiality could drop away.

Ecological and transpersonal visions provide a bridge between western and Zen psychologies and it is a good bridge to stand on. Although such bridges exist, it cannot be said that the integration of Buddhist and western thought, to which this book hopes to contribute, has yet reached the point where each tradition can draw on the other without a sense of crossing from one world into another. However, there is no doubt that the introduction of Buddhist ideas by many popularizing writers, from D. T. Suzuki (1949) and Alan Watts (1957) onward, has had an important impact on western philosophy and psychology and a genuine integration is now closer than ever before.

· 4 ·

Core Ethics

In Zen, ethics are not simply a matter of setting boundaries to
life, or to the therapy process. They are, rather, the central nub
of the therapeutic problem. To be psychologically healthy is to
return to and live from our core ethics. Actual ethical formulations, such as lists of precepts, are signposts pointing in the
direction of our happiness.

Consistent with the belief in buddhata, the Zen view of ethics
is quite different from that common in the west. Generally, the
western view is to see the person as naturally selfish and, therefore, potentially dangerous and destructive. Ethics are created
to put a boundary wall around this danger. The basic concept
is that the natural person is sinful and that ethics exist to protect
society. This leads to a legalistic approach in which ethics are
formulations of words which, if infringed, lead to punishment.
Much effort therefore goes into textual interpretation to see how
much it is possible to get away with. Ethics are thought of as
being like a fishing net with which to catch bad people and do
away with them.

The Zen view, and here we also see, I think, echoes of Taoism,
is that the natural person is ethical and that people often act in
unethical ways because nature (the buddhata) has been distorted
or clouded by conditioning. Conditioning arises from ignorance,
and ignorance is fostered by corrupt society. Thus what is
needed is to return to 'the face we had before we were conceived'. Ethics, far from being society's protection against the
natural person, are considered the signposts showing the person

the way back to their original pure blissful nature which exists prior to corruption. In this conception, ethics are not restrictive walls: they are the ladder by which an escape may be achieved – the signpost pointing back to our true nature. This leads to an intuitive approach. It is not so much the wording on the signpost that matters as the direction it points. Erudition and legalism just detain us at the crossroads when what is needed is to set out on the road that leads back home. The fishing net is woven of our own views and opinions. If we can let go of them, then we can swim in the ocean of buddha nature unhindered.

In passing, it is worth also distinguishing the Zen approach from another western theory. The Zen view does not coincide with the idea of 'the noble savage' derived from Rousseau, because, in practice, 'savages' are just as likely to live in societies and be corrupted by them as anyone else. The 'nature' referred to by Zen is not a feral condition, but rather the prior condition of mind itself when free from adventitious pollution.

The Buddhist Precepts to respect life, do no physical harm, take nothing which should belong to others, regulate one's sexual behaviour, speak kind words, never depart from honesty, avoid becoming intoxicated, adopt a simple lifestyle and so on, are thus a recipe for happiness and harmony: an antidote to the seductions of society.

This, of course, raises a number of interesting questions about the task of psychotherapy. If one becomes happy by living a morally wholesome life, then is it the role of the therapist to impart moral principles to the client, and if so, how? What becomes of client self-determination, if the therapist knows how the client should live their life? These are the kinds of questions likely to come to the mind of a western critic. In this respect, however, there is perhaps more of a coincidence of view between Buddhism and at least some western practitioners than at first appears.

Carl Rogers, for instance, clearly held that if the therapists themselves maintained a selfless attitude, the client would discover within themselves what was needed to bring them to a more 'fully functioning' state, and such a state would be one which was socially constructive (i.e. ethical). It seems, therefore, that people are not usually made more moral by persuasion so much as by inspiration. Rogers got into some difficulties squaring this part of his theory with the usual western concepts (Brazier 1993), but he clearly did believe that it was the therapist's function to live out a particular way of being, characterized by certain admirable personality qualities, and that when such a therapist was in psychological contact with a client who was unenlightened (i.e. 'incongruent'), then we could reliably expect the latter to discover a more constructive path.

Therapist and client alike seek inner peace and outer harmony. Together they seek the wisdom to achieve this in reality. Many of the 'problems' which clients present to therapists boil down to ethical dilemmas: 'Should I stay with my spouse even though he/she treats me badly?', 'My relative has become an alcoholic: should I care for them or look after my own interests first?', 'My parents were cruel: should I hate them or forgive them?' and so on. These are not the sort of problems which can be dismissed with a simplistic moralizing answer. They are *koans*.

Koan is a Japanese word for the tests life presents us with: problems not amenable to simple logical solution. Koan practice is meditation in which one holds such a dilemma in mind with great intensity, trying to break through to new clarity. 'New clarity' does not necessarily mean a solution. It means a new view of life which arises when the blocked energies within us find a way of release. Thus a client, after long agonizing over his marriage and whether he should leave or stay, had an extended break in therapy while the therapist was abroad. When therapist and client met after the break, it was clear that the client was less troubled than before. The therapist enquired how the client was faring and the client said: 'Well, when you went away I felt quite abandoned for a bit, but then I thought perhaps it was quite a good thing to have some time to get on with it on my own, and then, one day, it suddenly just came to me that happiness is a state of mind. Just that: happiness is a state of mind. It has got nothing to do with all this other stuff, has it?'

This illustrates a common process. A client brings an insoluble problem. They spend time with the therapist enquiring into it, half hoping the therapist can take the problem away. In Zen, however, we say that it is not compassionate to take such problems away since the koan is actually the means by which a person can get to a new stage. In fact the therapist probably sharpens rather than softens the edge of the dilemma. The client says, 'People say I am irresponsible,' and the therapist responds, '*They* say you are irresponsible: so, what is the truth? Are you irresponsible?' The client is understood and is also invited to be more honest, more direct in confrontation with himself.

So, in our illustration, therapist and client spend some time sharpening the edge of the problem, then the therapist goes away. The client is now left on the razor edge alone. Once this sinks in, a real shift becomes possible. Now the client may grasp the nettle. When the therapist is available again, the client comes to have his insight confirmed, but he comes with confidence and shares his insight as an equal. Therapist and client, at that moment, have disappeared. Simply there is one human being and another human being sharing what, deep down in their hearts, all human beings already know. Such sharing is marvellously affirming and constitutes a 'true word'. Truth, however, belongs to nobody in particular. It already belongs to everyone.

It is probably apparent by now that Zen is not always a particularly comfortable therapy. It attempts to break through shallowness. Daisetz Suzuki, in recounting some of the history of the koan method, tells us that the great Zen masters of the past 'Rinzai (–867), Reijun (845–919), Keichin (867–928) and others were strict observers of the Vinaya Precepts, but were never satisfied with being merely moral, blindly following rules of conduct which were set up by others, however exalted beings they had been. They desired to dig down deeply into the fundamentals of the so-called moral life; and this made them come to Zen' (Suzuki 1972, p. 152). Therapy is really about helping a client to dig down deep into the fundamentals of their own core ethical nature.

Almost all student therapists come into contact with a book by Rogers called *On Becoming a Person*. One might say: If I am not a person, what am I? Yet the title of Rogers' book holds our attention. Can we become fully a person? This question is a koan. It is no different really from the questions: Can we listen unconditionally? Or, can I become a buddha? There is a fully functioning buddha inside each of us, but how can we produce her?

Rogers' book title *On Becoming a Person* is a modern koan. How to be a person? Unless the question has freshness for us it does not demand anything and we do not take it seriously, so we must restore it to freshness in our experience. Rogers wanted us to take this question as a means, to help us become the most we can possibly be. The answer cannot be in words, but in the way we are. If we are a person, in the sense asked, then it will show. So solving a koan means changing our way of being and this generally means giving up some ideas rather than producing new ones.

Facing our koan opens up new spaces in our lives. Breaking through one koan is not the end of the story. Some shifts are small, such as giving up resistance to a fact that one had avoided for a long time. Some are of great consequence. All allow us to feel newly grounded. This ground is, in a way, impersonal. When we live from the very ground of our being, we do not live from self. We simply play our part in the universe, happily doing what reality gives us to do.

The way of Zen is thus supremely practical. Although we all tie ourselves up in knots with our ideas and feelings, the way through generally begins with acting purposefully now. Know your purpose at this moment and there is no difficulty knowing what to do. Paradoxically, perhaps, being able to act this way means letting go of trying to control tomorrow or yesterday. Simply do the right thing now.

WONDERFUL PRECEPTS

The precepts of Buddhism, then, provide a description of an enlightened person. They are not, however, merely descriptions of the goal, they are also an essential part of the means.

Precepts can be used at different levels. At the outer level, they guide action. At the inner level, they reveal the pure mind. The person who really understands them finds that they become their blood and bones. Working with the precepts at all three levels gives our training in Zen a cutting edge.

Generally, in a modern cultural context, it is not appropriate to instruct clients in the precepts, though to do so in some cases is valuable. Nonetheless, we can rely upon the client's buddhata. The precepts simply describe an ethical sense which everybody already has. It is not the therapist's part to help the client evade this reality. On the other hand, to impose a model of it would be counter-productive.

A very common state of affairs is that a client has got into ethical confusion as a result of being 'inoculated' against the truth already. The preceptual path, in its reality, is simply the life force. However, most people have been inoculated against catching real life. They protect themselves against it as though it were a dreadful disease. Inoculation can happen when one is quite young. What happens when we receive an inoculation is that we are injected with a half-dead version of some germ and this prevents us later catching the real thing, even when exposed to it. When our bodies sense the invasion by the half-dead version, they organize the production of antibodies on a large scale to keep the vaccine at bay.

Most people's initial exposure to morality is like this. It is injected into them in a restrictive form favoured by society and they become immune. When such a person later comes into therapy, it is no use telling them about moral behaviour since they are already well defended against any such ideas. This defensive structure contains false morality and opinionatedness. Discussing moral ideas in this circumstance is worse than useless. What is needed is to ground our work in actual experience, which is, in any case, always the main Zen approach. We look for situations in which the client's own inherent moral sense will appear. There are, therefore, important issues about timing. A person is not necessarily ready.

For a therapist, however, a grounding in at least the basic precepts is essential. They enable us to do a thorough spring clean of our personal, not just our professional, lives, and so rediscover their original beauty. There are five basic precepts common to all branches of Buddhism. The wording varies from school to school, but that, as we have seen, is not the point.

The first precept is to avoid doing physical harm to sentient beings. A little reflection soon reveals that to fulfil this precept legalistically is impossible, and so indeed it is with all of the precepts. We attempt to keep the precept fully. We live on a strictly vegetarian diet, say. Nonetheless, there were many insects killed in the harvest. We avoid working directly for military organizations. Nonetheless, we are still involved in social structures which destroy lives. The precept points the direction. If we can act in that direction in each moment of our lives, our life will be perfect. Although it may be sometimes like sweeping the floor in the middle of a dust storm, still we just calmly get on with the sweeping.

Zen posits no god, nor external judgement. We follow the precepts because it is what our heart wants us to do, fully knowing that we will frequently fail. The spirit of Zen is to live fully even though we die in the process. Zen Master Shunryu Suzuki taught that 'Even though it is impossible, we have to do it because our true nature wants us to. But actually, whether or not it is possible is not the point. If it is our inmost desire to get rid of our self-centered ideas, we have to do it. When we make this effort our inmost nature is appeased and Nirvana is there' (Suzuki 1970, pp. 45–46). Conventional psychology assumes that the ego must always be fed. In following the precepts, however, awareness of failure helps us give up self and so allows us experience of buddha nature.

The second precept is, in its full form, not to accept anything which has not been freely given, or, at the very least, to respect the property of others, and be generous. The direction here is to change our relationship with material things: eliminating the delusion of possession and realizing that whatever we happen to be responsible for at the moment is not really our property, but held in trust. Our best purpose is to use it well, for the benefit of all beings, thus opening our hearts and those of others. It is not possible to be a therapist without generosity of spirit. Nobody should be a therapist, doctor or any other sort of healer primarily in order to earn money.

The third precept is to eliminate wrong doing in connection with sexual desires. This, as many of us know from painful personal experience, is a minefield for therapists. In therapy we form close relationships. It is absolutely essential that a therapist has their sexual drive under control and does not allow relationships with clients to become contaminated by sensual appetite.

The fourth precept is right speech. Humans communicate all the time. Taking on an undertaking not to criticize others, even for a short time, can quickly reveal how habit-bound we are and how corrosive of happiness those habits can be. This book, for instance, is awash with assertions that such and such a course of action is preferable to some other and is, therefore, by direct implication, critical. Many statements in it are also probably untrue, since the author does not claim omniscience. Some parts of it are contentious and might contribute to conflict. All these are examples of the kind of wrong speech which this precept urges us to work diligently to eliminate. So I, at least, am not a very good example. If we take this precept upon ourselves, we undertake to practise loving speech, speech which heals wounds and draws people together, speech which inspires others in good actions and good states of mind, 'words worthy to be laid up in the heart', speech which helps people to think well of others. This is of the essence of the therapeutic art. As therapists, this should be our forte. It is also one of our biggest, and most revealing, struggles.

Many clients come to us feeling aggrieved. They want their anger understood. Part of them wants us to collude in condemning those whom they see as their oppressors. We may be in a constant dilemma. We have only partial information. We have heard only one half of the story. We have in front of us a person who is hurt and perhaps full of bitterness, who needs, indeed demands, that we take sides. To keep this precept in all its fullness presses us to develop great wisdom and we learn more from our every failure. There can be few professions which offer a better training ground for work on this precept.

Finally, the fifth precept is concerned with what we consume. In particular it enjoins us to avoid all consumption which is addictive or toxic, especially alcohol and similar mind-altering substances. One might think, what business is it of anyone else what I consume in my own time? That is, however, the ego speaking. Nobody exists in such independent separation. Alcohol, tobacco, marijuana and so on consume a great deal of our money which we could use far more compassionately and they serve only to distance us from experiencing the reality of our lives. They make us lazy and stupid, destroy our health, lead us to deceive ourselves and others, make us a burden upon the medical services and help nobody. More important even than this, however, they are the antithesis of the Zen approach, which is clarity of mind.

By extension, this precept covers not just substances but all forms of consumption such as what we read, what we watch and the conversations we take part in (Hanh 1993a). As therapists we are concerned with helping people overcome their self-destructive patterns of habit. So we must first make the effort to overcome our own. Compulsive behaviours poison the body and corrupt the mind. They do not contribute to happiness.

The essence of this precept is to search our own lives, to notice our compulsions and to break their hold as soon as we become aware of them. Helping others cannot be separated from doing something about ourselves. Giving up what we think we cannot do without is always a step toward freedom. There is a Zen saying: Gain is delusion, loss is enlightenment. 'For breaking the ego's grip, nothing is more effective than giving something up' says Zen Master Uchiyama (1993, p. 167).

THE BODHISATTVA AS THERAPIST

In Buddhist terminology, a bodhisattva is a person on the way to enlightenment whose effort is turned toward helping others. This is a good general description of a therapist: a person who seeks the truth and cares about people's suffering. The bodhisattva's practice is to help others. Thus 'it is essential for a psychotherapist to make ceaseless efforts regarding his own personality growth' (Chung 1990, p. 28).

The bodhisattva is not yet fully enlightened and even the most mature psychotherapist is not beyond personal problems. 'A mature analyst and a Bodhisattva have the trace of neurotic motivation but they are aware of it and are not influenced by this in helping others,' says Rhee (1990, p. 24). In looking at myself, I think I can confidently say that the experienced therapist may still have rather more than a 'trace' of inner disturbance left, but certainly there is an onus upon us as therapists to be 'on the way', to be actively doing something about ourselves, if we are to be able to assist others to do likewise.

My Korean friend, Chang Yong Chung, whom I have just quoted, has also written: 'Our text books of psychiatry and psychotherapy are, generally, giving more emphasis to the concept and technique than to the therapist's personality . . . hence, students are apt to satisfy themselves with knowledge alone without examining themselves' (Chung 1990, p. 29) and 'regrettably, it seems to me that not only Western people but also all human beings living in modern ages usually prefer the rational and intellectual thinking to self-mortification, so they minimize their ability of enlightenment. Thus they devote themselves to irresistible course of nature and leave their responsibility undone' (Chung 1968, p. 19). The most effective way of helping others is to make spiritual progress oneself and the best way to make spiritual progress oneself is by helping others.

SUMMARY

Zen insists upon action and experience and is a direct transmission of the truth outside of words and texts. The kinds of problems which people bring to therapy are the things which have stopped them in their tracks and so are the very same dilemmas which can provide the springboard for breaking through to a more direct contact with the real ground of life. The things which bring people to therapy are essentially the same moral dilemmas which we and all people have in our own lives. Simply, the client has the courage to start doing something about them. Therapists and clients are on the same path. Zen aims to sharpen the cutting edge of such dilemmas, for ourselves and others. I hope this book will convey some of the flavour of this style of work and reveal some of the thinking behind Buddhist psychological methods, but description alone does not do the work. Each of us has to find our own way back to our true home. Learning is of no avail without practice.

· 5 ·

Tranquillity

The safe space of therapy depends upon the therapist's inner calm. As therapy progresses, the client too becomes calmer. Tranquillity erodes the mind's conditioning. Conditioning makes us compulsive. Zen frees us from compulsive habits. When we stop being run around by things, then we are making some progress in Zen. It follows that a Zen therapist will carefully study his or her own life and seek to identify and eliminate compulsiveness from it. The person whose life is governed by 'I could not possibly . . .' 'I must never . . .' 'I always have to . . .' and so on, is not free and feels inwardly oppressed.

Just like the moon, the art of tranquillity has four phases: absorption (*piti*), poise (*samadhi*), mindfulness (*sati*) and equanimity (*upeksha*). Everybody has some degree of each of these. The art is to refine what we have got. Collectively they are called dhyana or zen. Refining the zen of our life can revolutionize our existence, helping us let go of old habits, choose purposeful activity, live confidently and bring peace to others.

Zen is tranquillity in action. In this chapter we will examine the method of stilling the mind. In the next chapter we will look at how that stillness is carried over into daily life. Inner calm is the base from which to grow the qualities of love, compassion and understanding which are the key to healing personal suffering.

SITTING

Our perception is blurred by conditioning. Go into a quiet room, sit down for half an hour in silence and listen to whatever arises: the sounds of traffic, birds singing, people moving about in other

54

parts of the building or the gurgling of one's body or whatever. Try to stay alert and attentive. When there are no sounds, listen to the silence. If you make a serious attempt at this exercise in unconditional listening, you will discover a number of things about consciousness and attention. In particular, however hard you try, unless you have trained your mind, you are unlikely to complete the half-hour without quite a number of lapses of concentration. Indeed, it is unlikely that you will complete the first few minutes. Yet, a therapist's basic task is to listen unconditionally for an hour. However hard we try to be in command, the mind is apt to wander. Our preoccupations crowd in and our attentiveness fails. We follow the tracks of the ego rather than staying with what is there. Similarly, when a therapist is with a client, it is our personal preoccupations which interfere with deep listening.

The basic exercise of Zen is to sit in meditation and quieten the mind. This is called *zazen* ('za' = sitting). A Zen therapist needs to use this practice regularly and, in suitable cases, it can be taught to clients. Zazen is a direct antidote to stress and a powerful aid in breaking habits. Zazen is like allowing a glass of muddy water to clear. The water will clear by itself if we stop agitating it for a while. Inner calm requires stillness. In particular, Zen practitioners have discovered, the best way to control the mind is to control the body. When the body is perfectly still, the mind quietens down.

Formal zazen is done sitting. The Buddha became enlightened while sitting. Of the four postures, lying, sitting, standing and moving about, sitting is most suitable because we can stay still and alert without undue fatigue for an extended period. The spine is upright to maintain alertness and allow a flow of energy through the body. The traditional leg position of the full lotus, with feet upon opposite thighs, is very stable and balanced. If one cannot do it, then any other posture which is upright, stable and nearly symmetrical will suffice, on a chair or on the floor. The important thing is to be able to remain perfectly still. A cushion under the base of the spine helps tip the pelvis forward. The power of the body is then concentrated in the lower abdomen, called the *tanden*. When the residual tension in the body is all transferred to the tanden, the quietest state of mind will be achieved.

This tranquil state is called 'body and mind dropping away'. An approximation to this condition can be achieved by most serious practitioners who adopt zazen practice on a regular basis. Generally, we sit for thirty or forty minutes at a time. Shorter sitting may be better for beginners. Longer sittings may be punctuated by slow walking meditation though there is also benefit in longer unpunctuated sitting if one can manage it physically. Many great teachers have found benefit in sitting for long periods and the Buddha is said to have sat for seven days immediately after his enlightenment.

When one sits, as a beginner, even for fifteen or twenty minutes, one is liable to find that there are all manner of discomforts which distract. This is in addition to the fact that the mind seems unable to stay concentrated upon one thing. When we stay still and alert, the compulsive, conditioned mind reacts. It tries its very best to regain control, but the meditator just sits still and watches. The more our life is subject to compulsiveness, the more difficult we find it to do this exercise.

Compulsiveness may be extrovert or introvert. If it takes the form of activities and addictions, then the struggle we will have with zazen is likely to be physical: the sheer effort to stay still will combat our habit. If, on the other hand, we are the kind of person who becomes lost in reveries, it will be the control of the mind which will challenge us most. In this latter case, however, a great deal can be achieved by paying particularly detailed attention to posture. Body and mind are a unity and when the mind wanders, the body loses tone.

Concentration can be aided by counting breaths. Alternatively, one can say to oneself, 'Now I breathe in, now I breathe out,' or just 'In ... Out ...' This improves concentration and gets us used to the interplay between body and mind. Soon, one dispenses with actual counting and simply keeps the breath in mind, observing the quality of each breath, long, short, rough, smooth, fast, slow, warm, cold and so on. The aim is to avoid intellection on the one hand and mind wandering on the other. Simply be there, observing. Stay in the here and now. Central attention is on the breath. Peripheral attention notices whatever else occurs, passing car noise, bird-song, etc., while holding to the utmost stillness of body and mind.

STONES ALSO LIVE

When I was a child of five our family lived abroad. We occupied a house with a large garden. There were very few other English-speaking children so I spent a lot of time on my own. It was a hot climate, so I was often outdoors. I was a rather introverted child, but also curious, as children generally are. I wanted to understand the world around me. In particular, I spent much time reflecting, with great intensity, upon a number of questions which seemed very important to me at the time. Some of those I remember were: 'Who am I?', 'Where was I before I was born?', 'Where do I stop and other beings begin?', 'What is the life of a stone?'

I did not know at that time that these questions are called koans. I simply knew that it was very important to ask. I can remember standing in the garden for long periods looking up into the sky, wondering, Was that where one came from? What was beyond the sky? Who was God? And ... I was full of questions, but the four listed in the last paragraph were my favourites. In particular, I spent much time looking at stones. I would fix my attention single-mindedly upon a stone and beg it to give up its secret. This seemed, somehow, to be the key question, the one which would give access to all the others. If I could understand the being of a stone, understanding myself would be a small matter.

So it was that I quite spontaneously taught myself to meditate. I do not expect that I am unique in having done this, but I certainly benefited from conducive conditions which were relatively uncommon. I learned to sit or stand very still, not as technique, but simply as a direct result of the intensity of my interest in obtaining the knowledge I sought with such passion.

In our garden there was an orchard at the back. This was a good place to play active games, make dens, climb trees and have adventures with imaginary friends and enemies. The front garden, however, was a complete contrast. It was a formal garden with low privet hedges around flower beds laid out with traditional symmetry. In the centre was a circular pond. At the front a white wall separated the garden from the road. Down the side of the front garden ran a driveway. At the head of the drive, a trellis separated the front garden from the back. At the end of the trellis was a pine tree.

Generally my most intense meditations occurred on the drive, because this was where a ready supply of stones was to be found. One day, while delving deeply into my question, I stood up and looked out across the garden toward the wall. All at once, I was overwhelmed by an experience of the scene becoming completely radiant. Everything appeared vivid and twice as real as before. Not only the garden: I had a strong sense that this state of perfection, which is what I experienced it as, extended far far beyond and, in fact, took in everything in the world. I stood transfixed. In that moment I knew that I had somehow broken through something, as though the whole world had, until then, been wrapped in some kind of camouflage which had now been taken away.

This early experience had a profound effect upon my subsequent life. I never forgot it and for many years I sought ardently for the means to return to it. I carried within me a certainty of its validity. This was how I came to be interested throughout my life in spiritual paths. As a child, I became devoutly Christian, that being the only form of spirituality to which I had access. My piety surprised my parents. Around puberty things changed. All my grandparents died at this time and this had some impact upon the atmosphere in our home, which never seemed so carefree again. More devastating, however, was my discovery through reading of all the blood that had been shed in the name of Christianity down the centuries. I was deeply wounded by this, as you might feel if your lover betrays you.

Although this was undoubtedly a crisis, I could not doubt my own experience. The result was that my search for spiritual truths soon redoubled. I read everything I could find on spiritual matters and struggled hard to make sense of it all. It was in Buddhism that I began to recognize what I was looking for. Here, it seemed, there were people who understood the kind of experience I had had, and who valued it. This seemed like a home-coming.

By the time I was in my early twenties I at last began to find people who could teach me how to meditate. My search was no longer totally dependent upon books. Eventually, I ventured upon the retreat mentioned at the beginning of chapter one, a fortnight which impressed me with the need to intensify my own training if I was ever to get once again in touch with the reality I had glimpsed as a child. That week, I sampled the power of an extended period of meditation and the profound effects that can come when one alternates between encounter with advanced practitioners on the one hand and solitary stillness on the other. During the week I got, as it were, a scent of what I sought. It was not until many years later, however, that I was really able to see behind the curtain again.

THE FOUR PHASES OF THE MOON

Drawing upon these experiences, let me highlight some of the important features of the four phases of meditation as described by the Buddha and by the Zen master Lin Chi who lived in the ninth century. The Buddha said, First prepare by finding a secluded place. Somewhere quiet, spacious, clean and beautiful is ideal. Conducive space enhances any kind of therapy and zazen is our own therapy for ourselves, so we make a good place for it.

We sit in a stable posture. Perhaps, initially, we focus upon an object, rather like a child at play, just as I, as a child, looked at stones. Thus, if one learned to concentrate by paying attention to the breathing, one might start to ask, 'Who breathes?' One observes the air come in, the abdomen rise, the air go out, the abdomen fall. 'Who is doing the breathing?' One starts to become aware of space between the breaths, and space within the breath itself. 'Who breathes?' We become happily absorbed. This playful absorption is piti, the first zen. Lin Chi called this the state in which 'circumstance is, self is not'. One loses oneself in thinking about a matter or observing an object single-mindedly. This is pleasant (*sukha*) and tantalizing.

The first dhyana can easily fade, just as a child's mind can wander away from the game. Samadhi requires a more complete stillness. The question 'Who breathes?' or, at least, its essential sense, remains palpable, and supremely important. One is now experiencing the question continuously, but no longer thinking *about* it. Rather, one is in it. The demandingness of the question still maintains a certain tension, or rapture. The feeling of pleasure increases, quietly approaching ecstasy. One remains very still, with a sense that even the slightest twitch would break the gradual build-up. This is the second zen. Lin Chi called this 'circumstance is not, self is'. One is self-possessed and attention has naturally withdrawn from the object.

Gradually one lets go of the tension of the question. Calm completely replaces rapture. It is not so much that we are *in* the question as that we *are* the question. We are the mystery of who breathes, yet the breath goes on. We are at peace with it and everything seems beautifully pure and complete just as it is. It is lovely that the breath is a mystery. Our whole being is suffused with ease. Self-consciousness has faded and we do not need to know anything, as if sitting on the edge of a dead calm lake which extends as far as the eye could see and beyond. We are at peace with everything in the world. Body and mind fall away. We are simply aware, mindful. This is the third zen, a samadhi which Lin Chi calls 'neither circumstance nor self'.

Finally, the question is no longer there at all. I am here. So is the breath. And the stones. Everything simply is. What is, is perfect just in itself. Stillness is no longer dependent upon body and mind. Lin Chi says: 'Neither circumstance nor self are missing.' This is the state of equanimity in which one returns to the world 'with bliss bestowing hands'. It is, in some ways, to have the naïve mind of a child. This is perhaps what Jesus really meant by being born again. A person in this state enjoys life and can readily become happily absorbed in helping others or in wonderment at the miracles of life: a leaf blowing in the wind, cold water on one's hands, the taste of an orange, whatever.

STILLNESS HEALS

We aim to arrest the compulsive gallop of the conditioned mind. Although the manifestations of trouble are myriad, all clients want to restore self-control and rediscover confidence and peace of mind: inner calm. This grows out of a natural capacity for attentive absorption which the person already has. Really we are talking about a vicious circle. When a person is happy, they do not find it so difficult to give attention to good things. As worries intrude we become more and more dominated by them and lose the original, childlike simplicity. Many people search for the happy absorption which they know they once had in childhood, but have since lost. Now they are just absorbed by worries. Stress creates suffering in the mind and destroys physical health.

The therapist models stillness and is not frightened by the client nor what they present. The client feels driven, but the therapist demonstrates that this is not inevitable. The therapist shows that she can hear what the client has said and is not panicked by it. Being inwardly still, the therapist is able to listen without reacting or jumping to conclusions.

The client is liable, unconsciously, to provide the therapist with a series of provocations and will watch, expecting to see the therapist jump in the same way that other important people in their life always did. The therapist whose inner calm is well established remains minutely attentive, but does not react in the predictable manner. When this happens, therapy is rather like a meditation for two.

When we first practise zazen, we remain still and all our compulsive states of mind do their best to disturb us: 'I shouldn't really be sitting here, I should be . . .', 'If I just scratch that itch, then I will be able to sit still,' 'I wonder what's on TV this evening . . .', 'Now I am doing this really well. I'm better at this than the other people here . . .', and so on. In therapy, the client's conditioned mind similarly mobilizes everything it has got to try to draw the therapist into its orbit, by seduction, provocation, pathos or whatever: 'I'm sure you are the only person who can understand . . .', 'I don't know if you have got children yourself . . .', 'My last therapist thought that . . .', 'I am hopeless, I can't do anything,' 'Do you think you will be able to help me?' and so on. In zazen, the body remains calm and the mind struggles with it. Eventually the mind becomes calm too. In therapy, the therapist remains calm and the client's conditioned self struggles. Eventually the client will start to calm down too.

I do not wish to be misunderstood here. The calm we are referring to is a deep inner stillness, the fruit of much inner work. It may manifest as immobility of body, but, in interaction with another person, it may just as likely appear as lively responsiveness or decisive action. A therapist who simply thinks, 'I must stay calm,' and clings to this, will just find themselves resisting the client and achieve little. There is an onus on the therapist, therefore, to deepen this inner quality as much as possible through sustained meditative practice.

The therapist's calm has a stabilizing effect. The client's own capacity for samadhi then comes out. Actually we never lose the childhood ability to enjoy happy absorption. When we seem to have lost it, it is generally because some attachment or aversion is preoccupying us. Therapy is the means for a person to rediscover their bliss and this can mean finding out what it is that is really holding their attention.

A client comes to see me and tells me that he cannot concentrate at work. It emerges that he cannot concentrate at home either. His record at school, when he was a child, however, was fairly good. This client does not need to 'learn to concentrate' as though this were a skill he had never had. It is not that he cannot concentrate: it is that he is preoccupied. So, with what? After some time of paying careful attention and picking up whatever he mentions in passing, it becomes apparent that the centre of gravity around which all this client's subliminal attention orbits is the thought of death. It is not that my client cannot concentrate. It is that his attention is absorbed by something more important than the day-to-day tasks set by his employers. It is thus quickly apparent that this client, who initially could have been judged superficial and ineffectual, is actually embarked upon struggling with a most important koan.

This is not uncommon. A person comes to see a therapist because they cannot cope with some of the mundane matters in life and, when we look just a little below the surface, we find that they are actually engaged with a spiritual or existential question that is more fundamental. A therapist needs an appreciation of the spiritual dimension of life. The first stage of cultivating the mind, therefore, is to learn the art of absorption and the best way to do this is to discover what it is that is actually absorbing us already: to discover our burning question.

In Zen, the insoluble issues become the means of penetrating into existence. We look, not for an intellectual solution, but a transformation of experience. At some level, we all know that we have to do this work. Our culture, however, instructs us that there are two main ways of dealing with things. One of these favoured paths is knowledge. If we can just know enough about the subject, then we will be safe. The other is denial. If we cannot solve the problem through knowledge, we will turn our backs upon it and keep our minds distracted with entertainment, work, drugs or whatever. Zen is a different strategy. By intensifying the problem itself and penetrating into it we find a much more durable peace.

In psychotherapy, a person works hard upon one object. This is the koan, the test, which brought them into therapy. Initially, perhaps they are only aware of the way their mind seems to be whirling around, seemingly out of control. Then they begin to realize that it is engaged in its own meditation, its own piti. The shift from piti to samadhi occurs when the mind begins to focus upon the centre of concern, rather than whirling. Once the focus comes into view, there is more to appreciate, but less to say. This is like entering into the eye of the hurricane. In the very centre, it is still.

In the next chapter, we will look at how this stillness can be applied in daily life, for the health and peace of mind of ourselves and those we help.

6

Mindfulness

ZEN GARDENS

Early in the morning, I stand in the garden. It is fresh and clear. I reach out my hand and touch a leaf. In a garden we are surrounded by what is natural. Gardeners do not construct plants. On the other hand, nothing in the garden escapes the gardener's careful attention. The gardener purposefully co-operates with nature, and does not simply allow everything to become overrun with weeds, nor fail to plant and harvest at the right times. The garden is constantly improved by this co-operative purposefulness.

Zen is the capacity we have for improving our minds in a similar way. The Buddha taught that everything in life comes from the mind. Act with a good mind: happiness will follow us. Act with a mind of greed or hate, a small or rigid mind: misery will follow in our wake. A peaceful mind is thus a great treasure: it will bring peace to the world.

A well-cultivated mind is like a well-cultivated garden. It has not been neglected and allowed to go to seed. The gardener pulls up weeds and turns them into compost, digs up rocks and makes them into paths and rockeries. In therapy we dig up the kleshas and transform them, thus embellishing life with love, compassion and understanding. The gardener feeds the plants which are beautiful and fruitful and finds good uses for as many different plants as possible. The gardener is always attentive and works hard. Often his or her back aches. The gardener of the mind, sitting on his or her Zen cushion, is just the same.

In particular, a good gardener creates good soil. When we look at a productive and beautiful garden, we might be tempted to say: 'How fortunate to have such good soil.' In reality, however, if the garden is established, there is very little of fortune in it. The soil is made by the activity of the gardener. 'As the gardener, so the soil.' Zen is the care of the soil of our mind. The mind is the ground of our being and we take care of it. This is the work of Zen. This is the ultimate therapy: to improve the ground of the mind.

The most valuable commodity in improving the ground is compost. To make compost, we need weeds. People who have many weeds in their garden can, with much hard work, achieve excellent results. We have seen how the peace of samadhi can be attained through intensive work with our koan.

A book recently published gives an account of the life of Issan Dorsey (Schneider 1993). Issan Dorsey's early life revolved around drugs, bars, performing as a 'drag queen', petty crime and high living. Through his encounter with the Zen teacher Shunryu Suzuki he began to practise meditation and train himself. Eventually he became a Zen teacher himself and founded the Maitri Hospice for AIDS victims. He became a deeply compassionate teacher, not in spite of his 'misspent' youth, but rather because of it. His feeling for those who were in trouble was real because he had been there. He was genuinely nonjudgemental in the face of others' offences because he understood.

Further back in history, a key figure in the growth of Buddhism was the emperor Ashoka. As a young warrior, Ashoka was ruthless and hot-tempered. He fought many wars and killed many people. Then he encountered Buddhism and began to think more deeply about what he was doing. He was particularly appalled by what he had done in a war against the Kalinga people who had been slaughtered. Ashoka resolved to change and began a process of self-reform which eventually led to his becoming one of the most tolerant and benevolent monarchs in India's history.

Nobody is too damaged to begin cultivating their mind, nor too overrun with destructive habits to be able to turn what they have already learned from life to good account. There is no denying, however, that Zen is hard work. Just like gardening. And it is work which does not end. A garden may be created by hard work, but if it is then neglected, it will soon revert to chaos.

Dhyana (zen) is the subject upon which the Buddha spoke most. He was constantly encouraging his disciples to spare no effort in training the mind. Train with all the energy you have, he would say to them. Make this your first priority.

LEARNING TO GARDEN

Many of the clients who come to see us do so because their mind gardens have become overgrown. They do not know where to start. Often they think that the garden should look after itself. The whole idea that it needs to be cultivated, or that this involves work, may come as a shock.

Nonetheless, the client also has intuitive understanding. We know, and if we do not then the fifth precept will remind us, that, in some sense, we are what we take into ourselves. If our environment is full of toxins – alcohol, drugs, pornography, violence, anger, criticism, dishonesty, selfishness, casual sex, erratic patterns of sleeping and eating, feuding and resentment – and we consume these, we are going to find that our minds will become full of rambling weeds which will cause us a great deal of trouble. The first stage in gardening generally has to do with clearing some of the undergrowth.

We should, however, never minimize the task. A therapy which implies that everything will be easy will rarely achieve much.

> The flickering, fickle mind, difficult to guard, difficult to con-
> trol – the wise person straightens it as a fletcher straightens
> an arrow. (Dhammapada 3, v. 1)

BREATHING

Mindfulness of breathing is one of the best starting points for the cultivation of the mind. The breath is a clear indicator of our inner life: a bridge between body and mind. The therapist notices the client's breathing. Is it shallow or deep, long or short, rough or smooth? How does it change as the client tells their story? By synchronizing one's own breath with that of the client, it is often possible to understand the client's suffering more deeply. Drawing attention to the breath can sometimes be helpful. As the client breathes into their pain, some relief may occur or an insight be triggered.

Learning to pay attention to the breath is the beginning of meditation. It is a means of noticing that we are alive, calming ourselves and returning to the here and now. Studying the breath makes us aware of our bodies and of their inter-dependence with the world. A little time devoted each day to conscious breathing, sitting in an upright alert posture, or walking slowly, or just as one happens to be when pausing in the midst of other activities, will improve health and calm one's life. Breathe from the abdomen. Do not try to alter the natural flow, just notice. The breath will naturally deepen. Many people breathe with only the upper part of the chest and this makes them more vulnerable to panic.

If, in the course of the day, a person can stop once in a while, perhaps when the clock chimes or the telephone rings, and enjoy breathing for a minute before returning to the task in hand, there will be less build up of stress and things will get done in a more balanced and caring way.

Meditation is a process of holding the attention upon a wholesome object. The breath is such an object. Mindfulness of breathing is one of the simplest and most profound forms of meditation and everybody can benefit from it. The Buddha taught this method in many of his discourses.

MINDFULNESS

Mindfulness (*sati*) rides on the back of samadhi. In samadhi the mind comes to appreciate all things by focusing upon one. In mindfulness, sati, we begin simply to appreciate all things. No one particular focus need be retained. Mindfulness is the miracle which transforms every aspect of life.

Most people miss most of their life. It passes by while they are doing something else. We get to work in the morning, having traversed a number of interesting and even dangerous events, like manoeuvring through traffic, hardly having been present for any part of the journey. The mind was not there. It had gone off on some other business, planning, dreaming, reminiscing, self-soothing or whatever.

Mindfulness is to harmonize the mind with the body: not the other way around. Generally, when we go somewhere, the mind arrives before the body. In mindfulness practice, the mind stays where the body is. The body remains full of the mind. Initially, this means slowing down. So, mindfulness is being here, with no particular object. Mindfulness does not hold on to particular things. But mindfulness is still a samadhi: the samadhi of this present moment.

What is the most important thing to do in your life? The most important thing is what you are doing right now. Whatever it is, if you do not live this moment fully, then an opportunity has been lost which will never return. Lived fully, this is one moment of complete enlightenment. If it is passed by in a haze, then it is just one more moment of fog.

Who is the most important person in your life? The most important person is the person who is with you right now. This person needs you. Perhaps they need your help, or your stillness. Perhaps they need a word from you or they need you to listen. Perhaps they need you to refrain from interfering. Whatever it is, this person is the most important person. That is mindfulness.

Knowing that the person that you are with right now is the most important person in the world is the essence of therapy. Although, in this book, we have many theories about life, the mind and enlightenment, in the moment of actual encounter with another person, the theories are no use. It is no use having theories about this person because that would make them a non-person. This person is special. They are more important than all the theories. The theories help us to understand people in general, but this person is not a person in general. This person is just what they are and that is fine.

What is the most beautiful sight in the world? Open your eyes and look. If we can see this object – the page of this book, the bubbles in the washing-up bowl, the excrement on the piece of paper with which one has just cleansed oneself, the teacup held between one's hands – whatever it may be, if we can really see it, we will see that it is the most wonderful thing in the world. This is how many people were led into spiritual practice by experimenting with drugs like LSD and mescaline. Such drugs, for all their pernicious effects, also enabled people to realize that there was a universe of wonder locked up in every moment of perception. The drugs gave some people a glimpse of the jewel island on which we live all the time. To have one's eyes opened by a drug, however, does not give one control over this process in the way that mindfulness training does.

What is the most wonderful music in the world? What is the best perfume? What is the most important sensation you will ever have? You know the answers. The most important sensations you will ever have are the ones you are experiencing this minute. It would be a shame to miss them.

EQUANIMITY

Equanimity (*upeksha*) grows out of mindfulness. The person who has upeksha is master of every situation, no matter what the situation is. This is why Zen includes many tests to practise on. When one reads Zen stories, there is often an element of mutual testing involved or of people being tested by naturally arising situations. One has not reached the stage of upeksha until one can take anything that arises in one's stride.

Taking everything in one's stride means that nothing matters to oneself personally. It does not matter whether we die or not. If we are going to die, let us do it well. Life includes dying. A good life includes dying well. We are talking here, then, of a state in which the survival passion called ego is out of the way. This is the state in which our relation to the rest of the universe is as the relationship of one hand to the other. The left hand does not seek its own benefit at the expense of the right. We are all limbs of one life.

Upeksha is generally translated as equanimity, but its significance is really that one lives unconditionally. We will look in detail at conditioning. Upeksha is its undoing. Conditioning is like a knot that uses the mind as a rope to strangle the heart.

Upeksha is the sword which cuts through the mind and releases the heart. It is thus the real basis of the qualities of compassion and love which we will discuss later. There is a great deal of confusion still about the teaching of Buddhism. The Buddha often spoke of the importance of detachment and equanimity. This does not mean to become a cold, aloof, distant person at all. It means that one is detached from the thing that holds us back from genuine caring – the ego passion.

The client who comes into therapy is probably, as we saw in the last chapter, already involved to some degree in piti-zen. They are worrying away at some important concern, like a person polishing a piece of old tarnished metal. This is hard work and slow progress. Through contact with the therapist, the object of concern comes more clearly into view and the possibility of samadhi-zen emerges. Zen, as we have seen, tends not to take the client's concern away from them, but to sharpen its edge, to clarify its challenge. The client is already focused upon one thing.

MINDFULNESS AS THERAPY

One day the Buddha gave a talk which has been recorded as the Four Grounds of Mindfulness (*Nian Chu Jing*, in Chinese; *Satipatthana Sutta*, in Pali). It continues to be used as a basic manual of mindfulness practice. The four grounds are: to observe one's body as body, one's feeling as feeling, one's mind as mind, and objects of mind as objects of mind. This means to be aware of everything just as it is. The teaching goes into considerable detail and provides a great many exercises for developing awareness of bodily and mental processes as they happen.

The therapist needs this moment by moment awareness to see the client just as they are and to appreciate their world as it is revealed. The therapist notices the client's bodily movements, feelings, mental states and world as experienced. The therapist does not look for faults and is not directly trying to change the client. Rather, the therapist makes the client and their world the object of mindful attention.

When a mindfulness practitioner moves his body, he knows he is doing so. When his body is still, he knows it is still. He is not lost in a dream. When he experiences a pleasant feeling he knows it for what it is and likewise when he feels an unpleasant feeling. When attraction or aversion arise in his mind, he knows straight away that this has happened. When his perception of an object is giving rise to a mental confection, such as pride or dejection, he experiences it happen. When anger or jealousy arise in his mind, he experiences them arising. When they remain, he knows they are remaining. When they cease, he experiences their cessation. When they are absent, he experiences their absence.

The therapist who is mindful notices every little shift in the client's demeanour and intention as well as what is happening inside herself. When we are carefully attentive to another person, a kind of resonance occurs. Listening to my client, I notice that I am beginning to feel irritable, say. If I identify with my feelings, I am likely simply to start thinking that this is an irritating client and my care for them will be eroded. If I am mindful, however, I notice the irritation and think, 'That's interesting – I wonder what that is.' Very commonly, if I then tell my client, in a non-judgemental way, what is happening to me: 'I have noticed some feeling like irritation – I am not sure where it has come from,' he will recognize it as his rather than mine and we will have made some progress. The therapist frequently gets infected, as it were, with the client's unexpressed mental confections. Noticing this happen gives the therapist something approaching second sight. The deeper the samadhi of which the therapist is capable, the less internal 'noise' there will be to interfere with this receptive process. The clairvoyant power of the Buddha was often noticed.

A great deal of the therapy dialogue is, in fact, concerned with helping the client become mindful. The therapist is a mirror. The mirror has no personal agenda but enables the client to see themselves more clearly. The client, however, does not always have the therapist present with them to act as mirror. There is, therefore, much to be said for helping the client to develop mindfulness on their own account.

This can speed therapy up enormously, since it gives the client the reins. Even an elementary level of mindfulness gives people enhanced self-control. Every compulsive behaviour is embedded in a sequence of other behaviours and impulses. If a person wishes to change a behaviour pattern, the first thing they need to do is to start to recognize the chain of events. This requires mindfulness. 'Through individualized mindfulness practices the client learns to be more aware of those situations, actions, feelings, and thoughts related to behaviors to be changed. A power of mindfulness is that it can be moved earlier and earlier in the chain of events' (Mikulas 1990, p. 154).

The young man who commonly finds himself embroiled in fights does not know how it happens. He is a victim of his own programmed behaviour. Through therapy he first discovers that when he goes into the bar he looks around, and, if someone is looking at him, he takes offence and challenges them. Through increasing mindfulness, he discovers that the chain of events begins well before he even reaches the bar. The whole evening's events are stereotyped (conditioned) within him. The therapist helps him to go through specific incidents pinning down how he behaved and how he felt from before he left home, through meeting up with a friend to walking down to the bar, and so on, in detail. Only when a person is aware of their actions can they choose to do something about them.

Bringing the client's attention to small details of everyday life, perhaps even getting them to record them in a structured diary, can be a valuable aid to the development of mindfulness. Many of the problems clients bring to therapy are couched in such global terms that nothing can be done. Once the attention comes down to practical detail, purposeful action becomes possible. Mindfulness is close to thoughtfulness. A client can talk endlessly to no purpose about what is wrong with their parents. What is needed is to examine, perhaps, how often the client says 'thank you', shows respect or listens to them. Attention to small acts of kindness can have a profound effect.

Mindfulness can change our sense of who we are in very fundamental ways: 'the most profound personal changes resulting from mindfulness come when a person disidentifies with the contents of his mind and stands back from the melodrama' (Mikulas 1990, p. 159). Zen does not erase the complexes in our minds: it enables us to stop being troubled by them and to see that 'they are not me'. This is a great liberation. Of course, if we cease to reinforce our passions, they will gradually fade and bad states will become less likely. It is important to realize, however, that we do not have to wait for this to happen before we begin to live our lives in a more sane way. The complexes fade when we live sanely, not the other way about. Zen is not about results in the future, it is about practice in the present.

CONCLUSION

The therapist is concerned with the quality of the client's life moment by moment. Generally, the therapist is not concerned whether the client stays with or leaves her husband, for instance. The therapist is concerned with how well she lives with her husband or how well she fares without him. Therapy is more about improving the quality of life than solving specific choice dilemmas. Improving life quality begins with mindfulness.

Meditation has been used for millennia to cultivate the mind. It is one of the oldest therapies. Although there are many different approaches, all involve quietening habitual energies: cleansing perception so that we can see what is going on. Mindfulness is an attempt to regain contact with the flow of experience.

Mindfulness is both radical introspection and direct connection with the phenomenal world. It is not simply inward looking. It is more a matter of being fully present in each step of life. By attempting it we throw into relief all the obstacles in our minds which prevent us making direct contact with experience. Simple degrees of mindfulness are immensely valuable, indeed essential, at all levels of personal growth. At its fullest development, mindfulness depends upon samadhi. It is the samadhi of every moment. The meditation practice described in this and the previous chapter is the necessary basis for liberating ourselves and others from conditioning and it is to this topic of conditioning that we will now turn our attention.

Part 2
Buddhist Psychology

7

Introduction to Part Two

Now we will embark upon a more detailed exploration of Buddhist psychology. Part Two is, in some respects, more technical than the rest of the book, as it presents the underlying theory derived from texts written over two thousand years ago. My intention is to make this material as accessible as possible. Nonetheless, I must ask the reader to accept that what follows includes some analytical material. Those who wish to gain more of the flavour of Zen before tackling the theory may prefer to proceed to Part Three first.

The key to Buddhist psychology is the analysis of conditioning. All ordinary mental states depend upon conditions. If conditions change, then the mental state also changes. To identify with conditioned existence is unsatisfactory (dukkha) since within it nothing can be relied upon. One is at the mercy of forces beyond one's control and simply goes round in circles under their influence. Real satisfaction depends upon breaking the hold of conditioning.

Conditioning can take many forms and we will examine the more important ones. The aim of therapy, from a Buddhist perspective, is to liberate the mind by enabling it to let go of the conditioned states. The differences between different Buddhist schools are differences of technique rather than principle in this matter. The liberated state of mind is called *nirvana*. The conditioned state is called *samsara*.

The Buddha's teaching (*Dharma*) points out the way to liberation, the ultimate goal. Within samsara, however, conditioning is a matter of degree. Delusion can be built upon delusion, like a house of cards. The higher the tower, the more unstable the structure. The more conditioned our minds are, the more neurotic we will be and the more we will suffer. It is therefore definitely important to reduce conditioning in ourselves and others as far as we can.

Since everything is dependent on conditions, nothing exists independently from its own side. When conditions change, whatever is dependent upon them changes as well. All phenomena are, in turn, the conditions for other phenomena. The universe is like a net, sometimes called 'Indra's net', after Indra, the creator god of Indian mythology. In this net all the knots are interconnected and a movement in any one will affect all the others, be it ever so slightly. The aim of Buddhist practice is, nonetheless, to go beyond conditioning: to let go of all bad states of mind, and thus manifest nirvana. It follows that complete nirvana implies freedom from attachment to all phenomena.

In samsara, all mental states are unstable and unsatisfactory because they are attached to or identified with dependent phenomena. Even 'successful' states are unsatisfactory if they rest upon unreliable conditions for their occurrence and continuance. The samsaric mind goes round in circles. The theories examined below describe how such conditioning operates and how to overcome it.

The Buddha taught the principles of dependence upon conditions in many different ways according to the needs of those who came to him. One simple formulation is the 'Four Noble Truths' (see figure 1, chapter one). The Four Noble Truths appear in the Buddha's earliest teaching given to the ascetics who had practised with him for a long time. These ascetics were advanced in yogic practice already, so a short instruction pointing out the basic human predicament was enough to liberate them.

Another well-known presentation was given in the form of a twelve-link chain, called the teaching on dependent origination, some explanation of which appears in most basic books on Buddhism. On other occasions the Buddha gave more extensive explanations and it is to one of these that I have turned for a framework for Part Two.

The primary source books on Buddhist psychology are called the Abhidharma. Buddhist sacred texts are in three collections:

Sutras, which record the talks and conversations of the Buddha and his close disciples; Vinaya, which lists principles of behaviour for monks and nuns; and Abhidharma, which presents an analysis of the mind. Each collection has several subsections.

The seventh book of Abhidharma is the Pattana, or Book of Origination. It is an extensive analysis of the subject of dependence upon causes and conditions. It lists twenty-four *paccayas*. Paccayas are conditions or relations: the ways in which one thing can depend upon another. The Pattana thus provides a catalogue of our conditioning.

The last six paccayas in the Pattana list actually constitute a separate classification, which simply re-sorts the previous eighteen into new arrangements, so I intend here only to use the first eighteen categories. They are listed here for convenience, and explained in the remainder of Part Two.

The Eighteen Theories of Conditioning

1.	Root Relations	(Hetu paccaya)
2.	Object Relation	(Arammana paccaya)
3.	Predominance	(Adhipati paccaya)
4.	Association	(Anantara paccaya)
5.	Orderly Association	(Samanantara paccaya)
6.	Co-birth	(Sahajati paccaya)
7.	Co-Dependence	(Annyamannya paccaya)
8.	Dependence	(Nissaya paccaya)
9.	Inducement	(Upanissaya paccaya)
10.	Pre-condition	(Pure-jata paccaya)
11.	On-going Dependence	(Paccha-jata paccaya)
12.	Habit	(Asevanna paccaya)
13.	Karma	(Kamma paccaya)
14.	Extinguished karma	(Vipaka paccaya)
15.	Food Relation	(Ahara paccaya)
16.	Indriya	(Indriya paccaya)
17.	Dhyana	(Jhana paccaya)
18.	Path	(Magga paccaya)

These eighteen are not mutually exclusive. Rather, each presents a different perspective on the topic. Here I will reinterpret them as propositions. I hope this will make it easier for readers with a background in western thought to see what this is all about. Each paccaya proposition has therapeutic implications, and I will try to briefly indicate some of these as we go along. There is not room to cover everything in detail, and I have grouped some of the propositions which are similar.

In the next two chapters we will look at the first three propositions, Root Relations, Object Relation and Predominance. These three constitute a complete theory in their own right. The foundation for a complete system of phenomenological psychotherapy is revealed in these three paccayas and we will see how western psychotherapy has rediscovered significant parts of this material quite independently. This is as it should be, since we are talking here about the fundamental principles upon which the samsaric mind operates. The truth is always being rediscovered. One of my hopes is that this book will contribute to an emerging east–west synthesis.

After that, we will look at each of the other paccayas and we will see how the whole eighteen gradually build up into a comprehensive psychological theory which has direct applications in many different aspects of psychotherapy and personal and spiritual growth work. By way of preparation, as the second half of this chapter, we will now have a preliminary look at the Buddhist view of personal growth and introduce a model of the mind generally used in Buddhist psychology. This will help to set the scene.

PERSONAL GROWTH

The principle that one's ability to help others is proportional to one's own progress along the path of psychological maturity is common ground between Zen and western therapy. However, the notion of what personal growth means in the two approaches is not always the same.

For instance, a very common axiom used in the west is the idea that 'I cannot love others until I love myself' whereas the Zen attitude would be better represented by the phrase 'The best thing I can do for myself is to discover my love for others.' If a person genuinely loves others, then it is likely that their hang-ups about themselves will diminish, since they will have repeated experience of doing something worthwhile with their life. On the other hand, the person who only loves themselves is likely to use up whatever stock of good they have without having anything to show for it and so will end up loving neither self nor others. The Zen idea of personal growth, therefore, is not that I must learn how to listen to and obey 'me' so much as that I need to do something about the tyranny which the self-passion wields over my life.

In Buddhist psychology, the word 'self' is the collective noun for all our conditioning. In the west, most psychology is concerned with the level of the mind called 'consciousness' or ego. Most psychology is ego psychology. There are psychologies which try to reach deeper than this and go into the unconscious layer. Then there is what is called 'depth psychology' which attempts to fathom the collective unconscious. Zen is the attempt to go even further than this:

> We have unknown layers, or realms of consciousness within us. And through meditation, we can perceive how states of consciousness can be altered . . . We begin to realize that we are, in fact, a storehouse for all human history. Jung termed these deep layers of the psyche as 'the collective unconscious', and asserted that they were the most profound parts of our nature. With continuing experiences in meditation, however, we come to realize that this theory is not quite right. We can actually penetrate beyond the depths of the collective unconscious of human nature and there come to the bottomless sea of Buddha-nature. If we go beyond the collective unconscious, thereby breaking through the final barrier of the unconscious layers, we experience true birth completely anew in the ocean of true emptiness. This is infinite freedom of no-self, no-mind, no-idea; this is life itself, completely unconditioned. Here in the infinite no-mind we find flowers, the moon, our friends and families, and all things just as they are; we appreciate our everyday lives as miracles. But please confirm this for yourself. (Hogen 1993, p. 27.)

The bottomless sea of Buddha nature described above by the Zen monk, Hogen, is the precondition for our freedom from conditioned states of consciousness. This bottomless sea is called *jnana*. We could also call it universal mind or primordial consciousness. All the separate layers of consciousness are called *vijnana*, the syllable 'vi-' implying 'divided' or 'partial', but jnana itself encompasses all. Jnana is unbounded. The ordinary mind, vijnana, is dualistic, even in its depths. Even the archetypes of the collective unconscious represent ways of dividing the world of experience. Often enough, the contents of the unconscious are the 'other halves', the split-off parts, of our consciousness which we have repressed. Discovering them can thus be an important step on the road to wholeness. Rather than putting ourselves back together item by item, however, Zen offers the more demanding route of rediscovering the original unity directly through experiences of 'sudden awakening'.

THE MODEL OF THE MIND IN BUDDHIST PSYCHOLOGY

The map of the mind implied in what we have said so far is summarized in figure 4. Any diagram of this kind is simply an aid to thought. A map is only a partial representation of the actual terrain. The mind is not just two-dimensional. Nonethe-

Fig. 4. A model of the mind

	Six senses	Sensory data
	Chitta conscious cognizing mind	Perception, recognition
Vijnana consciousness	Manas the censor mind	Ego, attraction and rejection
	Alaya storehouse consciousness	Karma, passions and mental formations (complexes and archetypes)
	Buddhata	The light within 'the bottomless ocean'

less, a two-dimensional representation can be a useful starter.

Here we see that *chitta* and *manas* together roughly correspond with what in western psychology is called the conscious mind. Chitta is the perceiving, cognizing mind: the mind which pays attention. The *alaya* corresponds roughly to the unconscious. It stores all our passions developed over beginningless time. Between chitta and the alaya is manas. Manas acts as the organizer and censor, allowing some passions to rise up and keeping others suppressed. Generally, manas is a bit like a closed fist, keeping the mind in a firm grip.

Manas is ordinarily controlled by the ego complex which exerts a dominating influence over the whole psyche and constantly struggles to maintain this supremacy. Through the faculty of manas it strives to keep everything organized in a self-defensive or self-expansive way. The alaya stores our karma. Manas and the alaya together, in their conditioned state, ensure that chitta never gets a clear view of the buddhata. When conditioning is abandoned, manas relaxes, the alaya settles and the mind fills up with radiance from below. Chitta is then able to turn this light upon the world. The mind in this radiant condition becomes jnana.

The reader of translations of Buddhist texts always needs to be careful when the word 'consciousness' is used, since, as can be seen from the above chart, it can be a reference to chitta, manas, vijnana or jnana and the resulting confusion can be considerable. One will thus find statements to the effect that enlightenment brings about a loss of consciousness, for instance. This does not mean that on awakening to buddhahood one goes into a fainting fit. It means that the dualistic consciousness, vijnana, clears like morning mist to allow the sun of primordial awareness, buddhata, to shine through.

In western psychology the terms 'conscious' and 'unconscious' are rather confusing. In Jung's system, the ego is the conscious mind. In Freud's, the core of the ego is in the unconscious. In the Buddhist system, all the layers are 'consciousnesses' of one kind or another and it is the whole system that becomes obscured by conditioning rather than just one part of it. Jung divides the unconscious into two parts called personal and collective respectively. Buddhism also regards the alaya as a repository of material both from this and from other lives, but these are not thought of as occupying different areas or levels. Whether Jung's 'archetypes' and Buddhist 'traces from previous existences' can be equated, is a question I will not need to go into.

THE SKANDHAS

Another important model used in Buddhist psychology is the idea that ego process is made up of five *skandhas*. The word means a heap. The implication usually taken from this teaching is that a person is not such a unified entity as at first appears. The skandhas are form, reaction, recognition, mental confections and consciousness. Generally we talk about the five skandhas but in fact they are innumerable since the fourth, *samskara*, is a collective term for many mental formations. The term consciousness here refers to vijnana.

Fig. 5. The Skandhas

Sanskrit	English
Rupa	form
Vedana	reaction (feeling)
Samjna	recognition
Samskara	mental factors (confections)
Vijnana	dualistic consciousness

The analysis of the mind into skandhas can also, however, be taken as a description of how vijnana arises and continues. In this interpretation, the skandhas represent five steps in a process. The mind cognizes forms (*rupa*), has an instant reaction (*vedana*), and then labels the phenomenon (*samjna*). This label indexes a whole history of associations – the confections of the mind (samskara) – thus stirring up the alaya and clouding our consciousness so that we can no longer think straight and deluded consciousness (vijnana) results. Each step of this process operates under the influence of conditioning.

Thus, for instance, a person's attention is drawn to an object (rupa), a bar of chocolate, say. Immediately a reaction (vedana) occurs: attraction, perhaps. The mind now seeks to gain control over what is happening by classifying the experience (samjna) – 'Chocolate!' This promptly brings into play a whole range of mental confections (samskaras), such as glee, guilt, self-reproach, greed, excitement, visions of gluttony, getting fat, getting slim, punishment, reward, and so on. Once the mind is full of all these samskaras, it becomes opaque. It is like stirring up the mud in water. The primordial awareness, jnana, is obscured. This obscured condition is vijnana.

Vijnana is thus kept in business by conditioning. If the person were free of such compulsiveness, the bar of chocolate would simply have been perceived as no more and no less significant than anything else and the original clear mind, jnana, would have stayed untarnished. Also, we can see that all the conditioning is related to the person's belief in self. The energy that stirs up the samskaras derives from the belief that 'this concerns *me*.'

In other words, in the bottomless ocean of buddhata, where self does not figure, there is no cutting up of the world into pleasurable and unpleasurable objects. There is one seamless purity in which all the ordinary things – chocolate, flowers, the moon, our family and friends – occur just as they are, free from the skandha process.

Jnana appears as soon as we disidentify with the skandhas. Although we usually think we are them, really they just arise spontaneously from the natural workings of the universe and none of us can really say that they are 'me' or 'mine'. In the Alagaddupama Sutta the Buddha says that letting go of the skandhas will bring us happiness and well-being for a long time, that we should no more regard them as ourselves than we would so regard swept-up leaves which have been thrown on the bonfire. If we can disidentify in this way, then when chitta espies a bar of chocolate and a pleasurable reaction occurs, we can just notice: 'Oh yes, the mind is interested in chocolate again.' We do not have to run the whole sequence of mental gymnastics which usually follow.

The Buddha says that if we let go of the skandhas we will feel much better. We hang on to them, however, because fundamentally we are attached to the sensual pleasures they involve us in. Self and sensuality are deeply implicated in each other.

In order to be an effective therapist, therefore, one needs, at least at the moment of therapeutic encounter, to be empty, clean and open to the flow of whatever may arise from the bottomless ocean, willing to observe each phenomenon cleanly: neither attached nor rejecting. One must guard against the stickiness of samjna and the samskaras, the preconceived sentiments that create vijnana. The therapist establishes the clear mind of meditation as the prerequisite for true understanding.

The client too, studies these processes as they operate in their life and seeks freedom from them. Often, what brings a person into therapy is some major manifestation of the trouble which the disturbed mind (vijnana) can cause. The work of therapy may, however, have to begin with tackling smaller, more everyday instances first.

This, then, is a sketch of the Buddhist concept of how the mind works. We will refer back to these models from time to time as we now go on to examine the conditioning process itself from a number of different perspectives.

· 8 ·

Root Relations

The theory of root relations states that all dukkha (mental suffering) can be traced back to three bitter roots, greed, hate and delusion, and that all wholesome states can be traced back to three sweet roots which are the opposites of the bitter ones.

The ordinary mind is obscured. The obscurations are called *kleshas*. A klesha is any mental factor which produces turmoil in the psyche. Kleshas are whatever seems to prevent us thinking clearly or acting sensibly. Collectively they constitute what Freud called the Id. In Buddhism, Freud's Id is represented by 'basic ignorance' (*avidya*). This basic ignorance can have a positive, negative or neutral valency. Thus we arrive at what are generally called 'the three poisons', *lobha*, *dosa* and *moha*. These three terms are usually translated as greed, hate and delusion respectively. They are the roots of all the thousands of kleshas.

Let me repeat these basic points so that this is clear, because it is so fundamental. Buddhism aims for a clear, clean, unimpeded state of mind called enlightenment. An enlightened person perceives the world without preconception, without distortion. This quality of clear perception is called *vidya*. When it is lacking, we talk of *avidya*. Avidya, 'ignorance' or 'non-clarity', then, is the root of all trouble. In the grip of avidya, we respond to experience unrealistically. This may take one of three forms. We may feel overly attached to things and have distress separating from them. This is called *lobha*, roughly 'greed'. Or we may feel overly detached, separated, alienated, and experience distress when we have to connect with them. This is *dosa*, roughly 'hate' or 'aversion'. Or, again, we may be in the grip of fixed ideas, prejudice or confusion which paralyse our better nature. This is *moha*, variously translated as delusion, confusion or dullness.

There is thus ultimately one wholesome root condition, vidya, and one unwholesome one, avidya. From these, as more practical working principles, we derive six roots, three wholesome or sweet and three unwholesome or bitter. The three bitter roots are lobha, dosa and moha, greed, hate and delusion, and the three wholesome roots are their opposites, *alobha*, *adosa*, and *amoha*, which we may call non-greed, non-hate and non-delusion, respectively. Although the sweet roots are described in negative language, they are nonetheless positive forces in our lives and in therapy as we shall soon see.

Fig. 6. Hetu

Bitter tap root	Avidya Closed mind		
Three poisons Bitter roots	*Lobha* greed	*Dosa* hate	*Moha* delusion
Antidotes Sweet roots	*Alobha* non-greed	*Adosa* non-hate	*Amoha* non-delusion
Ultimate antidote, or Sweet tap root	Vidya Open mind		

This, then, is the theory of root relations. Virtually all mental states derive from one or other of the six roots. These, then, are the prime conditioning factors in samsara. The Buddha says that the unfortunate consequences of lobha are mild but last a long time, those of dosa are severe but do not last so long, while those of moha are both severe and long-lasting.

Diagnostic Implications

This theory can be extended into a system of diagnostics. Thus, for instance, in the field of eating disorders, three conditions are generally recognized. Compulsive eating is, fairly clearly, a lobha condition. The person wishes to incorporate more than is realistic into themselves. Such people commonly have difficulty with separation. Anorexia, on the other hand, is a dosa condition. The person wishes to be separate and purified, not contaminated by the material world. Such people commonly have difficulty with closeness or contact. Finally, there is bulimia, a condition which has the drawbacks of both the others. This is the moha condition. We notice too that, in general, just as Buddhist theory suggests, compulsive eating tends to be a condition that goes on for a large part of a person's lifetime, but has, compared with the other two, milder consequences. Anorexia tends to have severe consequences but, in most cases, patients grow out of it at a fairly young age. Bulimia is both severe and long-lasting (Beech 1994).

Whether the major categories of mental disturbance such as neurosis, psychosis and hysteria, or narcissism, megalomania and hypochondria, can also be mapped on to this system is perhaps more uncertain. The difficulty is in that no condition generally manifests in pure form and definitions are disputed. We all suffer from all three forms of obscuration of consciousness all the time. What we are talking about, therefore, is an imbalance or particular excess being the characteristic of a condition. Nonetheless, some such classification as that shown in figure 7 may be useful.

Fig. 7. Diagnostic categories

Tap root	Avidya		
Root Relation	Lobha	Dosa	Moha
Type of obscuration	Compulsiveness and reactiveness	Dissociation and fright	Perplexity and fixed ideas
Eating disorder	Compulsive eating	Anorexia	Bulimia
Melancholic manifestation	Existential depression (anomie)	Reactive depression	Endogenous depression
Functional disorder	Neurosis	Hysteria	Psychosis

The matrix suggested here departs from conventional psychiatric thinking in locating reactive depression with hysteria, rather than neurosis. This seems, however, to better fit the symptomatology. Reactive depression is readily converted into anger and often begins with an angry phase. Reactive depression is severe but short-lived. Existential depression is milder but endures. Endogenous depression is both debilitating and of long duration.

If we think about aetiology, dosa conditions are liable to be associated with trauma, whereas lobha conditions are more likely to be associated with deprivation. Of course, circumstantial conditions are only half of the equation. Depending upon temperament, what is experienced as depriving by one person, may not be so by another, and different personalities also have very varying resilience in the face of shocks and losses.

Therapeutic Implications

The implication for therapy of root relations theory is, in essence, that we need to find ways to convert the bitter roots into sweet ones. Now one way for this to happen is simply that people learn by experience. Since the ultimate results of avidya are invariably unpleasant, one would expect that a learning process would go on such that it would be eliminated. This does happen to some degree. Most psychological distress shows a tendency to spontaneous remission and to some extent people do get wiser as they get older. The learning process is, however, often exceedingly slow, for reasons which will become apparent when we consider karmic relations later on.

The Japanese Zen Master Kosho Uchiyama has likened this process to the maturing of a persimmon tree (Uchiyama 1993, pp. 14 *et seq.*). A persimmon tree growing naturally produces bitter fruit. It does not begin to produce sweet fruit until it is about a hundred years old. Consequently, in order to obtain sweet persimmons sooner, cultivators take branches from very old trees and graft these on to younger trees. The branches then continue to grow and produce sweet fruit. Uchiyama draws the analogy thus: 'If you leave humanity as it is, it has an astringent quality no matter what country or what part of the world you look at. It just so happened, however, that several thousand years ago in India, in the culture of that day, a sweet persimmon was born; that was Buddhism. Or, more precisely, it was Shakyamuni Buddha who was born – like a branch on an astringent persimmon that after many, many years finally bore sweet fruit' (ibid., pp. 15–16).

In therapy, we aim to speed up a process which would otherwise take much longer. Our client will, no doubt, given enough time, learn whatever is necessary to convert bitter roots into sweet ones. We would like to hasten that process, to, as it were, graft a sweet branch on to the existing tree. How can this be done?

To answer this question, I will turn to western psychotherapy theory. For the analysis which follows I am much indebted to a western scholar, Campbell Purton (1994). Purton refers to the theory of Carl Rogers that there are only three 'necessary and sufficient conditions' of therapeutic personality change and asks why it should be, in principle, that there are only three such conditions. It is a fact that there have been a number of attempts to demonstrate that Rogers' list should be extended, but none of these have been successful. Rogers' original theory remains intact and is broadly supported by research. The three 'core conditions' in Rogers' theory are empathy, unconditional respect and congruence or genuineness.

Purton points out that these three core conditions map on to the three roots in the Buddhist theory of root relations. Empathy is, in fact, the antidote to hate, dosa. The person afflicted with dosa-mind pushes things away, rejects them, does not want to understand them. Empathy is the opposite of this. It involves achieving deep understanding of what is other, as though from the inside. Empathy overcomes aversion.

Unconditional respect is the antidote to lobha, greed. This may not seem immediately obvious because of the translation, but when we remember that the meaning of lobha is essentially to do with hanging on to and trying to incorporate the other, giving it no space nor independence, we see that respect is precisely the antidote to this condition. Unconditional respect or positive regard means that I am willing for the other to *be* other, without stipulations or restriction. It is the opposite of the clinging, suffocating lobha-mind.

Finally, congruence is the antidote to moha, delusion. This is fairly obvious. Moha could just as well be translated by the word 'incongruence'. The moha-mind is the mind of deception and confusion. The person who is congruent is clear about what they are and does not conceal it. They do not cling to fixed views, but flow from moment to moment, 'being their organism', as Rogers puts it.

Fig. 8. Hetu and core conditions

Sweet root	*Vidya*		
Root relation	*Alobha*	*Adosa*	*Amoha*
Core conditions	Unconditional respect	Empathy	Congruence

Thus, according to Purton, Rogers' three core conditions are simply the three sweet roots. Empathy is adosa. Unconditional positive regard is alobha. Congruence is amoha. The therapist is enjoined to adopt these three core conditions when with the client. This will enable the client's actualizing tendency to begin to work. It may also, of course, in a more direct fashion, model a different way of being for the client (Brazier 1993) and thus enable a sweet branch to be grafted on to a bitter tree.

Rogers, like Buddha, clearly spelt out that none of the three beneficial conditions works in the absence of the other two. It is not therapeutic for me to be congruent if I have no empathy nor positive regard, for instance, since this would simply mean acting out my hate and greed, and so on. Nonetheless, both theories also assert that a preponderance of one or other condition is appropriate in particular circumstances.

Putting this together with our theory of diagnosis suggests the possibility that compulsive conditions call particularly for unconditional positive regard and dissociative ones for more empathy, while the moha conditions of denial especially require a congruent response. This conclusion does seem, in general, to tally with clinical experience.

As Purton makes clear, this exposure of the deep structure of the core conditions as based, unknowingly, upon the theory of root relations does explain why there are just three core conditions. The three roots exhaust all logical possibilities. Avidya can only have a positive, negative or neutral valency – there are no other options. What Purton does not mention, is that this analysis also explains why Rogers himself and his followers insist that these three conditions are all that is necessary while other therapists continue to espouse a variety of different approaches. The theory of root relations is the first item on the Pattana list because of its fundamental nature. If we can transform the roots, everything else will look after itself. Nonetheless, the Buddhist analysis goes on to show how there are also many other aspects to conditioning which are just as pernicious. Buddhism thus concurs with Rogers that these three antidotes do strike at the very root of the disease in the human condition, and it also explains why many other theories also hold.

The terms empathy, positive regard and congruence are drawn from western psychotherapy. In Buddhist psychology the terms alobha, adosa and amoha are variously translated by different scholars, but in this book we will come back to them in detail in later chapters where they will reappear as love, compassion and wisdom respectively.

Fig. 9. The roots of enlightenment

Positive root (Pali)	*Alobha*	*Adosa*	*Amoha*
Close western term	Unconditional positive regard	Empathy	Congruence
Zen equivalent (Sanskrit)	Love (maitri)	Compassion (karuna)	Wisdom (prajna)

In the Buddhist definition of these terms, hate is the desire that others should suffer. Compassion is the desire that others be relieved of suffering. Thus compassion is the antidote to hate. Greed is the desire to have all good things for myself. Love is the desire that good things happen to the other person. Love is therefore the antidote to greed. Delusion is to turn away from and deny reality. Wisdom is to turn toward, affirm and understand reality. Wisdom is the antidote to delusion.

If we remember the theory of mind presented in chapter seven, we see that the theory of roots thus applies to the operation of manas. By applying the antidotes to the three poisons, manas may be induced to relax and so it may be possible for more communication to take place between chitta and the alaya at least, and even the buddhata, the buddha nature beyond the passions.

Because of their fundamental importance, the three qualities of maitri, karuna and bodhi require a chapter each. For the present, however, let us turn to the second kind of conditioning, the theory of object relation.

Perception and Will

THE THEORY OF OBJECT RELATION (Arammana)

The object relation theory tells us that all mental states are conditioned by the objects, real or unreal, which hold their attention. Mind is that which cognizes objects. As the object is, so will be the mind which clings to it.

We have seen that the mind of enlightenment is vidya, clear perception. Mind is that which perceives. A clear mind perceives clearly, an obscured mind perceives badly, but all mind is concerned with perceiving. The object relation theory in Buddhism is the principle that all mental states are defined by their object.

This theory is similar to but not identical with the theory of similar name in western psychology. A number of Freud's successors developed a theory called object relations, according to which we all, over the course of our lives, internalize images of 'objects' and continue to relate to them even after they have ceased to be present. The term 'objects' includes people as well as things. Western object relations theory thus envisages us as having a great range of 'internalized others' and talks about the psyche in terms of relations between them and our images of ourselves.

The idea that all mind has an object is also the fundamental axiom of the branch of western philosophy called phenomenology. 'Consciousness is always consciousness of something,' said its founder, Edmund Husserl (1929, p. 13). Husserl also saw, however, how the definition of a consciousness by its object is a reciprocal event. Objects define consciousness, but consciousness also defines ('intends') objects. Indeed, every consciousness of even a single object implicitly intends a whole world. The fact that perception of an object is shot through with intending-a-world is what makes perception meaningful.

The Buddhist object relation theory incorporates both these features. Mental states all hang upon the perception of objects. Such objects may be really present, as when fear arises upon the perception of a snake, or not really present, as when a person is depressed about something remembered from the past. In this respect, the Buddha's theory of object relation is parallel with the psychoanalytic idea. Our lives are full of images of objects which are not really present and these influence us in most of our activities. Indeed, it is not uncommon for people to live their whole life in front of an imaginary audience. In a conversation with his disciple Ananda, recorded as 'The Shorter Discourse on Emptiness', the Buddha points out that the first step toward peace of mind is to rid ourselves of all the trouble caused in our heads by things which are not actually happening.

The objects we perceive, therefore, are, unless we are completely enlightened, all shaped and coloured by a personal agenda or intention. They are conditioned. This personal agenda constitutes our attachment to self. In Buddhist psychology, particular attention is paid to the pivotal significance of one particular object. It is the fact that we hold this particular object in mind which distorts all other perceptions. This pivotal object is ourselves. It may seem strange, at first, to think of ourselves as an object. Surely our self is the subject who perceives, rather than the object perceived, we might say. In fact, however, Buddhism asserts, the self as perceiver is not something we can ever directly perceive. Such a self cannot be found. Nonetheless, even though we never really see ourselves, we do all hold many images of ourselves in mind. These images are imaginary objects. They are not really present, but are images which we use to make sense of our experience. In Buddhist psychology, then, self is an unreal object which tends to dominate our perception and distort our relation to the world.

William James, the great nineteenth-century psychologist, when writing about how our minds choose some things and reject others and how such choices can be much the same for many people, goes on to say: 'There is, however, one extraordinary case in which no two men ever are known to choose alike.

One great splitting of the universe into two halves is made by each of us; and for each of us almost all of the interest attaches to one of the halves; but we all draw the line of division between them in a different place. When I say that we all call the two halves by the same names, and that those names are "me" and "not-me" respectively, it will at once be seen what I mean' (James 1890, p. 289). Zen, and all Buddhism, is an attempt to overcome the 'great splitting of the universe' to reveal its delusionary nature and to restore us to the original cosmic unity, not just as a piece of academic knowledge, but as an experienced reality.

Thus we act as though we are something separate from the world. Yet, in truth, none of us actually has any separate inherent existence. This is true in quite simple material ways. As a body, we are constantly in process of exchanging material substance with the 'not-self' world around us: this happens every time we eat, every time we breathe. The body is made up of not-self substances. Our bodies are warm. Is the heat ours? No, it is simply an impersonal quality in which our bodies happen to be sharing at this moment. And so on. Buddhism devotes a good deal of effort to techniques to help us shift the universal delusion that we are each a separately existing self entity. The delusion of self is, in fact, the corner-stone of the whole house of avidya. To realize non-self is to realize the Buddha nature: our identity with the universe.

The object relation theory describes how chitta operates. Either chitta is fixed upon something in the environment or upon something which manas has let through from the alaya. When we are asleep, chitta is almost completely preoccupied with alaya material, which is why dreams provide insight into the basis of our passions.

Object relation theory and root relations theory work together. One shows how perception conditions feelings. The other shows how the kleshas condition perception. Root relations arise according to the way we cling to some objects and reject others. This clinging and rejecting is just our effort to construct and maintain one particular object, the self. While I hold on to self as the most important star in my firmament, everything that I perceive will be distorted since it will all be perceived in terms of such categories as 'useful to me', 'not useful to me', 'pleasant for me', 'unpleasant for me', and so on.

Buddhism offers many techniques for unhooking ourselves from attachment to self-building. These generally involve setting up objects for our mind which draw us away from attachment to self. Thus there are meditations upon the self as an aggregate rather than a unity; upon the decomposition of the body; upon our unity with the cosmos; and upon caring for others. All these practices aim to exploit the fact that mental states are determined by their objects.

Fig. 10. A meditation on the dissolution of the physical body

Each step of the meditation is held for the space of about ten breaths. The guidance may be read out by one member of the meditation group.

1. Breathing in and breathing out, I am aware of my body, warm and alive.
2. Now I imagine my body as a corpse, lifeless and cold.
3. Now I imagine my corpse invaded by maggots.
4. Now I imagine the flesh falling away. I see my skeleton exposed.
5. I see my skeleton white, the flesh all gone.
6. I see my bones separated and scattered.
7. I see my bones disintegrate to dust, blowing away in the wind.
8. I feel the dust becoming part of the earth and the sea.
9. I am aware that my body has completely disappeared.
10. Knowing everything is impermanent, I smile.

The first few times, this meditation may bring up unpleasant feelings. Some variation of it, however, is widely used by Buddhists to help free ourselves from attachment to the body and fear of death. If one does it frequently, one learns to go through the sequence of stages without having to think about the instructions.

Meditation is to dwell on a wholesome object. A wholesome object, in this sense, is anything which leads to clarity and bliss, anything which helps free us from kleshas.

To summarize, object relation theory states that all mental states hang upon the perception of some object. The objects may be real or imaginary things, circumstances or abstractions. People will go to their deaths on behalf of an abstraction like 'the fatherland'. In particular, our construction of ourselves as the most important object in our perceptual world acts as the root of all distortions. This root may be cut by fixing our attention upon objects which bring home to us the real nature of our situation: transience, selflessness and inter-dependence.

Therapeutic Implications

The implications of object relation theory are that the substitution of a wholesome object for an unwholesome one will improve a person's state of well-being. A person who masters the art of transforming displeasing circumstances into blessings has the secret of contentment.

Consider the following dialogue with a client:

Client: I want to talk about the fact that I feel lonely all the time.
Therapist: So some trace of that feeling is with you now.
Client: Yes, yes, it is.
Therapist: You can feel it.
Client: Yes (gestures toward heart area).
Therapist: Now that you are attending to it, I wonder if it brings anything with it . . . a word . . . a picture . . .
Client: I have a picture of a little girl sitting on a big rock . . . a long way away from the people.
Therapist: (speaking slowly and gently) A little girl on a rock . . .
Client: Yes, quite high up . . . there is nobody else there. The other people . . . there are no other people.
Therapist: There aren't any other people there.
Client: No (cries).
Therapist: That image brings a sadness.
Client: (still crying) She's all alone.
Therapist: She's all alone. A little girl all alone.

Client: That's how I feel a lot of the time, even though I'm hardly ever alone. I don't let myself ever be alone. I've had that flat quite a while now and I think I have only been there on my own in the evening twice since I've been there. I always get a friend to visit or I go out.

Therapist: So now you are thinking about your present life, seeing yourself there on your own, feeling desperate to go out.

Client: I don't know why I hate being alone so much. After all, I chose this situation. When I was living with my mother, I could not wait to get to my own house.

Therapist: It is what you wanted then. You wanted to be alone.

Client: Yes, when I was first there, that first week, it was great. It was all wonderful. I was really positive then. I felt free.

Therapist: So this is a different story about yourself. In the first story you hate being alone, and now this is a memory of a time you really enjoyed it.

Client: Yes, it's funny, isn't it? I was so pleased then to be on my own. I wanted lots of space. Now I am just afraid of making a mess of my life.

Therapist: So at that time, you made the decision, you chose to be alone. Now, you are afraid of making the wrong decisions, with nobody to help you.

Client: Yes, I can't bear being alone now.

Therapist: I am still remembering the image of the little girl on the rock.

Client: (smiles faintly)

Therapist: There is something about that image that is important for you.

Client: Yes, I think so. I don't think she *really* minds being alone.

Therapist: (firmly) She's on her rock . . . and there is no one else there.

Client: Yes, that's it. I want to be like that.

Therapist: You want to enjoy being alone, being self-reliant once again.

Client: I do, yes. I don't know where I got the image from. I don't think it is me. I don't have a memory of that.

Therapist: (spontaneously) I have a sense that she is your guardian angel.

Client: (suddenly with tears) Oh! That somehow seems right. Yes. Perhaps she is.

Therapist: So when you are alone, she is there with you, looking after you.

Client: Yes, yes she is.

Therapist: You seem more peaceful now.

Client: I feel calmer. I think this will help me do what I want to do in the future.

Commentary on the dialogue

The therapist focuses upon the here and now. In the now, there is a feeling: loneliness. Is there then an 'object' conditioning this feeling? Yes. The loneliness is conditioned by an image: the girl on the rock. This shift of attention from feeling to perceptual object gives access to the client's experience. It also makes her experience more vivid.

Bringing the image of 'girl on a rock' into my own mind, I also start to feel some of the feelings which the client is experiencing. By setting up the same conditions for myself, I replicate the client's process. Western therapy calls this getting into empathy. Getting into empathy depends upon a replication of the client's experience. All experience is conditioned. If you want to understand the client's experience, replicate the client's conditions for yourself and see what happens.

I repeat the details of the image slowly, letting it sink in both for myself and for her. Dwelling upon the image, we both savour its full flavour. I try to open up as completely as possible to the experience.

As I go back and forth between the image and the feelings it evokes, she starts to talk about her contemporary life. The image of her present life and the image of the girl on the rock are superimposed in her mind. I help to conjure the second image: the image of being at home alone. Feelings always arise in relation to something: they are not an expression of a person's separation from their world, but of their participation in it.

To work with feelings generally implies keeping attention upon whatever it is that gives rise to them, otherwise vitality is lost.

The client remembers that this is not the only image that she has of herself at home. A second story emerges through association. We can have numerous stories around a single scene or set: different mental dramas (actions traces) we can play around the same props. I notice the second story. With it comes another image.

I still have in mind the image of the girl on the rock, intuitively sensing that that part of the story is not yet complete. At this point, I do not know what will transpire from a further consideration of that image, but I offer it. She takes it up again, but this time comes to it directly from her 'second story'. From this changed vantage point, she sees the girl on the rock in a different way. This is an example of association theory which we will look at later. Now, the girl on the rock does not mind being alone. This, then, is a parallel second story of the girl on the rock. I enter into the spirit of this and restate the image adding a tone of voice which reflects the new interpretation which she is putting upon the image. 'She is on her rock' now indicates a position of strength rather than one of weakness.

The client goes on to say that she does not think that the image is herself: it is not a memory. Clearly, however, it is a powerful object in her subjectivity. It plays a magical, poetic or fairy tale role in her life, we might say. I give some flesh to this notion with the phrase 'guardian angel'. This is an intuitive leap. The image of the girl on the rock has transformed into something which can help rather than distress. It has become a guardian spirit.

Some would say that in therapy one should never go beyond what the client has given us. On the other hand, the whole purpose of therapy is to help the client go beyond what they have come with. In order to tune into the client's world, the rule of staying within what the client has expressed is vitally important. Once one has tuned in, however, therapist and client are together occupying a privileged space in which new possibilities may spontaneously occur to either of them. What is crucial then is whether they ring true to the client rather than whether the client actually spoke them first.

One never does actually know the full extent of what the client has given because therapist and client are not two inherently independent systems. The client–therapist is also a unity just as client–client's world is a unity. If one can tune in with all one's attention and care to what the client is expressing and if one can appreciate the delicate interplay between the 'objects' of perception and the 'felt-sense' to which perception gives rise, then the whole of one's own subjectivity begins to resonate with the client. The sequence ends on a calmer note. The sense of self has shifted. It has not disappeared, but it has become looser. This client achieved a great deal in her life over the next two years.

Therapeutic issues illustrated by this dialogue

The client speaks of loneliness. Loneliness is her constant companion. Paradoxically, in an important Zen sense, this client was actually never alone, because she always had this preoccupation with 'loneliness' as her companion, her 'second'. If she were truly alone, there would be no problem. The meaning of aloneness has been examined in an earlier chapter. In this dialogue she did not discover true aloneness, but she changed her companion for a more helpful one.

In the client's subjectivity it is immaterial whether the image is of something real or not. The therapist tunes into the client's images without any particular discrimination in favour of fact or fantasy. The conversation takes place in the therapist's consulting room, so whatever the client tells us about her 'real life' is, at this moment, also fantasy. So, for my client, the girl on the rock and her mother are two characters in her subjective world, both illusory. Exploration of either will unlock important experiences and may generate shifts in how she perceives her world. As we perceive, so do we feel. Consequently, a perceptual shift generates a change in a person's general well-being.

Many therapies fail to make the shift from feeling to perception and so stay locked into an examination of feelings as if they existed in their own right, but in Buddhist psychology all phenomena depend upon conditions and the condition for a feeling is generally a perception.

The images of self, according to Buddhist psychology, are the key determinant of the ways in which perception is distorted and suffering generated. We all hold a considerable stock of self-images. There are many different inner dramas we can each play before our mind's eye and with each of these goes a different set of emotions and behaviours, a different adjustment to life. As we go through the day, we play different films of ourselves to ourselves, and as different images flash before us, so our mood and confidence go through many transformations. These films obscure reality. Therapy may sometimes be concerned with changing the film, sometimes with letting a film go completely.

As films become superimposed one upon another we become more and more removed from clarity. Therapy sometimes offers the opportunity to, if not actually stop the films running, at least separate one from another. This helps the client to return closer to clean, fresh contact with actual experience. The therapist helps by taking each image as no more and no less than it is. Each is taken seriously and its message heeded without allowing its power to be unduly exaggerated. There are greater powers available to the client.

OTHER THERAPY USING THE OBJECT RELATION

In the dialogue considered above, the images were amplified by painting pictures with words. Pictures can also be put on paper or enacted. Sometimes clients bring 'objects' to the session with them. We have evolved a wide range of ways of using art, poetry and creative craft work for therapeutic ends. Work with natural materials, especially, has therapeutic effect. The methods of psychodrama, too, can be readily harmonized with this Buddhist object relation theory (cf. Holmes 1992).

Zen thus leads us to a therapeutic attitude which has great respect for the client's world: what they see around them, not just what they consider to be 'inside' themselves. Although we might think a meditation-based therapy would be completely introspective, Zen is actually very practical. Subjective experience is experience of a world, so we must pay attention to that world. The idea of what is 'inside' and what 'outside' begins to dissolve. A person's conscious life is a succession of perceptions of 'objects'. If the therapist is to tune in, it is necessary not so much to see the client as to see the client's world. If, as therapist, I simply focus upon the client, and keep saying, 'Yes, but what about you?' I am likely to strengthen their self-preoccupation rather than weaken it and this can be sterile, leading to interminable analysis. From a Zen viewpoint, much contemporary therapy may be counter-productive.

The koan method too attempts to shift a person out of self-centredness. The mental construction of a self-centred universe inevitably generates contradictions. These crystallize as koans, life tests, which may drive a person to seek therapy. The client wants the therapist to remove the source of discomfort. The koan, however, represents an opportunity for bringing matters to a head, and the Zen therapist is likely to approach it with this in mind. In Zen temples special koans are designed for trainees to study. The best koan, however, generally emerges naturally out of daily life.

THE HERE AND NOW

Zen Master Dogen advocated that we forget our selfish selves for a while and let our minds be natural. Then we will be close to the mind of the bodhisattva (Kennett 1976, p. 125). Clear seeing is not something abstruse. The basic practices of Zen are very simple. Master Lin Chi said: 'The true miracle is to walk upon the earth.'

Many of the recorded statements of the great Zen masters are poetic. They bring ordinary experience to an exquisite pitch. When we are in touch with this present moment, cares about the past and future can evaporate. If we were suddenly unable to breathe, we would be desperate and the only thing that would hold our attention would be the necessity to get air. Our mind would be focused with great intensity upon one object. We would, at such a moment, know that being able to breathe is

Fig. 11. Ten points on Buddhist object relation theory
1. Feelings (and other states) are conditioned by perceptions.
2. Ascertaining the object of perception helps us understand the inner state.
3. Amplifying the object, e.g., by drama or vivid language, intensifies the experience.
4. Replicating the client's conditions using our own imagination generates empathy.
5. Clarity is aided by separating out different objects which are superimposed.
6. A therapeutic gain can come from substituting a helpful object for a malign one.
7. Attachment to objects supports some aspect of self-complex.
8. Loosening the hold of particular objects loosens the hold of self.
9. Focusing attention on objects which are real and immediately present, such as the breath, or a flower, helps the mind to return to its natural home and allows the self-passion to cool.
10. Natural objects (mountains, rivers, clouds, the sea, etc.) are naturally therapeutic.

the most precious thing in life. And yet, this miracle of breathing is available to us all the time. Why then not appreciate it?

Zen Master Nhat Hanh (1993b) offers us this simple meditation exercise:

> Breathing in, I calm my body.
> Breathing out, I smile.
> Breathing in, I dwell in the present moment.
> Breathing out, I know it is a wonderful moment.

By returning to the breath we unhook ourselves from the objects that give rise to dukkha, ill-being. Similarly, a great deal can be achieved by consciousness of natural objects. In Zen literature there is profound respect for the natural world and the peace of mind that arises from communing with it. Thus, Yoka Daishi wrote:

> Since I understood the unborn
> I have had no reason for joy or sorrow

When honoured or disgraced.
I have entered the silence and beauty of the mountains;
In a deep valley beneath high cliffs
I sit beneath the tall pines.
Meditating in my rustic cottage
I have peace, solitude and true comfort.

A person who is suffering may sometimes be helped more by a gentle walk through beautiful countryside, by seeing smiling faces and beautiful flowers, than by recounting a catalogue of misfortunes which have beset them in life. We do need to do something about the weeds which grow in our garden, but it is necessary to water the good seeds too.

THE THEORY OF PREDOMINANCE (Adhipati)

Predominance theory tells us that our lives are conditioned by those forces which predominate in our mentality. Further, although the mind is commonly dominated by the self-passion and its associated kleshas, there are more powerful forces available which, when mobilized, can exert a more wholesome influence.

When something is esteemed particularly it will dominate our perception. In the uncultivated mind, dominance is determined by the illusion of self and the kleshas. However, the real predominants are intention (*chandra*), energy (*virya*), attention (*chitta*) and enquiry (*vimamsa*). These, which collectively we may call purposefulness in the moment, have the power to override the unwholesome roots.

This theory extends those of object and root relations. We have already discussed how the object 'self' tends to dominate and distort. This basic distortion gives rise to the three bitter roots and soon the garden of our mind is overrun with weeds. Predominance theory shows that this is not an inevitable state of affairs. It reveals the tools at the mind gardener's disposal.

Zen harmonizes 'self-power' and 'other-power'. This does not mean that self is cultivated. It means we rely upon our own purposefulness rather than divine intervention or luck, but we believe that when we put energy out in this way, the universe unfailingly responds. Vigorous self-training without thought of reward is the result: what Zen Master Dogen called to train 'using the same energy we would employ if our hair were to catch fire' (Kennett 1976, pp. 123). Predominance theory is an assertion of the value of purposeful action. Purposefulness in the Zen sense, however, is not the same as becoming attached to a goal. It means being responsive, in a wholesome way, to whatever reality asks of us. This is a kind of spontaneity akin to that described by Jacob Moreno (cf. Moreno 1985) in which action is always adequate to reality.

In therapy, therefore, it is a major step forward when the client's sense of purpose becomes apparent. Listening for the client's motives and aspirations, we can sense the direction of their energy, seeing what holds their interest, intrigues or perplexes them. From these seeds a change of heart may emerge.

A client comes to see me feeling apathetic. Her successful career was interrupted a few years ago by a near fatal car accident. She continues to receive substantial income and lacks for nothing, yet she feels completely unenthusiastic about her life. What becomes apparent is that this person has lived, as many do, completely under the influence of acquisitiveness. Then, a brush with death brought home the pointlessness of her existence. What is the use of all she has accumulated if she might die any time? She thinks she knows no other way of being, such is the spiritual impoverishment of our times. Yet, as she talks, it becomes apparent that there are some things which still hold her attention – music, animals, dancing. These are not, perhaps, ultimate satisfactions, but they are positive objects, things beyond herself into which she may invest some care. As such they may provide a basis for new intentions and energy, new direction in her life.

MORITA PSYCHOTHERAPY

Morita psychotherapy is a Japanese approach which incorporates many elements from Zen. It does not attempt to remove the client's troubling symptoms. It aims to help clients live well in spite of them. 'The goal of therapy is to help the clients achieve satisfactory control over what they do in life . . . character growth rather than symptom reduction . . . as the clients take proper control of their behaviour, attending to what reality brings them to do and doing it well, their suffering and complaints diminish' (Reynolds 1989, p. 11).

Morita is a mixture of education and self-training, meditation and action. The client engages in self-study with guidance from the therapist who focuses upon the practical concrete detail of daily life. How can a person improve their marriage? Take home small presents. Perform secret services for their spouse. Say thank you more often. Tidy the house. How can I cure my neurosis? Try going to the park and clearing up some of the litter, or going to help out on a soup run for the homeless. If this is too much, try really looking at flowers or noticing the people who walk past. Morita therapy helps people to improve their lives by improving the quality of each little thing they do, undertaking purposeful activity in a good spirit.

'Life, in the Moritist view, is lived moment by moment. Reality presents itself this way. The problems and emotions associated with victimization are present concerns for a victim only when they are actually noticed in a given moment. There is an ebb and flow to emotions. There is no repository of anger, fear or anxiety "bottled up" or hidden within. There are no angry persons, fearful persons or anxious persons, only persons who have moments of anger, moments of fear, moments of anxiety . . . One of the goals . . . is to help victims attend fully to what needs to be done in their lives rather than exclusively focusing on how they are feeling' (Reynolds 1989, p. 75).

Morita includes several specific methods. One of these is a week of secluded bed rest with no distractions. The patient is not allowed to read, write, listen to the radio or anything of the kind. From this, as from Zen meditation, one learns to observe the uncontrollable comings and goings of feelings and thoughts, and develops an appetite for activity.

A second method is engagement with a wide range of practical activities. After the secluded rest, this mobilizes energy constructively. A third method is the keeping of a structured diary of daily activities with separate columns for what cannot and what can be controlled. Feelings and thought go into the first column and behaviour goes into the second. The therapist reads and annotates the diary. These notes challenge the client's morbid life philosophy. Seminars and lectures are also given. Thus the client learns through experience that although feelings are not directly controllable, new patterns of action can be established which will lead to quite different and much more satisfactory feelings in the future.

Morita therapy has a distinctly Zen flavour in: 1. helping clients pay attention to the quality of ordinary daily actions; 2. stressing the value of service to others; 3. not being primarily centred on feelings; 4. valuing tranquillity; 5. not accepting a victim mentality; and 6. putting the client in situations where the opportunity for experiential learning (*taiken*) will be maximized. Therapy does not necessarily take place in a clinic or counselling room. The therapist may go for a walk with the client, or go with him to a restaurant or join her in other activities where there will be opportunity to observe how the client goes about the details of daily life.

Zen is an approach in which the will plays an important role. The Buddha was helped by many teachers, but finally achieved enlightenment on his own. He started with a strong determination and went through many hardships in his search for truth. His dying words to his followers were: 'Seek out the Way with all diligence.' Nothing is achieved by allowing our lives to drift except that the three poisons become stronger. There is a story of a man who loses control of the horse he is riding being asked where he is going. He replies, 'I don't know, ask the horse.' When our lives are like that, predominance theory tells us that although we may feel we are being swept along by factors beyond our control, the important things in life are controllable. We can establish a wholesome approach to life. The universe will respond.

SUMMARY

In chapters eight and nine we have looked briefly at the first three theories of conditioning listed in the Pattana. These are simple psychological principles with wide-reaching implications.

We have seen how they relate to psychotherapy practice and how they begin to provide a framework for understanding the mind. We have examined:

1. Root relations (hetu paccaya)
2. Object relation (arammana paccaya) and
3. Predominance (adhipati paccaya)

Object relation theory shows how all mental states depend upon perception of objects and in particular how one object, the self, exerts a particularly distorting influence. Root relations theory shows how the myriad obscurations of consciousness brought about by attachment to objects can be reduced to three basic forms and how each of these has a corresponding antidote. Predominance theory shows how the mind has resources by which the dominant and distorting effects of some objects can be overcome.

We have seen how root relations theory gives some pointers toward a system of psychiatric diagnostic categories and also how it keys in with the person-centred theory of core conditions. We have seen how object relation theory corresponds in some ways with psychoanalytic ideas and also with the principles of western phenomenology. Predominance theory establishes the importance of 'purposefulness in the moment' in Buddhist psychology and we have briefly looked at how this works out in the distinctive methods of Morita therapy. In the next chapter we will continue our exploration of Buddhist psychological principles.

· 10 ·

Association

THEORIES OF ASSOCIATION
(Anantara and samanantara)

The theory of association (anantara) states that each mental impulse is conditioned by those which immediately precede it and the theory of orderly association (samanantara) states that impulses flow from one into another in a natural sequence according to their nature.

Consciousness flows in an unending stream of thoughts, feelings, images and sensations. Each holds our attention briefly. Impulses arise from nowhere and go nowhere, yet looking back we can generally see how we got from A to B to C. When we experience a sequence of impulses repeatedly, a track gets worn in our mind, like a path across a field. Our minds are a maze of such trackways. Association theory studies how each impulse stimulates something related to itself in the next thought moment. As soon as we start off in one direction, a whole sequence of impulses arises: we are on a track. A positive impulse sets up more of the same. Similarly for negative impulses. Each shapes the next. There is inertia in the human mind.

This accords with general experience. The most difficult step in any attempt to change our mental habits is the first one. The sooner we start the more experiences we have which point us in the right direction. The life process is self-reinforcing whether headed for heaven or for hell. Thus, in therapy, it is very important to notice every positive impulse the client has. One will lead to another.

Association is not determination, however. Nobody is all

good nor all bad, so there is always freedom to choose. In the last section, Predominance, we learned the importance of finding and using our will. By doing so, we can choose positive associations rather than negative ones. With mindfulness, we can always choose good associations if we wish, whatever has gone before, and with wisdom, we can transform bad associations too. Mindfulness and wisdom are thus the tools with which we cultivate the mind.

Association theory is used differently in Zen from its equivalent in western psychology. Although we westerners tend to think of ourselves as active and of Buddhism as a passive religion, the western concept of a person has become more and more that of a victim, whereas the Buddhist view is that everyone is the gardener of their own life. This latter perspective is held particularly strongly in Zen.

In the west, we take refuge in material conditions. We are only active in the sense that our first thought is almost always about our material interests. This is essentially a victim mentality, full of distrust. We remain at the mercy of conditions. The tendency to regard ourselves as victims, however, goes even deeper than this. We have come to think of ourselves as victims of our unconscious mind.

Therapy is commonly seen as the recovery of memories from the distant past which are thought to determine our current life. The earlier the memory, the more powerful the effect is held to be. This is a rather fatalistic view which Zen rejects. What association theory does predict is that the longer we have lived negatively, the more ready our mind will be to fall into negative states if we simply allow it to wander unchecked; but we do not have to let it do so.

Radiant mental health is not achieved by casting blame at people from one's distant past. The act of blaming is itself a negative impulse which will set the ball rolling in a negative direction. Positive conditions include appreciation of one's life as it is, with all the different impulses it now includes, which make us fully human. If these include bitterness, we must face that too.

Our task is to look deeply into our nature and discover that it is not cut off. Some therapies mistakenly lead people to feel more cut off by, for instance, encouraging conflict between clients and their parents. Yet, by inevitable association, our parents live in us and we will not find peace by hating them. Our ancestors and we ourselves all need to be understood, not condemned. Modern society has, in fact, become quite callous in its disregard of older people who are no longer productive, as if a person's only worth were what they give or gave us. Productivity is no measure of a person. Whatever their lives may have been like, and however much we may resist the idea, we will always be associated with our forebears in our own mental continuum. To deride them is to deride ourselves.

ONE GOOD MIND LEADS TO ANOTHER

So, association theory is used in Buddhist practice, not to expose and reinforce enmity, but to set the mind on a more positive course. The remedies it indicates are often quite straightforward.

Thus those who are suffering from bad experiences need care and kindness. This is simple and obvious, but all too often ignored. Consider our treatment of offenders, for instance. Our general idea is to punish. We think that a person who has done wrong will suddenly start doing right if we give them more bad experiences. It does not work. If we consider our prisons and so-called 'reformatories', the more punitive they are, the worse their recidivism rates tend to be. This is well known, but ignored by public policy because of our anger. The klesha of hate obscures the facts.

Punishment has no place in a Buddhist psychology. Foolish actions have naturally unpleasant consequences enough. Wrong-doers need rescuing, not hurting more. A person who is out of control may need to be confined for their own good and they may find this irksome, but if those who do the confining are motivated by a wish to harm rather than help, how are they themselves better than criminals? The offender is not separate from ourselves.

We can seek ways to make others successful. Such consideration dispels helplessness (cf. Seligman 1975). Marriages, for instance, only flourish when each partner thinks about how to make the other successful in their own way. Each person is a flower which needs the best possible conditions in which to bloom (Hanh 1992, pp. 11 *et seq.*). When those around us bloom, we will live in a beautiful garden. Ideally we should try to create such conditions for all sentient beings. At least we should do so for those we love. Yet, too often, relationships become a battleground. Obscured by kleshas, we convince ourselves the other person can be made nicer to live with by our saying the most hurtful things to them. If we want a flower to grow beautiful and smell sweet, we have to water it. And we are all flowers.

Therapy begins with finding ways to give good experiences. This may begin with a smile. It grows with our efforts to understand. There is a place in therapy for small acts of genuine kindness. Depression may gradually be overcome by exposure to beauty, nature and pleasing relationships. As new experiences accumulate they gradually reach a point where they outweigh the bad. This is how people recover. Put balm upon the wound. The best therapy is compassion, love and understanding.

WESTERN ASSOCIATION THEORY

At the turn of the century, psychologists were very interested in the flow of consciousness. William James (1890), in very Zen-like style, wrote:

> The first fact for us, then, as psychologists, is that thinking of some sort goes on. I use the word thinking . . . for every form of consciousness indiscriminately. If we could say in English 'It thinks,' as we say 'It rains' or 'It blows,' we should be stating the fact most simply and with the minimum of assumption. As we cannot, we must simply say that *thought goes on* . . . How does it go on? . . .
>
> 1. Every thought tends to be part of a personal consciousness.
> 2. Within each personal consciousness thought is always changing.

3. Within each personal consciousness thought is sensibly continuous.

4. It always appears to deal with objects independent of itself.

5. It is interested in some parts of these objects to the exclusion of others, and welcomes or rejects – *chooses* from among them, in a word – all the while. (pp. 224–225)

This reads very like Abhidharma. James offered two theories very similar to those we are looking at: the 'law of contiguity' and the 'law of association'. The law of contiguity states that 'objects once experienced together tend to become associated in the imagination, so that when any one of them is thought of, the others are likely to be thought of also, in the same order of sequence or co-existence as before' (ibid., p. 561) and the law of association that 'when two elementary brain processes have been active together or in immediate succession, one of them, on reoccurring, tends to propagate its excitement into the other' (ibid., p. 566).

Shortly after this, C. G. Jung embarked upon researches into word association. This was an experimental method for exploring mind tracks. He studied sequences of spontaneous thoughts and thoughts evoked by given stimulus words. Stevens (1990, p. 32) tells us that 'the *laws of association*' were worked out by academic psychology at the end of the nineteenth century. He calls them 'the *law of similarity* and the *law of contiguity*'. Jung used them to explain how an 'archetype' gets translated into a 'complex'. In Jung's system, archetypes are the instinctive expectations we have of life, born out of the experience of our species over millennia, and complexes are the personal mental constructions we unconsciously hold which shape our individual lives. Stevens explains: 'Let us take, for example, the development of the mother complex in the child's maturing psyche. The complex is formed and becomes active as a consequence of the child's living in close *contiguity* to a woman (usually the mother) whose behaviour is *similar* to the child's built-in anticipation of maternity (the mother archetype) . . . Later in life, the same complex can be *projected* on to other older women, or on to institutions or public figures, which perform the maternal role' (ibid., p. 32).

Jung discovered that just as roadways converge upon major centres of population, so tracks in the mind all converge upon conglomerations of mental contents which he called complexes. Using this geographical analogy, we could say that the Zen method helps us return to the open country of the mind and not spend all our time in its cities. The more dominated by 'complexes' a mind is, the less open it is to new experience. In Buddhism, these complexes are called the 'passions'.

Jung showed how spontaneous associations reveal the mind's secrets. This is what lies behind the so-called 'Freudian slip' (Freud 1901). Every good therapist notices the associations which a client makes in the course of dialogue, as this provides a route into the 'cities' of the client's mind. If the client has been talking about her church and then suddenly is talking about her boyfriend, we know this is not just a random sequence, even if we do not yet know what the connection is. We know that these two topics will prove to be like two planets orbiting a single deeper concern which may emerge into clarity in due course.

The extent to which we are dominated by passions is the measure of our madness. Were this development to become complete we would lose touch with reality altogether. Writing about madness, Jung says: 'The alienation from reality, the loss of interest in objective events, are not hard to explain when one considers that schizophrenics are permanently under the spell of an insuperable complex. Anyone whose whole interest is captivated by a complex must be dead to his environment' (Jung 1907, p. 98). This statement becomes even more telling when we realize that the ego is a complex and we ask ourselves how much of our own interest is not captivated by it. We ourselves are, as we saw in the last chapter, our most dangerous passion.

TRACKLESS ZEN

To counteract the effect of the passions we need mindfulness (*sati*). When practising mindfulness, we notice what we are doing. Each noticing becomes a new starting point which could, if followed, be the beginning of a track leading back to one of the metropolises of the mind. However, when one is being mindful, one does not take a second step along the track, since there is a new observation of reality to be made. Each moment of time requires us to notice something new. Thus we stay in touch with reality rather than being pulled into inner circlings. The word sati originally meant 'stop' – stopping the habit of circling down into the passions.

In Zen we practise a particular form of meditation called 'just sitting' (*shikantaza*). Shikantaza is to sit without letting any train of thought develop. Generally, when a person sits with nothing to do, the mind wanders. Once it starts down a track, it can be some time before it returns to awareness. We become oblivious to our surroundings as a day-dream or line of thought unfolds. In shikantaza, no wandering. We keep returning to the immediate present, so that what gets reinforced is not track-building, but awareness.

Shikantaza opens the windows of the mind in a new way. Following tracks we miss a lot. We just see the same old things again and again. In fact we do not even see them. We take them for granted and life just passes us by.

So Zen is like living every moment as both the first and last moment of existence. In the first moment, we are fresh, alive, vital, and clear. We are in a state of awe. In the last moment, we know nothing else matters. We do not treat what is happening as a step on the way to somewhere else because we are not going anywhere. Each step is all there is. So, when doing Zen, we are not on a track. We are simply sipping the delicious nectar of this very moment. Zen Master Dogen wrote: 'Mountains, rivers, earth, the sun, the moon, and the stars are mind. At just this moment, what is it that appears directly in front of you?' (Tanahashi 1985, p. 88).

ZEN TANTRA

In Buddhism, there are three main approaches to self-training. First is the path of the renunciant. This person trains by changing the circumstances of their life quite radically. They cut off all distractions and fill their life solely with experiences which reinforce commitment to the spiritual path. Buddha recommended that renunciants spend lengthy periods away from cities in the forest or mountains and adopt a simple lifestyle. On a lesser scale, we all know how refreshing it can be to 'get away from it all' for a time. All Buddhists try to find at least some periods for retreat. Once, when the stress of modern life was becoming particularly burdensome, I was fortunate to spend several months away in the country, living out of doors for the most part, meditating and engaging in practical tasks. The effect was wonderfully restorative. Even if we cannot live outside, there is much to be said for making our home environment peaceful and beautiful, with space and plants and objects around us that remind us of our Zen practice.

The second approach relies not so much upon changing our circumstances as on changing the way in which we act. This is the bodhisattva path. A bodhisattva is someone who feels the suffering of others. A bodhisattva is active in the world. Bodhisattvas train by service to others. A modern bodhisattva might be a therapist. The bodhisattva sees the world through the eyes of others. Even if someone robs her, the bodhisattva understands the need of the robber.

Finally, there is a third approach, called tantra. Tantra means to go directly to the 'pure land' by reconstructing every experience as a blessing. We ourselves thereby become divine beings. 'Through the practice of dharma we can come to change the way in which we experience things because, given that they have no ultimate reality in and of themselves, there is no reason for [negative] aspects of experience to dominate us. We are perfectly able, with the practice of dharma, to know the benefit that comes from being able to take control over our own experience,' says the great Tibetan lama Kalu Rimpoche (Kalu 1987, p. 16). Tantric practitioners consider the peacock a good symbol of their path, since it flourishes eating berries which other species find poisonous.

When we first read about tantra, we may think it is just pretending, but this is to overlook the influence manas already has on our perception. Liedloff, for instance, gives this account of an occasion when her expedition, consisting of Europeans and South American Indians, had to portage a large boat round a set of rapids:

All were doing the same work: all were experiencing strain and pain. There was no difference in our situations except that *we* had been conditioned by our culture to believe that such a combination of circumstances constituted an unquestionable low on the scale of well-being and were quite unaware that we had any option in the matter. The Indians, on the other hand, equally unconscious of making a choice, were in a particularly merry state of mind, revelling in the camaraderie. (Leidloff 1986, p. 25.)

We are conditioned to regard anything hard as undesirable. But it could just as well be fun. We are already colouring all our experience. If we can colour it one way, then we are just as capable of colouring it differently (cf. Apter 1989).

Zen integrates all three approaches. It is firmly based in the renunciant tradition of early Buddhism. It has developed the bodhisattva path in all its fullness and it incorporates the tantric (or *shingon*) method. Thus an important Zen text is the Lotus Sutra chapter on Avalokita, bodhisattva of compassion. According to the text, Avalokita appears in any form, anywhere, any time. This is basically a tantric text. The method it enjoins upon the practitioner is to regard everything that happens as a manifestation of Avalokita, which is to say, as an act of the utmost compassion.

Three ways this kind of transformation practice can be used in therapy are:

1. Finding the good seeds
2. Changing our sense of identity
3. Establishing a helpful vision

Finding the good seeds means looking deeply. A client tells the therapist that she was sexually abused by both parents. Now she has a child of her own and her mother is threatening to abuse this child too. The client says, 'I hate my mother.' Where are the good seeds in this situation? The fact that the client has come to discuss this hints that 'I hate my mother' is not the whole story. The client actually does not want to hate. However, overriding her concern for her mother is her maternal instinct. Two powerful human instincts, that of being a daughter and being a mother, are in conflict and being a mother has to prevail. As we begin to understand, we see that here is a person who is functioning very appropriately. She has to separate from her mother for the sake of her child. This is difficult to do, so she has to generate a powerful head of emotional energy. This finds expression in the statement 'I hate my mother.' When the client says this, she does not really want the therapist to reinforce the hatred. She needs the therapist to understand the dilemma she is in. When the therapist does so, and the client's very proper urge to protect her child is affirmed, there is less need for her to keep the hate going. It now transpires that the client's mother was also sexually abused. The client actually has some understanding and compassion for her mother; just, she knows that she must not let this prevent her from protecting herself and her baby. This case illustrates a situation which is inherently extremely distressing. However, it also shows that even in such difficult circumstances, the client is generally trying their best to act in a wholesome way.

Changing the sense of identity: A client in conditions like those just described is liable to be aware of a great range of kleshas in themselves: hate, envy, rage, misery and so on. It is easy to conclude, when one finds such things, that one is a not very good person. However, according to Buddhist psychology, all the energy in the kleshas is good energy. Kleshas are only illusory. In a recent popular cartoon film, one of the characters is given the line: 'I'm not really bad, I'm just drawn that way'(!). The kleshas are like that. This client's hate is not a sign that she is an evil person. It is simply one interpretation of the very proper impulse to separate and thereby save her child. It is a good energy. Although the client may begin by believing that evil forces are at work in them, the therapist sees nothing of the kind. In time, the client too accepts what they have always intuitively known at some level, that the source from which their life energy all flows is immaculate.

Through Zen practice we learn not to identify with any of these things. If hate arises, that is interesting. If joy arises, that is interesting too. Neither of these is me. When we disidentify with the kleshas we can have compassion for them too and understand their true function.

Establishing a helpful vision: Zen trainees may learn to visualize the traditional form of Quan-yin as ever close at hand. Sometimes Quan-yin is depicted with a thousand hands, each able to reach out and help. In each hand there is an eye so that the help given shall not be blind. This visualization helps us to reconceptualize the kleshas as the helping hands of Quan-yin. In a more general way, having the sense of a helpful presence can support us through many difficult situations. The precise symbolism of an oriental figure does not have to be used. A client of mine learned to carry with him an image of a mountain he had visited on holiday. This vision brought with it a particular quality of serenity which he had experienced there. The mountain helped him cope with many difficult situations at work, and so was Quan-yin for him. Visualization practices are often taught as formal meditation exercises. They are also, however, a very useful aid to daily living. All day long our imagination affects our actions and moods. By deliberately cultivating a helpful image and building up many associations with it, we take charge of this natural process and redirect it for the benefit of ourselves and others.

SUMMARY

The mind is conditioned by association. Habitual mind-tracks develop, blunting our awareness of immediate reality. These tracks converge upon and sustain the passions, particularly the capital city of the deluded mind which is the self-passion. Zen practice counteracts association conditioning in four ways:

1. deliberately creating good associations by surrounding ourselves with wholesome things and separating from unwholesome ones;
2. adopting patterns of action which set us on a positive course;
3. transforming adverse circumstances into blessings; and
4. undermining the whole process of track formation by mindfulness meditation.

Association theory brings our attention to some basic facts about how to make a person better: facts which one might have said were obvious were it not that they are so often ignored in our treatment of one another. Good moments matter. If we can bring our client a good moment, this is never wasted. It will always be there as a good association.

· 11 ·

All Change

(Sahajati and Annyamannya)

The theory of co-birth (sahajati) states that all the elements of samsara, although seemingly separate and interacting, are actually part and parcel of one another, all arising together. Each dimension of samsara is conditioned by the others. The theory of co-dependence (annyamannya) states that these same fundamentals are also coterminous. When one ceases, they all cease.

There are times in life when everything changes. Life does not proceed in a neat, linear, orderly way. Every so often we turn a corner. The approach adopted by Zen is strongly influenced by the fact that Gotama Shakyamuni, who became the Buddha, trained himself for many years with different teachers, undergoing many tests and hardships and learning many lessons, but his enlightenment, when it came, was a sudden event. It happened at Buddh Gaya in northern India, on a particular spring night, when the Buddha, who had been sitting in meditation for many hours, saw the morning star rise. This kind of transformative experience is called *kensho*.

It had been clear that Gotama's struggle to understand the question which most deeply concerned him, the question of human suffering, was coming to a head. Long practice of austerities had taken him to its very depths but was not, of itself, going to yield him the goal he sought. He therefore began to accept food once again and set himself to sit in meditation in a final supreme attempt to gain the truth. He sat under a pipal or *bodhi* tree on a grass mat and meditated into the night.

What then happened was that he was assailed by 'Mara'. Mara is a character who appears in the Buddhist texts in a rather similar way to the devil in Christianity. His name means the one who snatches our life away. Enlightenment can also be called *amara*, the state in which we never let life get snatched away from us. The appearance of Mara, therefore, is a graphic way of saying that all the forces which stood in Gotama's way marshalled their strength against him. The hosts of Mara are the kleshas: lust, aversion, hunger, thirst, graspingness, laziness, cowardice, doubt, hypocrisy, foolishness, desire for gain and glory, and disparagement of others are some of those listed in the classical descriptions of the enlightenment. Gotama stood firm against them and, as he did so, they disappeared, to be succeeded by a rain of heavenly flowers. This breakthrough was accompanied by a flood of profound insight. Within a few hours, at most, there came to him a clear understanding of the real nature of the universe. He saw the roots of his own existence back into the depths of time past, and understood how all things arise interdependently. Seeing the dawn, that spring morning, he saw the unity of the cosmos.

This event changed his life and, indeed, was a turning point in world history. Similar things could be said about the experiences which Jesus had in the desert, which are described in the Bible in very similar terms:

Jesus was then led away by the Spirit into the wilderness, to be tempted by the devil. For forty days and nights he fasted, and at the end of them he was famished. The tempter approached him . . . and showed him all the kingdoms of the world in their glory. 'All these,' he said, 'I will give you, if you will only fall down and do me homage.' But Jesus said, 'Begone, Satan; Scripture says, "You shall do homage to the Lord your God and worship him alone."' Then the devil left him, and angels appeared. (Matthew ch. 4)

According to Zen, these descriptions tell us not just what happens to spiritual super-heroes remote from our lives. Rather, they give us a picture of the essential elements of how every person can radically change the direction of their life. Often the experience involves passing through a relatively short period when the person experiences an 'altered state of consciousness' as a result of abandoning a self-centred position. It is like scales falling from one's eyes. Everything is seen with a clarity and radiance never experienced before. Not everyone will necessarily have an experience which conforms to the classic descriptions of kensho, since each of us is different, and there is no point in seeking such experience for its own sake. Nonetheless, everybody is capable of sudden changes of heart, which can be of remarkable profundity and generate lasting improvements in quality of life. Zen practice aims to increase the likelihood of such a radical breakthrough occurring.

Interdependence theory alerts us to the fact that our lives in samsara are built like a house of cards. When one card falls, they all come down. Thus radical change is possible for anybody who seriously sets out to do something about themselves. We are talking here about a change of heart and mind: the experiential realization that there is an altogether better way to be.

Of course, we all know that when we make an effort to change, we immediately run into obstacles. Anyone who has tried to diet knows the pitfalls. The problem with dieting, however, is that the dieter is generally not trying to bring about a wholesale change in their way of being, they are just trying to lose some weight. The dieter wants everything else to stay much the same. According to interdependence theory, this does not work.

When the spiritual practitioner decides to fast, they do so, not to lose weight, but to bring the kleshas out into the open where they can be seen and dealt with. The quickest way to bring Mara's hosts to battle is to give something up. If we are conditioned to surrender as soon as Mara appears, however, our diet will not get very far. If we confront Mara joyfully, he is soon transformed into a rain of flowers (or angels). To use this principle it is not necessary to believe in Mara or the devil as metaphysical beings. We are not talking here about ghosts and goblins. We are creating a picture of what happens in everybody's mind when they decide to make some changes.

What we are talking about here, therefore, is the way to break our conditioning. Generally, we find that changes do not stick when they are just based on information. There have been many campaigns to get people to give up smoking, for instance. Everybody now knows that by smoking they greatly increase the likelihood of dying sooner in a very unpleasant way. Very often, however, this information, in itself, only has the effect of frightening people. If the person's conditioned reaction to feeling fear is to light a cigarette, this kind of information may not help them. To give up smoking, or any other addiction, one has to change a whole pattern of life. The lifestyle and the habit are born together, die together. This is the interdependence theory.

Another common illustration is that people come into therapy and do begin to change one aspect of their lives; then, if the change is serious and sustained, we soon find the client reporting changes in many other areas of life as well. In some ways, this is a problem. A client comes into therapy in order to deal with what at first seems a straightforward and encapsulated problem, like anxiety at work, for instance. Quite soon they may be reconsidering their marriage, relating differently to their parents and children, seeing less of old friends and finding new ones. This can be quite disruptive for the other people in their life. The client, although now making these changes themselves, probably did not realise quite what they were entering into when they came for their first therapy consultation.

So a way of life is made up of interdependent parts. The mind too is, as we saw in the last chapter, dominated by a network of interdependent passions (complexes). When one changes, they all change. When a new one comes into being, all the others have to adapt. When one is given up, all are weakened.

Zen transforms the passions. It is more useful to talk here of transformation than of abolition. In the temptation of Jesus, the devil disappeared and angels appeared. In the enlightenment of Gotama, Mara vanished and celestial flowers cascaded down. When we observe the kleshas with the clear eye of enlightenment we see that they all actually are creative energy in disguise. When this energy finds its natural path, it no longer appears in an evil guise. According to Buddhist theory, therefore, strictly speaking, there is no such thing as evil, only ignorance. When we understand, we can forgive and feel genuine love and compassion.

Passions are transformed by self-study. This does not mean self-indulgence. It means that we undertake to study the way our heart and mind work by developing mindfulness. We aim to achieve complete awareness. We watch the kleshas arise, see how they affect us and watch them depart again. We study them with a degree of dispassion, but also with enthusiasm for the task, just as we might set about studying the habits of a timid or stealthy animal. The client is encouraged to embark upon the investigation of how their own body-mind functions, by simple non-judgemental observation.

i) Jealousy

A client came to see me suffering from compulsive jealousy. He cannot bear his wife to so much as glance in the direction of another man. This condition is ruining his life. Most of his energy is consumed trying to prevent his wife doing anything which will bring her into the vicinity of men. In modern society, this covers just about everything she might ever do. Consequently he is always desperately unhappy and flies into a rage with her over small actions on her part which were completely innocent. Talking to me he knows that he is being irrational, but when he is out of my consulting room he is unable to control himself. His is not a particularly unusual condition and it is certainly one which therapists need to know how to respond to.

From what we have learned of Buddhist psychology so far, we can have confidence that this client can indeed control and change his behaviour and that, once a different pattern has become established, the present distressing cycle will fade. However, the client will not be able to avert his usual pattern so long as he does not see it coming. The first task for the client, therefore, is not so much to learn a method for averting the jealousy, but rather to devote some energy to studying it. When he has studied it carefully his way of being will probably shift of its own accord. This study can happen to some extent during the therapy sessions – client and therapist working together – and to some extent will be carried on by the client on his own. He learns to watch the symptom without in any way attempting to alter its course.

As the client's concentrated study of the symptom continues, he will begin to develop mindfulness. He will notice times when the jealousy is *not* present. He will begin to notice what signs occur when it is coming on. He will notice other emotions. Since this client is already motivated to change, once he has developed some capacity for mindfulness he will probably effect the remainder of the therapy himself without my assistance. Awareness induces natural change. Thus he will discover experientially the capacity he has for change and for inner calm. This will stand him in good stead, not only in this crisis, but in life generally. Not only will his jealousy change, but his outlook on life as a whole will shift. He will stop conceptualizing himself as a victim of circumstance.

ii) Anger

Another client comes to see me, also to talk about marital problems. The situation is complex, but within it we identify one strand which is my client's burning rage. 'My spouse has a bad temper, but I am even worse,' she tells me. The story unfolds and there are indeed many pretexts for anger in the way these two people, who once loved each other enough to marry, now relate to one another.

In addition to specific incompatibilities between the marital partners, she also mentions repeatedly the injustice of the modern wife's position, needing to have a career while still being expected to do all the housework: a valid point. I stop her and say I have noticed that, even though she knows I agree with her, she is still becoming very agitated in her manner while talking about this subject. She agrees. In her mind's eye she is not talking to me, she is addressing her husband.

Now, there are, no doubt, many ways to work with this case. One could see the husband and wife together and work toward mutual understanding. One could work with the woman and help her identify the roots of her rage in her identification with her mother who lived a singularly down-trodden life with a domineering husband. One could affirm the justice of her views and support the growth of her self-esteem through her identification with a just cause. All and any of these approaches might be useful and one could think of many other ways of helping.

Nonetheless, from a Zen perspective, whether her cause is just or not, whether her husband is unreasonable or not, whether it is possible for her circumstances to be changed or not, this client needs to do something about the mental poison of hate which devours her from within. If she can do something about her self-defeating vitriolic temper, she will be happier and she will be much better equipped to live the reality of her life, whether this proves to be with her husband, in the divorce court or on the barricades.

I ask her to tell me again about the position of women and this time to try to do so more calmly. She grins and makes the attempt. She grins because there is good rapport between us at this point. She can see the relevance of what I am asking her to do and is acutely aware of her own difficulty in complying. She starts to speak again. After a few sentences I stop her again and ask what is happening with her feelings. 'I am burning hot in here,' she says, pointing to her chest area. 'So, even though your voice has become somewhat calmer, the hot feeling is still very fierce.' 'Yes.'

We go on experimenting for a while. I keep stopping her and each time we stop, she checks her visceral experience. This is mindfulness training. *Sati*, remember, means 'stop'. Mindfulness training means to keep creating stops in which one stands aside from one's process and has a look to see what is happening. We can only do a certain amount in the session and the client needs to learn to create her own stops. She is confident that she can do so, however, because the whole process has now caught her interest. Remarkable as it may seem, she had not, before this session, ever noticed the hot sensation in her chest which arises whenever her anger is beginning to be roused. This is because she is, as she put it, 'too busy in my head at those times to notice'. Now, however, she wants to study this heat: to notice when it arises, what qualities it has, how intense it is in different circumstances, and so on. I encourage her not to try to change it, simply to work at enhancing her awareness.

This work with the woman with hate in her heart is essentially no different from that with the man who suffered from jealousy. In both cases self-study depends on learning mindfulness. Mindfulness is cultivated by stopping (*sati*). Stopping enables the client to discover and study their own process. As they study it, they learn to stand back from it (*upeksha*).

Even though the client's life is in the grip of dominating passions manifesting as greed or hate, there are stronger powers available to the person through the mobilization of their intention, energy, attention and enquiring interest. For these powers to predominate, however, the person needs the skills of concentration and mindfulness, and these can be learned.

To do this, the client does not necessarily have to sit in the lotus position on the floor. The methods of mindfulness are available all the time in all the situations of life. Concentrated practice, of course, can take us further, but even a small enhancement of *samadhi* (concentration) and *sati* can yield great benefits in terms of the client's happiness, ability to exercise self-control and liberation from passions. It does not matter all that much which passion we study first. We just follow the client's interest. But, as therapist, we know that if the client pulls out one brick in the wall, a lot of others are likely to come loose and a more wholesale shift in the person's life will be under way.

NAIKAN

Naikan therapy was developed in the 1950s by Ishin Yoshimoto, a follower of the Jodo Shinshu school of Buddhism. It is based upon a method used in the training of Jodo priests which also has parallels in a number of other schools of Buddhism. Naikan involves a retreat-like period of intense introspective examination of one's past life in relation to others. This period lasts about a week. In Japan, the physical arrangements are generally that one is allocated a small area in a large meditation hall where one is to spend almost all one's time doing naikan. One is allowed times to bathe and to go to the refectory for meals, but is asked to keep one's naikan work going in the mind even during these times. The aim, therefore, is to fill all of one's waking hours with the work of responding to the naikan questions.

Questions to reflect upon are given to the *naikansha* (client/student) by the *sensei* (therapist/instructor) in an interview called a *mensetsu*. The Sensei, or another naikansha, comes around every few hours to conduct the mensetsu. This interview takes a particular form. The sensei's task is not to pass any judgement upon what the naikansha says, but to ensure that the naikansha does stay on task. If the question has been avoided, the sensei will point this out and ask the naikansha to try to stay with the task. Generally, however, the naikansha shares with the interviewer their thoughts from the immediately completed hours of reflection and the sensei simply thanks them. Both bow to each other and the sensei asks the naikansha to continue with a further question. Being in the role of sensei can sometimes be as therapeutic as doing one's own naikan, since one is receiving accounts and confessions from others of matters very close to their heart. The approach, thus, aims to create a situation where a person can come and undertake naikan work, conducting a detailed self-examination and drawing their own conclusions about their life. It is not necessarily easy to get into the work at the beginning, but as participants begin to penetrate more deeply into the questions and confront themselves more honestly, cathartic reactions often occur. There are many accounts of how naikan work has sent a shock wave through the world view of participants such that they emerge from the experience with a completely new outlook on life.

The questions which one is asked to reflect upon in naikan follow a fairly standard pattern. There are generally three questions to consider at each session, all three relating to one's relationship with a particular person during a particular period of one's life. The three questions are: 'What did this person do for you?', 'What did you do in return?' and 'What trouble and worries did you cause them?' One is advised to spend most time on the last of the three questions. The first session is generally focused upon one's relation with one's mother during the first few years of one's life. Subsequent questions take one through the same relation in subsequent periods: age six to nine, age ten to thirteen and so on. Then one works on one's relationship with father, other relatives, friends and associates whose names we know. If there is time, one can consider wider and wider circles of people including those we have never met (like those who grew the food I ate for breakfast this morning) and eventually even inanimate things. Commonly, during the retreat, some time is also given to considering the questions 'What thefts and deceits have I indulged in?' for particular periods of life.

For many people, there is a strong initial tendency to resist the questions altogether, to try to deal with them in an abstract or psychologized way, or to spend all the time being self-justifying. The sensei will point out that the task is more straightforward than this. One is to think about what the person actually did for us: she fed me, she clothed me, she got up in the night when I cried, she changed and washed my nappies, she worried when I was ill, etc. It is irrelevant what the other person's motives might have been. The point is to reflect upon our debt. Someone cared for us or we would not have survived.

Naikan leads to a deep sense of gratitude for the concrete and specific ways in which we are supported by our world. It helps us recognize the ways in which we have taken from others in the past without gratitude or even recognition that we were taking. This method of self-reflection helps us to realize the fallacy that we could be 'self-made'. The desire to serve in order to begin to repay the world naturally wells up within the *Naikansha*. The self-centeredness of neurotic suffering finds release in the giving of oneself to others. (Reynolds 1989, p. 36.)

The naikan method can be used in contexts other than those of a week-long intensive retreat. Systematic naikan can be done using a journal. The naikansha works in their own time, spending some time each day thinking about one of the naikan questions and writing down their reflections in a journal which is then discussed with the therapist at their weekly session. Or this can be done as a personal exercise outside the context of a therapy relationship. Or it can be done as part of a self-help study group in which the participants agree to support each others' naikan work. In a less systematic way, the naikan questions can figure in the context of other forms of therapy, helping to ground the work in the practical and specific and assisting the client to enter into the reverse role position, learning to see him or herself as they were seen by parents and other significant people at particular stages of life. Naikan challenges our tendency to deceive ourselves and to build up a self-justifying story. It undermines the ego.

GRATITUDE, CONTRITION AND FORGIVENESS

The western reader is likely to be immediately struck, in reading about naikan method, by the difference of underlying assumptions here from those ruling in most western forms of therapy. The perspective that prevails in most western therapy advocates the importance of supporting ego development, helping the client justify themselves and building up self-regard. Many clients come to me and say that what they have learned from other therapy to date is how to be more selfish. It is commonly asserted that one cannot give to others until one has received for oneself: one cannot love others without spending more time learning to love oneself first. These assumptions are at odds with Buddhist psychology.

In order to justify ourselves we blame others, but blaming others does not change them for the better nor improve ourselves. We have all been hurt by others many times, but hanging on to blame does not heal wounds. It is common to think that nothing will ever improve unless we fight for improvements, but it is fighting which is tearing the world apart and making human life ever more combative and destructive. The only real way to change our lives is to have a change of heart ourselves. When we lay down our own weapons, we will begin to live a better life.

The three qualities to cultivate, conducive to fundamental change in our way of being, are gratitude, contrition and forgiveness. Many western therapists regard shame and guilt as useless emotions. Gratitude is derided as old-fashioned. Forgiveness is allowed some place, but the cultivation of anger and self-righteousness is often given priority. From a Zen perspective, such ego-supporting attitudes are seen as doing far more harm than good.

Sustainable positive change comes through gratitude, contrition and forgiveness. These three are, from a Buddhist perspective, inestimable treasures and definitely worth cultivating. The person who experiences them is able to let go of defensive posturing. To feel any of them deeply is to experience a turning around in the seat of consciousness. They allow us to return to being what we are. Inevitably we run up debt in relation to the world around us much faster than we could ever hope to repay. Inevitably we make mistakes in life and hurt others. Inevitably we ourselves get hurt by the mistakes made by others. These things are happening so often in our lives that it is crazy to disallow ourselves the appropriate feelings to go with them.

Gratitude, contrition and forgiveness are thus essential equipment for living a real life. They are the outward signs of necessary catharsis (= cleansing). If we cannot allow ourselves to feel them, we will never become clean, never be able to let go. The false ego syndrome, which is the root of all our neurosis, is simply the attempt to avoid these realities. Gratitude, contrition and forgiveness dismantle the ego, allow our natural feelings to flow once again, and begin to heal our relationship with the world, reconciling us with others. Far from being a useless emotion, genuinely felt guilt can be the essential impetus needed for positive change. To really do something *for* ourselves we have to start by doing something *about* ourselves. Until we experience the need to do so, nothing will really change.

· 12 ·

Body Zen

THE THEORY OF NISSAYA
(Nissaya paccaya)

Nissaya theory highlights the fact that everything depends upon or grows out of something as its base or source. In particular, the mind has the body as base, just as later generations have ancestors as base. This is the relationship of one thing growing out of another.

The relationship called nissaya is like that of a tree depending upon the ground. In our case, as humans, we have the body which we have received from our parents and ancestors. Many relationships of the nissaya type exist, but in this chapter I am going to concentrate upon the body-mind unity because this is so important in therapy and essential to our attempt to understand what Zen is all about.

Buddhism emphasizes our supreme good fortune in having a human body. This is the essential basis for enlightenment. Buddhism is, in fact, different from most other faiths in asserting that the human embodied state is the most fortunate. This is not because it is the most comfortable, but because it is the only state which has the opportunity for full spiritual enlightenment. Thus the Zen text called Sandokai asks:

If from your experience of the senses basic Truth you do not know, how can you ever find the path that certain is no matter how far distant you may walk? (Kennett 1976, p. 280.)

The physical basis of mind is six sense organs: the eyes, ears, nose, tongue, body surface, and brain. Correspondingly there are six different modes or channels of mind activity corresponding to these six 'sense doors' which yield data of six different kinds: form, sound, smell, taste, touch and consciousness. Each sense door opens on to a different world of experience. Enlightenment can occur through any of the sense modes. When it is complete all the sense worlds are experienced as 'empty', that is, clean of any kind of clinging or obstacle.

Mind depends upon body. The relation of body and mind has been a subject of endless debate in western philosophy due to belief in the idea of a soul capable of living independently of the body. The body-mind split has been a constant source of difficulty for western thought. Some western psychologies, like behaviourism, have tried to ignore the mind dimension altogether; others have come close to ignoring the body aspect. In Zen, there is no place for such division. Mind is body, body is mind. This is also the inseparability of practice and enlightenment. Here, practice refers to the body and enlightenment to the mind.

Gotama was enlightened by seeing something. Other famous teachers have been enlightened by hearing something. The Surangama Samadhi Sutra states that hearing is the easiest. Most kensho experience, by all accounts, is triggered by something seen or heard. The other senses can, however, also awaken the mind. We have probably all had the experience of smelling something and being immediately transported into a different frame of mind. The use of smell and touch in therapy with elderly people, whose sight and hearing may be failing, can have powerful effects, not only bringing back memories, but also opening minds which had become sealed into subjective circlings. For people of all ages, exercises which awaken our senses are enlivening and bring us more fully into the here and now.

Buddhism advocates a middle path. The Buddha had tried indulging all his senses in the pursuit of pleasure and had also tried extremes of asceticism, trying to live as though the body did not exist. Neither produces a wholesome life. If we get out of touch with the body, we move too far in the aversion direction and become alienated. If we give ourselves up to bodily pleasures, we move too far in the attachment direction and make ourselves dependent. Either of these maras can snatch our life away. In the former case, we miss most of what life has to offer. In the latter case we live it up, but with a constant subliminal fear of death and a progressive erosion of the powers of the mind.

ZEN IS PRACTISED BY THE BOWING BODY

Zen aims, therefore, for harmony of body and mind, a middle path. Since most people err on the side of becoming lost in their heads, Zen practice is physical. Meditation is a physical exercise. In sitting meditation, one adopts a cross-legged upright posture, spine erect, chin tucked in, eyes half closed, hands in the lap in a particular position, called the cosmic *mudra*, as though one were holding the whole universe in one's hands. Generally meditation is done on the floor on a cushion, but for those who cannot manage the posture, an upright chair may be used. The mind is brought into harmony with the body, rather than the other way about. Between sittings, the same practice can be carried on in the form of walking meditation. Here again the posture is carefully specified and one proceeds by very slow steps. The mind is harmonized with the body movement and the breath. There is a verse sometimes used at the beginning of meditation which brings home this body-mind unity:

> Sitting here
> Is like sitting under the Bodhi tree.
> My body is mindfulness itself
> Entirely free from distraction.
> (Hanh 1990, p. 22.)

The bodhi tree means the tree under which the Buddha sat on the night of his enlightenment. The Buddha was a person, an embodied being, not a disembodied spirit. He sat on the ground under a tree. The transmission of Zen through the centuries has been through actual lived lives. The Buddha transmitted the Dharma to Mahakashyapa. Mahakashyapa transmitted it to Ananda, Ananda to Madhyantika, Madhyantika to Shanakavasin, Shanakavasin to Upagupta. With Upagupta, in the fifth generation of teachers after the Buddha, the Dharma underwent a great surge in popularity. The emperor Ashoka became a pupil of Upagupta. From Upagupta, the Dharma was transmitted through many further generations of teachers in India, finally reaching Bodhidharma who took the Zen life to China. Bodhidharma is famous for his insistence upon the importance of two practices in particular, both essentially physical: sitting meditation and bowing.

The importance of bowing is something which western people often have difficulty with. However, Bodhidharma said: 'When bowing ceases, Buddhism ceases.' Nothing is more important in Zen than bowing. So we must ask what does bowing mean. Bowing means to bend our bodies. We put our palms together so that the hands are in a position called *anjali*, as in prayer. It is also like the shape of a lotus blossom. In a full bow we bend right down so that our knees and forehead touch the floor. Bowing is physical. There are also abbreviated forms of bowing. One can bow from the waist or one can simply make the anjali with the hands without bending the body, but touching the head to the ground is the full form and this posture has great consequence.

It is important to learn to bend and it is important to touch the earth. One might then say, 'So really bowing is about adopting a particular attitude of mind and the posturing of the body is just symbolic,' but if we think like that then we have missed the real Zen spirit. In Zen it is not enough to do something with the mind only. Zen training begins and ends in the body. It is the body which bows. The mind's job is to harmonize with the body. What the body is doing is the reality of our lives. It is for the mind to harmonize with the reality of our life.

When we work with the body, we find that particular postures and actions will evoke particular feelings and experiences. The act of bowing in itself generates a sense of surrender. It is an action found in one form or another in cultures all over the world. It taps into our basic instinctive experiencing. The learning is not in thinking about it, but in doing it.

Zen is experience. Many people who may acknowledge that having a flexible mind is important nonetheless find themselves very stiff when it comes to bowing. Similarly with sitting zen: it is easy enough to realize that we are run around by our mind, but it is another matter to just sit still, as one impulse after another arises unbidden. Yet it is in our bodies that we actually confront these things and unhook ourselves. It is the same with bowing.

> Usually to bow means to pay our respects to something which is more worthy of respect than ourselves. But . . . when everything exists within your big mind, all dualistic relationships drop away. There is no distinction between heaven and earth, man and woman, teacher and disciple . . . A master who cannot bow to his disciple cannot bow to Buddha. Sometimes the master and disciple bow together to Buddha. Sometimes we may bow to cats and dogs . . . Bowing is a very serious practice. You should be prepared to bow even in your last moment; when you cannot do anything except bow, you should do it. This kind of conviction is necessary. Bow with this spirit and all the precepts, all the teachings are yours, and you will possess everything within your big mind. (Suzuki 1970, p. 44.)

It is a hallmark of Zen that meditation does not only take place in the meditation hall. All activity becomes meditation. Thus we have working zen, eating zen, sleeping zen and so on. The Zen Master Pai Chang, who established this idea, worked in the fields every day even when eighty years old. When his disciples tried to stop him, he said that if he did not work he would not eat, and this saying has come down in the tradition as a reminder of the important place of physical work in the Zen life.

Bodhidharma transmitted the Dharma to Hui Ke, Hui Ke to Seng Tsan, Seng Tsan to Tao Hsin. Tao Hsin transmitted it to Hung Jen (601–674 CE) who thus became the fifth 'ancestor' of Chinese Zen. When Hung Jen was growing old, he told his disciples that he would transmit the Dharma to whoever could produce a poem demonstrating their understanding. His most senior disciple Shen Hsiu submitted the following:

Our body is the bodhi tree,
And our mind a mirror bright.
Carefully we wipe them hour by hour,
And let no dust alight.

Hung Jen liked this poem, but was not completely satisfied with it. He said that if people learned it and practised its message they would obtain great benefits. It showed that its author was on the threshold of awakening, but had not yet entered. He invited Shen Hsiu to reflect for a few days and then submit another poem. Shen Hsiu went and meditated but was unable to improve on his original verse.

In the same monastery, there was a monk from distant parts staying, who was called Hui Neng. Hui Neng heard Shen Hsiu's poem and realized that it did not quite hit the mark. Since he himself was illiterate, he asked one of the other monks to write a poem which he dictated, to submit to Hung Jen. Hui Neng's poem, which gained Hung Jen's favour, was as follows:

There is no bodhi tree
Nor stand of a mirror bright.
Since all is void
Where can the dust alight?
(Price & Wong 1969.)

Shen Hsiu's poem still shows traces of belief in the body-mind split and in the attainment of enlightenment by a process of accumulation, whereas in Hui Neng's poem, the body-mind split is transcended to the point where nothing can be a cause of trouble any more. We could say:

Whether we see a bodhi tree
Or a mirror bright
Let us welcome everything
Whether it be dust or light.

Zen Master Thien An writes: 'In the West, knowledge is considered a key virtue and the rational mind the peak of man's development, but this is not so in Zen Buddhism. In Zen, actions speak louder than words. Doing is more important than know-ing, and knowledge which cannot be translated into action is of little worth . . . Many people, especially in the west, try to intellectualize the state of enlightenment. But enlightenment can-not be realized through the intellect, but only through practice . . . The practice of Zen should not be confined only to periods of sitting in meditation, but should be applied to all the activities of daily life. If we are diligent in cultivating the Way, we will find that every day is a good day' (Thien An 1975, p. 116).

THE WISE BODY

A western therapist, Gene Gendlin (1981), has developed a psychotherapy method which relies upon the nissaya principle. This method is called Focusing. It relies upon the fact that our mental activity actually grows out of the body. As a therapist, one repeatedly has the opportunity to see how the client's body expresses something before the client's mind becomes aware of it. Gendlin says that when a person changes in some way – develops a new idea, a new feeling, or a new attitude of some kind – the change first manifests in the body. He began his research by looking at which clients in psychotherapy did best. He came to the conclusion that there was something which successful clients did which others did not do. What they did was to attend to 'a distinct physical sensation of change' (p. 7), a 'body shift'. I do not intend here to give a description of the whole focusing method. There are plenty of such descriptions available (e.g. Cornell 1993). The point is that it is our physical being which instructs our mental being. The wisdom is in the body.

This statement is true enough, but we can go a step further. The physical body is part of the physical world. The wisdom which we need is not simply 'in' the body: it is in the body's co-functioning with the world around it. It is, in fact, embedded in awareness (Brooks 1982). The Buddha became enlightened when he saw the morning star rise. This statement is not just a way of telling us what time of day it happened; it is a crucial indicator of what enlightenment is. We are told that the content of the Buddha's enlightenment was largely made up of understanding the nature of conditioning and dependent origination. This whole book is a commentary upon these principles. I do not think, however, that the Buddha produced this material by spending the night thinking out a set of abstract propositions. No. He had a deep, that is to say, body, experience (*taiken*) of being in direct unity with the cosmos. He experienced the morning star. Later he talked and produced his wonderful teachings according to the needs of all the different people who came to see him. Even his teachings, however, were not meant to fill up textbooks. They were designed to encourage people to experience directly for themselves. 'Try it and see,' was his style. If our consciousness is not going to be expanded by the use of our senses, what way will it be? There is no other way. It is through awareness that we transform our relation with our world and ultimately discover that we were never anything other than unified with it from the very beginning.

MUDRA: GESTURE AND TOUCH

A mudra is a posture, gesture or touch which has an effect upon our state of mind. Since body and mind are a unity, the attitude of the mind and the attitude of the body reflect each other. This can work as cause and effect in either direction. When one's mind is dull, the posture of the body is likely to become more slumped. When the mind is alert, we 'perk up'. Similarly, if we physically move toward an antagonist, we are likely to start feeling more confident than if we edge backwards. The English language contains a great many words and phrases which reveal our intuitive understanding of this body-mind correspondence. Thus we talk about 'keeping our feet on the ground', or 'being caught off balance', sometimes 'our heart sinks' or we 'put some backbone into a task', and so on. The language of emotions and relationships is full of references to the attitudes of the body. We speak of being 'close' to someone, and 'seeing eye to eye' with them, or of being 'distant' and feeling 'cold' toward them.

In Buddhist meditation, one sits with the back upright. This is important. It is not just symbolic. Having a straight back not only symbolizes the mental attitude of zazen, it creates it. Zazen is, essentially, a matter of letting our mind harmonize with this bodily posture. This is the posture in which the Buddha was enlightened. Zen principles suggest that this fact is not just coincidence. Kensho experiences may occur to people in many bodily attitudes, but the posture of meditation is particularly conducive to the state of samadhi. It is stable, balanced, alert and close to the earth.

Zen advocates staying close to the earth. Nowadays we tend to do our meditations sitting in well-insulated buildings. We should not forget, however, that the Buddha generally sat separated from the earth by no more than a grass mat. With our modern convenience and comfort-conscious mentalities, we tend to dismiss these details, but we lose something important by doing so. At the height of the mental turmoil which immediately preceded his awakening on the night of his enlightenment, Gotama reached down and touched the earth. Often statues of the Buddha show him in this 'earth witness mudra'. He sits in meditation posture, legs folded, spine erect, with one hand in his lap and the other reaching forward and down so that his fingertips touch the ground. He is grounding himself.

Getting grounded is therapeutic. There are many ways to apply this principle. Commonly clients may be lost in a mental fog. Putting them in touch with the earth in quite practical ways heals. We can work with clients directly making contact with the ground through their feet, helping them focus attention on the subtle qualities and variations in contact. A great variety of body awareness exercises are possible and useful in bringing the person into awareness of immediate bodily connection with the earth. Sometimes, the therapist has to act as a kind of 'lightning conductor' when the client has become lost in the nightmares of the mind. Enlightenment is also called 'awakening'. Therapy is often a matter of helping a person wake up from their bad dream.

Ellen had been in therapy for a year. She had lived with an aunt from age two, when her mother went away to work, until age eleven. The aunt had tortured her with a hot poker repeatedly, keeping her in a state of terror. Ellen was only able to talk of these experiences in a very fragmentary way. As soon as she started to recall them, she would begin to re-experience the pain in her body, which would writhe uncontrollably. On one occasion she had been talking about an experience in a particularly vivid way when she passed into a state of extreme distress, becoming convinced that her aunt was in the room. Screaming, she shrank against the wall in the corner, covering her face with her hands, trying to escape from the imagined instrument of torture. At this point there is a dilemma for the therapist. The client is in a state which is difficult to reach. Touching her by, say, taking hold of her hand, may achieve the contact necessary to bring her back into communication. On the other hand, she may take it as a further invasion and turn against the therapist. Ellen seemed to be moving in and out of her fugue state as the image of the aunt became more or less real to her. The therapist, taking advantage of one of her brief more lucid intervals, said firmly, 'Ellen, I am going to put my hand on your arm. Is that OK?' She nodded and the therapist did so. The therapist then concentrated primarily upon achieving the deepest possible degree of calm within himself, slowing and deepening his breathing and letting his stillness convey itself to her. Gradually she regained control.

Very valuable work can also be done using stones. Susan experienced repeated panic attacks which had come to dominate her life, preventing her from carrying on everyday activities such as shopping or taking her daughter to school. One day, Susan arrived for her therapy session in great agitation. Her breathing was fast. She seemed unable to sit still in the chair, but kept tossing her head from one side to the other. She complained of pains in her chest which terrified her. As she described her panic and spoke of how she had felt like this on several occasions during the past week, the therapist suggested that she choose a stone from the collection which always sits in our consulting room, asking her to hold the stone. She was encouraged to feel its texture and concentrate all her attention on getting to know its surface features. The therapist suggested that Susan shut her eyes and really get to know her stone, so that she would be able to recognize it among hundreds on a beach. After several minutes of intense concentration, during which the therapist became aware that Susan's breathing had become slower and her body seemed calmer, he asked her what she was experiencing in her body now. At this point Susan laughed, realizing that her panic attack had disappeared. The therapist suggested that Susan take the stone away with her and keep it in her pocket so that she could again use it to focus her attention if she felt panic returning.

Other clients find considerable release through working with clay. Clay is earth. Holding it in one's hands, shaping it and feeling its texture and resistance, is very satisfying. People can discharge a lot of stress in this way. Gardening, too, is an activity to which many people owe their continued sanity. Simply getting into the open air and walking is very valuable, but it becomes many times more so when it is done with a deliberately meditative attitude, in full consciousness of each step and with focus upon the contact which each footfall makes with the ground.

Touch heals. We use a practice based upon the earth witness mudra. A person reaches out and touches an object, the leaf of a plant, say. The touch is very light, just the fingertips touching with no pressure at all. The leaf should barely move. The touch is held, still and calm, for the length of time it takes to breathe three breaths. This very simple exercise develops mindfulness and grounds us. Gentle touch conveys love. One can go around the house touching things in this way, giving out love to everything in the house. At the end of such an exercise, one feels energized. This is quite a simple example of the principle that the well-being we feel is in proportion to the love we give out.

This touching practice can also be used with people. Of course, we should only touch people if we know that we have their permission. To touch a friend in this way is something very special. We have found that such very light touch can often be much more powerful in conveying love and caring than a hug or more forceful gesture. We touch the other person just as the Buddha touched the earth, and we feel ourselves involved in a flow of energy which warms both our hearts. This touching practice develops mindfulness in both people and reduces stress.

In Chinese medicine, the various mudras found in Buddhist iconography are related to the meridians of acupuncture and to flows of vital energy. There are points along these meridians where touch or massage can be particularly effective in stimulating tension release and restoring harmony. This is the basis of a wide range of massage and 'acu-touch' techniques, known as *anma*. It is beyond the scope of this book to go into these anma arts in any detail. The important point here is that touch plays a very important part in the restoration of harmony between body and mind with which Zen is primarily concerned. According to the nissaya theory, mind and body are a single functional unity and the conditioned state of mind is always a consequence of some degree of separation having opened up between the mental and physical dimensions of our being. One way of understanding the disharmony in our lives is to realize the extent to which we are 'out of touch'.

· 13 ·

Support

THEORIES OF SUPPORT
(Upanissaya, Purejata, Pacchajata, Asevanna)

The theory of inducement (upanissaya) states that we become conditioned to act in particular ways by following inducements. The theory of pre-condition (purejata) states that some events are not possible unless something else already exists. The theory of on-going dependence (pacchajata) states that growth depends upon on-going supplies and support. The theory of habit (asevanna) simply states that through repetition and cultivation mental states become habitual.

These theories can be used to explain many phenomena. They refer to the fact that in our samsaric condition, we rely upon support and inducements. They describe the ordinary worldly way of carrying on. We do whatever seems likely to be to our advantage. We find it hard to continue unless we are supported, especially in the early stages of something new. Eventually, however, as we go on, new patterns become established and are like second nature.

There are two sides to this. On the one hand, as we become stronger in character, we become less dependent upon conditions. On the other hand, insofar as we are not yet completely liberated in this way – and how many of us are? – we remain vulnerable to circumstance, which means that we can be helped or hindered by the conditions we encounter. Zen does not expect us to be enlightened before we start. So this group of conditions describes ordinary life, and the aspect of it which I want to focus upon here is the question of how people can help and support one another.

The fundamentals of therapy are not terribly esoteric. We have seen that the antidotes to the three root delusions are kindness, love and understanding. I am sure that you, the reader, knew this before opening this book. You might not have formulated it the way it is set out here, but we all know that what people in distress need, indeed what the whole world needs, is kindness, love and understanding. We can help one another. Therapy is a situation in which one person, the client, opens themselves to receiving such help. Therapists, for our part, need to think deeply about what is really kind and loving in particular situations. We have to try to really understand the whole situation of the client coming to us, and this invariably leads us into seeing the necessity to deepen our own practice, our own liberation from conditioning, our own effort to let go of self.

Therapy relies upon the fact that people can help one another. A client comes to a therapist because they need support during a period when they hope to see some changes in their life. The therapist is there to offer such support until the changes which the client wanted have become self-sustaining. The therapist does not withdraw too soon: that would be giving up on the client. Nor does the therapist hang on when no longer needed. The therapist offers support without any expectation.

THE NATURE OF THE THERAPY RELATIONSHIP

The therapist supports the client, but does not do so in the manner of someone who is superior. It is very central to the Zen view of things that we are all in this together. The client and I are both just people with the same basic hunger and thirst. Today I am supporting him, but who can say what tomorrow will bring? The kind of relationship which is needed for Zen work is one in which the therapist stays very firmly in touch with her or his own humanity and frailty. Both therapist and client are on the same sort of path. We are both afflicted by suffering caused by our conditioned state of mind. There naturally arises, therefore, a sense of fellow feeling.

The Buddha in fact said that to be a good friend to others is the whole of the spiritual life. A great deal is often made of the idea that some people are *mahasattvas*, 'great beings', and that one's spiritual progress is greatly enhanced simply by being in the presence of such a person. This is undoubtedly so. However, it is not always easy to know who they are and guru cults certainly have their pitfalls. Anyway, gurus need our compassion too. A truly great being, from a Zen perspective, is one who puts their ego aside and is a good friend to everyone they encounter. Such a person does not necessarily have an entourage, nor, even, a certificate.

When help is given, the real gift is the spirit of selfless being, rather than the gift itself. Therapists in private practice receive payment from their clients and those in clinics receive a salary. This does not, in itself, mean that what they provide to the client cannot be done in a spirit of selflessness. Traditionally Buddhist monks provided spiritual support to their community and the community provided material support to the monks. This kind of interdependence is practical and wholesome. It only becomes contaminated by self when greed arises, or when the helper is just going through the motions in an insincere way in order to qualify for their salary cheque.

Our ability to help others depends upon our first having made some progress in doing something about ourselves. Helping does not happen except insofar as the helper, the therapist, has attained some maturity and insight. As the client gains insights and maturity of their own, the therapist loses nothing.

This is not to say that it is impossible for a client to make progress in spite of having a poor therapist. Such things do happen. But in such cases the client has drawn strength from elsewhere. We all have such other sources of strength available to us. The real source is the buddhata, which partakes of the 'other power'. Other people enable us to actualize our buddhata in two ways. Firstly, through a relationship with one or more other people – therapists, sangha, friends, parents, teachers – we come to a realization that we do ourselves have access to 'the source'. Secondly, it is mostly through our interactions with others that we are able to put our progress into practice.

First, let us think about finding the source through relationship. In Zen there is a saying about climbing to the top of a hundred foot pole and then taking another step. I prefer to change this a little and talk of climbing a hundred-step ladder and then taking another step. We can see that this is an image about having the courage to act unconditionally. The client puts in a lot of effort with the help and support of the therapist, but then has to take a step on their own. Here, the ladder is the relationship. It gets the person to the point where they can step off on their own. The therapist is always willing for the client to take an extra step. This means that the therapist does not hang on to nor insist upon a particular action, interpretation or direction.

There is another point, however. When we consider the ladder itself, we also see that although the ladder reliably gives continuous support, the person on the ladder can only use it if they are willing to step off each rung in order to move to the next one. There is a stepping off at every stage. What does this mean in practice? A therapist does their very best to understand the client, empathizes and feels warmth for them, supporting in an unconditional way, just as the ladder remains solid. Nonetheless, however skilled the therapist is, their understanding is never perfect. There are gaps between the rungs. The client shows the therapist something of their life. The therapist tells the client what they have understood. It is not perfect understanding. A little bit of the client feels misunderstood. In the past, when they felt misunderstood, maybe the client habitually blamed the other person. However, in this situation, it is clear to the client that the therapist *is* doing their very best and really cares, so the client is reluctant to write them off. The habitual blaming response is blocked. Thus there occurs an inner crisis in which the client has to find some strength that they have never accessed before. This is a moment of real growth. Momentarily the client experiences the ability to stand alone without disaster occurring. At this point, the client may reach into the buddhata and forgive the therapist. The moment they do so, they find their foot firmly upon the next rung. If the client cannot unilaterally forgive the therapist at these points, the therapy will fail.

This also restates the principles established earlier that (1) the client makes real progress when they are truly alone, and (2) it is when the client discovers the source of good qualities within themselves that they grow. Every relationship is built up out of

moments of aloneness: actions which are, in themselves, unconditional. No real intimacy arises from trading and negotiation.
There has to be a unilateral giving (*dana-paramita*).

This is true in the large sense of attaining enlightenment
experience and it is true at every level of scale down to the most
detailed element of interaction. Heinz Kohut (1971, 1977) was
a psychoanalyst who worked with clients who felt extremely
fragile. He found that the best way to respond to such clients
was to be constantly and scrupulously empathic and always
warm and positive. The client should be able to see the gleam
in the therapist's eye, he would say. As we have explained,
however, he found that the clients actually made progress not
as a direct result of such unremittingly empathic attention, but
as a result of the therapist's occasional small lapses. However
hard the therapist tries to be understanding, they will not always
be successful. The client who wants to be perfectly understood
will, therefore, from time to time at least, be frustrated. It is in
such moments of frustration that the client has the opportunity
to grow. The client is only likely to do so, however, when such
points of frustration occur against the background of the therapist's very clearly apparent constant effort to be empathic. Kohut
called this 'optimum frustration' and this is very similar to the
Zen principle that it is dukkha itself which provides the opportunity for enlightenment.

This pattern operates at every level in the process of personal
growth. The relationship is the necessary *pre*-condition. Many
therapists believe that it is the relationship which effects change.
This, however, is not quite right. The relationship sets the stage
upon which something important can happen. But the important
thing occurs when the client draws it up from the buddha nature.

When talking about the relationship, therapists use the term
transference. This refers to the tendency of the client to see the
therapist as their parent. In theory, psychoanalysts attempt to
'analyse' transference, thus standing above it, while humanistic
therapists try to avoid transference arising, by acting congru-
ently. Both these modes of work are useful. In Zen, however,
we have the principle of *roshin*, 'parental mind', which, at first
sight, seems to contradict the western view. According to the
principle of roshin, we should view all beings as though they

were our only child. Does this not set up a difficult 'counter-transference' relationship?

It is quite clear that throughout Buddhist literature, the unconditional positive regard which a parent, especially a mother, has for their child, is viewed as a prototype for the way in which the bodhisattva views all beings. The Zen therapist, therefore, has the attitude of a parent. But here, we are not talking about the kind of parent who insists upon superiority. Rather, we are talking about the fact that the person with real parental mind loves, understands and feels kindly disposed toward the person, no matter what they do or have done or have become. It is an attitude of all acceptance, in which one only wants the best for the other person. To the parental mind, nothing is changed by success or failure. The therapist never gives up on the client.

Although western therapy is doubtful whether the therapist should be like a parent to the client, it is quite clear that many of the great therapists, like Heinz Kohut, whom we have just referred to, and Carl Rogers, whom we have referred to often, were, in practice, very warm people who did indeed enter into relationships with their clients which were parental, in the sense of roshin. This kind of parent does not cling on. They are a genuine good friend. They are reliably there for the client, but they are also willing to let go at every step. The client may feel a kind of dependency for a time, but it is like our description of the ladder. Every step depends upon the client lifting their own foot. The parent only wants the child to discover how to walk and climb in their own way.

GOOD HABITS

A plant needs watering and a baby needs feeding if they are to stay alive and grow. Similarly, some pattern may become established through a therapeutic relationship, but it may not be possible to sustain the new pattern unless the relationship remains in being or unless some alternative and equally effective support for the new state of affairs is found. Eventually, however, changes tend to become self-sufficient and find their own sources of vital supplies. There is generally in psychotherapy a problem of transferability of learning from the therapeutic to the natural situation and a constant danger that therapy will be terminated too soon. In general, even when the client has achieved all that they set out to do, there is wisdom in maintaining some continuing relationship with the therapist or other group members as support.

In spiritual training, if one works diligently, it may be possible to attain a breakthrough quite early in some cases whereas in others it may take a long time. Whenever it occurs, however, very little is achieved if one does not maintain one's training or if one neglects the conditions which help one's understanding to deepen and one's effort to strengthen. It is a fallacy to think that *satori* in Zen is a final point beyond which one need make no effort. It is just the same with insights gained in therapy. They are just the start of the real work.

Satori is the point at which one realizes clearly for oneself why one makes effort and how this effort will later come to be effortless. Nonetheless, there are many who obtain the satori who then try to cling to the experience rather than continuing with their training, and so the newborn buddha is starved in its cot, never reaching maturity. Therefore, in Zen, one talks about endless training.

Wholesome actions and thoughts can be deliberately cultivated and become established as good habits. The use of affirmations, for instance, relies upon this relation. It is a great aid to have reminders, and generally Buddhist practice includes many ways of building them into the programme of one's day. This is one reason why Zen values ritual. For instance, Zen practitioners learn by heart short verses (*gathas*) which we can say to ourselves whenever we perform certain everyday activities. This imparts a special quality to everything we do, beginning with getting up in the morning:

> Waking this morning
> My heart bows to the new day:
> May all beings awaken
> And be filled with new life.

A great range of verses exists appropriate to all the everyday activities such as washing, dressing, cleaning, entering and leaving buildings, seeing a flower, ringing the meditation bell, and so on. One can make up one's own gathas.

> Sweeping the floor
> I sweep away the dust of delusion:
> It was always clean
> From the start.

A person who is trying to change the pattern of their life must make repeated effort and this means starting again each moment with all one's will. Making effort has become rather unfashionable in some quarters, but if something is to be achieved, effort is necessary.

Undesirable habits can be displaced by the establishment of new preferable alternatives. Addictions can be overcome. A bad pattern can generally only be renounced by establishing a replacement. This is why dieting often fails – it is simply an attempt to stop doing something rather than to do something else. This is important in planning a strategy for personal change. Simply attempting to *not* do something is unlikely to be successful. Rather one should establish a desirable activity which is incompatible with the behaviour one wishes to extinguish. Zen training is very thorough. It enters into every aspect of a person's life.

> I wash the dishes
> With the power of pure mind:
> Each plate shines
> Like the Buddha's smile.

Every time one repeats this verse, one averts the resentment which might otherwise take hold as one approaches a 'chore' and replaces it with a realization that this is a precious activity through which to express love.

In modern life, we have lost much of the respect which society used to have for character training. This is unfortunate. Good habits become a springboard for high achievement. Thus a painter will reach a stage at which many aspects of their skill have become second nature before they produce their master-piece. In the same way, Zen training needs to be established not just through intellectual understanding or the reading of books, but by the repetition of good actions and good thoughts until the mind has become thoroughly cleansed. When we read the stories of the moment of enlightenment of a particular Zen master in the past, we should not forget that this moment almost invariably came as the culmination of many years of serious training, as, indeed, it did for the Buddha himself. A client will be inclined to tell us about the most difficult moments of life, the times when anyone would have difficulty coping. If we are to deal well with these difficult times, it is important to start doing something about the way we live our life during the easier periods, when we can build up our habit of mindfulness. Then we will not be caught off guard when the more difficult challenges arrive. The therapist will, therefore, be keen to help the client live even the most mundane aspects of life in a higher quality way.

In therapy, what is often needed is that the client learn some new pattern and then be supported while it is repeated again and again until it becomes second nature. This is like the training of a practitioner of martial arts. Each move has to be repeated again and again until it is second nature. When our second nature has been thoroughly trained, our first nature may show itself. While our second nature remains unruly, however, first nature tends to remain hidden. What is happening here is that while second nature remains untrained, it holds all of our attention. First nature is always there, but we do not see it. When second nature has been trained and become calm and obedient, then we are free to give ourselves to our true master, which is the buddhata. We should not think that we will be more spontaneous if we remain untrained. The most original painters, like Van Gogh, for instance, had trained themselves for many years with great diligence and would never have been able to produce such originality without this grounding. The same is true in the art of living.

In the world of western psychotherapy there has grown up an unfortunate split between those methods which advocate behavioural change and those which advocate deep psychological transformation. From a Zen perspective, this is a case of each school having got hold of a different part of the elephant. When the Buddha was asked why there are so many competing schools of thought in the world, he told the story of a rajah who had a number of blind beggars brought into the courtyard of his house where an elephant stood. Each beggar went up to the elephant and got hold of a different bit of it. When each was asked to describe the elephant, of course, each gave a totally different account from any of the others, according as they had held the tusk, the trunk, the foot, the tail and so on. So it is with schools of psychology. In Zen it is stressed that we need behavioural training and we need deep psychological change and these two go together. Each supports the other. To attempt one without the other is probably not going to work very well.

SUMMARY

Good spiritual friends are a strong supporting condition for progress upon our path. This is the basis of therapy. Each important step nonetheless always has to be taken alone with only our buddha nature for company. This involves reaching down to the very deepest levels of the psyche, beyond what is personal, to the sources of life itself. This is not something which only happens in big spiritual events, however. The day-to-day work of Zen training can transform every activity of our ordinary lives, changing our habits of body, speech and mind. In the next chapter, we will develop this theme further, examining what is needed to transform our karma.

· 14 ·

Karma

Karma is the law of moral consequence. All deliberate actions of body, speech and mind produce immediate effects in the life continuum, which are like seeds stored for future germination. They will bear pleasant or unpleasant fruit according to their nature when they are activated at some future time.

The word karma means action. It is related to our word 'drama'. Before the Buddha's time, karma referred primarily to ritual actions. People believed that by performing rites, which generally involved offering a sacrifice, reciting particular words and carrying out particular actions, the gods could be pleased, disasters averted and blessings obtained. The Buddha, however, gave new meaning to karma.

Firstly, Buddha taught that offerings should be made to good people rather than to gods. In practice, the sacrifice went to the priest. Many priests were not particularly virtuous or spiritual. The Buddha repeatedly taught that offerings only brought blessings if they were given to someone who lived a pure life. While never denying the gods, the Buddha made them less important in the scheme of things. What mattered was to support those who led genuinely virtuous and spiritual lives. That was the way to regenerate society and improve the quality of life.

Secondly, the Buddha saw that the value of the rites was that they were action deliberately undertaken to deepen one's life. He therefore set up the aim that all action might have this same quality. In a ritual which has not degenerated into stereotyped formalism, actions are deliberate, careful, conscious and intentional. They also generate a sense of community. Each individual has a part to play, but the collective action transcends the individual contribution and lifts people out of themselves. At such memorable and important occasions, one is no longer acting in a narrow or selfish way, but has become part of a larger dance. The Buddha saw that it was possible for the whole of life to have these qualities, not just those occasions when special ceremonies were performed.

Modern life has based itself upon principles of utility and pleasure seeking: upon self rather than community. In consequence, the appreciation of ritual has declined. This has left a sense of hollowness and fragmentation in life. On the other hand, there are also dangers in ritualizing life in a mechanical way. Nothing is gained by just 'going through the motions' mindlessly. Zen avoids these extremes by pointing out a middle path emphasizing the sacredness of everything we do. Training in selfless and mindful action effects a therapy of the individual and of society simultaneously.

Thirdly, the Buddha taught that actions have consequences not because of divine intervention, but simply as natural effect. Buddhism does not teach us to be good in order to please the gods and get to heaven. To do so is still basically selfish. The Buddha pointed out that selfless actions are what come naturally to the enlightened person and that we should all seek to enlighten ourselves about this. As long as we continue to think that acting selfishly is the best policy, we continue to create hells for ourselves and others. That is, we create bad karma. If we act virtuously in the hope of a reward here or hereafter, that is better, but still not ideal. It is to create good karma. Ideally, when we act in an enlightened way, we create no personal karma at all, because our action, being selfless, is not for ourselves, but for the community. Good communities are not built by everyone serving themselves, but by serving one another.

In Buddhist psychology, as we saw in the introductory chapter to Part Two, the mind acts as though it had a 'store consciousness' called the *alaya vijnana*. In this storehouse are held the traces of all our past actions, good and bad. All self-willed actions of body, speech or mind leave traces in the alaya which bear fruit later.

According to the karma theory, insofar as we act upon self-centred notions, to that extent will the delusion of self continue into the future: there will remain the potentiality for further self-centred distortions: anger, greed, jealousy, envy, pride, dejection and all the other mental confections to which the self passion gives rise. Karma is this circular process. Every person has an accumulated store of seeds waiting to ripen when the appropriate conditions arise.

This means that all mental suffering is actually the result of our own past actions. Here we can distinguish between 'mental suffering' and physical pain. We might call mental suffering 'anguish' or 'bad states of mind'. According to some schools of Buddhist thought, both forms of suffering are a result of karma. According to that theory, there are no accidents. Everything which befalls us in life is the consequence of something we ourselves did in the past, either in this or a previous life. I do not intend to put forward arguments for or against that theory. Here I shall confine discussion to the question of mental suffering alone. For practical purposes we often cannot control what happens to us, but we can do something about how we react.

There is pain in many life situations intrinsic to being human. We fall ill. We get injured. We go hungry. The Buddha himself suffered from a very painful foot at one time as a result of stepping on a thorn. This is the level of pain that we can do nothing about. Even if it is the result of old karma, we cannot avert it.

Then there is the layer of unnecessary suffering which arises from our attitude of mind. If the Buddha had thought, 'Why does this always happen to me?' or 'Somebody's to blame for not sweeping those thorns up,' he would have suffered mentally as well as physically. This is the area where therapy has a part to play and where liberation is possible by letting go. It is important to distinguish what we can do something about from what we cannot.

Since karma is created by wilful behaviour, it concerns both attitude and action. Therapy similarly must be concerned with both areas: what the client holds in their heart and what they act out in their life.

HOW KARMA WORKS

Karma has five phases. First, there is the establishment of a general attitude to life. Second, there is the genesis of karma through specific volitional activity. Third, there is a latency period during which the effect of the karma is not apparent. The fourth phase is the re-presentation of the karma as a result of a trigger experience or simply through the passage of time. The re-presentation takes the form of perception of a possibility for further action presented to the mind in a literal or symbolic form. If this invitation to action is taken up, that is to say, if it is invested with new volition, a new karmic cycle is set in motion. In any case, after this phase the old karma then falls into its 'final condition' (*vipaka*) which is a state of inactivity.

This theory has important implications. In particular, it is commonplace for people to misconstrue 'triggers' for causes. Thus, if someone insults me, according to the theory of karma, the ire which may arise in me is not caused by the insult. The insult is simply the trigger which has brought my pre-existing susceptibility to anger to the surface. If I am to extinguish this misery-generating habit, it is important that I learn to recognize the true state of things in situations of this kind. If I do so, I may be able to let my anger go. If I do not do so, I am likely to act in an aggressive manner and so set up the same karmic pattern all over again ready for the next trigger.

Karma, then, is a law of moral effect which does not rely upon divine intervention. Karma does not happen at the seat of judgement after we are dead. It happens immediately, now. All action which springs from self-will produces karma. An enlightened person produces no new personal karma, but still reaps the effects of seeds already sown.

Understanding this can radically change our response to life and its trials. As long as I believe that my upsets are caused by others, I am likely to blame and react to them in ways which will continue to set up more karma for my future. It is in this sense that samsara is a circle. We go round and round repeating the same pattern because our efforts to cure situations simply set them up to repeat. This is why it takes us a long time to learn how to handle our lives constructively. When we no longer see others as responsible for our upsets, instead of blaming them, we may be able to feel grateful that they have brought our negativity into the open where we can deal with it and let it go.

This theory has considerable implications for therapy. As therapists we will see how our clients continually recreate the same kind of problem for themselves and then try to get out of it by making the same mistakes. We will also see how states of misery are related to previous actions. At the same time, in most cases, it will be inappropriate to point these processes out to the client immediately because the client is liable to see this as blame. It will thus just act as a trigger for more trouble. The therapist may, therefore, often be in the position of having insights which they cannot yet use.

If, however, the therapist can create an environment in which people can candidly examine the contents of the karmic storehouse without creating new trouble in the process, great good may be done. Thus many forms of therapy create conditions in which a person can explore their hate, anger, jealousy and so on, without harm coming to others. For instance, in psychodrama, a person may enact the worst aspects of themselves without doing damage either to their loved ones or even to their enemies, since the whole process takes place within a group of people who understand. Therapy is to do something about one's karma. Thus a person may come to a deep reconsideration of the way they have been living their life. There may be new understanding of self and other, forgiveness, reconciliation and contrition.

THE BODY AS ALAYA

In many ways, it is the body which acts as the storehouse of past karma. Most people have characteristic physical weaknesses which reflect their particular history of pain and trouble. I myself suffered for many years from a variety of troubles of the throat. When under stress, my throat would go into a rather painful state of spasm. Even today, when I find myself caught up in a stressful encounter, I notice a trace of this discomfort return. I can track this back to a time when, as a child, I had just moved to a new school where the children were rather rough. I was frightened. In particular, I felt very uncomfortable being crowded together in morning assembly with all these other alarming children. When it came to singing the morning hymns, I was so tense that my larynx would not perform. Ever since, I have been prone to the same painful symptoms. It is also possible, of course, that this karmic loop goes much further back in time.

We all carry bodily tensions which reflect our particular history of experience. The times when we have found it difficult to cope are etched into our physical being. These ideas are not new. There are many branches of western psychotherapy, from the work of Wilhelm Reich onward, which have explored how the body stores stress as 'character armour'. All I wish to do here, therefore, is to acknowledge this concurrence of theory between Buddhist psychology and western body-oriented therapies.

VALUES IN THERAPY

It is a common idea that the therapist should not try to influence the values of the client, but I have yet to hear a description of any lengthy piece of therapy in which all such influence was absent, however 'non-directive' the therapist might have been in theory. The more non-directive, that is egoless, the therapist's style, the more influential they are likely to be. Forcefulness is generally counter-productive. All therapies implicitly or explicitly offer a life-way.

It is for clients to decide for themselves what is right and wrong. When we consider the theory of karma, however, this idea is not as straightforward as it seems. According to the karma theory, the client's suffering is the result of their own action. It is not inconsequential what they think. They will not escape from suffering just because they did not think what they were doing was wrong. We cannot remake the world just by wishful thinking. Whatever harmful things people do, they generally manage to convince themselves that they were justified, but such conviction does not avert the consequences. Therapy may be about discovering how one has deceived oneself in this way.

A client came to me suffering from a haunting fantasy of having stolen something. When the symptom was active, he could not leave a building without believing that he had unconsciously taken something while he had been inside. He had constant nightmares of being arrested, taken to court and sent to prison. In reality, he never stole anything, but he could not convince himself. He would stop and search his own car, just in case, but even when he had done so and found nothing, he was still not sure that he had not hidden the stolen goods somewhere else. This obsessional fantasy caused him a great deal of trouble.

In therapy we uncovered various childhood incidents which provided material for the form which this fantasy took, but knowing where something originated does not necessarily make any difference to its occurrence. What also came to light was that he had relationships with a number of women over the period he was coming to see me and these relationships were of various degrees of honesty. Sometimes, he went out with a woman because he felt genuine affection for her. At these times, I began to notice, his symptoms diminished. Commonly, however, he took up with a woman because he thought she would enhance his image. He liked to be seen in public with a beautiful woman, and achieving this often meant pretending affection which he did not feel. When a relationship of this kind was in progress, his symptoms would become far more disruptive. Although he himself was very resistant to any such interpretation, we can see that his fantasy that he was a thief, at such times, was not such a fantasy after all. Even though he had convinced himself that what he was doing was perfectly all right, he could not escape the immediate karmic effect.

The theory of karma predicts that we will have happier lives if we are good. If this is true, then living a good life is therapeutic. It follows that questions of good and bad are not matters of indifference in the therapy, but are quite central to it. If a client describes how they are causing trouble and suffering to others, then I can be confident that they are storing up trouble for themselves. Equally, if I hear a client describe how they have found it in themselves to be kind to others in ways which they had never before thought about, then I can be fairly sure that things are likely to start to improve for them. Since I care about my client, I will be pleased in the latter case and concerned in the former, and the client is bound to pick this up at some level even if it does not seem prudent to discuss the matter immediately.

Some will no doubt say that it is arrogant for the therapist to think that they know better than the client what is right and wrong, but if the client is harming others, no matter what the provocation or justification, there will be a price to pay. It may often, in practice, be outside the therapist's power to prevent the client creating karma for themselves in a specific instance and one might, like a parent watching their child grow up, have to stand by as the client experiments with life, learning the hard way. The therapist's job is simply to understand and not to judge; to be there willing to go on believing in the client's basic buddha nature no matter what they may do along the way. In Buddhism there is no judgement: just, the world is so constructed that we bring joy or trouble upon ourselves. Sometimes the most compassionate course is to stand by and wait for the opportune moment. Sometimes one can help the client explore their own doubts about what they are doing. In the last analysis, the client must decide for themselves, but this does not mean that the therapist has no insight into the matter. Therapy is an intrinsically moral process.

THE THEORY OF EFFECT (Vipaka paccaya)

Following on from the theory of karma, the theory of vipaka states that exhausted karma exerts a background effect which calms the mind and strengthens future positive actions. It provides a backdrop of 'effortless calm', like that which may descend after a storm has blown itself out, which is conducive to self-pacification.

Karma is action. Vipaka is the aftermath of action. The final effect of any karmic sequence is the karma's own extinction. We experience the fruit of our actions and then what? So long as we have not acted in such a way as to restart the same karma all over again, we have brought something to an end, to an extinction. Such extinction is difficult for the ordinary person to achieve yet much to be desired. We know from our own lives and from those of our clients, how much history tends to repeat itself. A client who has been in a violent situation, apparently through no fault of their own, reappears a few weeks later having been in another similar situation. A little later the same thing happens again. From the client's perspective, they are just unlucky. We know, however, that they are in some way acting to keep the wheel of karma turning. Their way of resolving each situation is somehow setting it up to happen again. One day, however, after we have worked with this client for some time, it occurs to us that we have not heard any accounts of such violent situations for a while. The client still perhaps does not understand what is going on and now thinks their luck has changed. Something more than this has occurred, however. A karmic process which used to condition their life has become extinct. It has reached its final vipaka. This will be because the person has learned to respond differently to the events in life which formerly germinated their karmic seeds.

The basic technique of Zen is zazen, also called 'just sitting' (*shikan-taza*). Shikan means 'nothing but'. Shikan is the quality we need if our karma is to exhaust itself. We could translate it as 'whole-hearted'. Anything can be done with this shikan quality. When walking, just walk. When cleaning, just clean. If, when sitting, we just sit, then it is like a glass of muddy water. The particles of mud all gradually sink to the bottom of their own accord and the water becomes clear. When we live shikan, our whole life settles upon itself and clarity results.

There are times in therapy when one can feel that something which has previously caused trouble has now finally been let go of and there is a palpable sense of new-found calm. Becoming conscious of such moments strengthens the client's confidence in a manner which they may experience as slightly uncanny, but which is nonetheless quite recognizable. Such extinctions have a positive effect. We tend to think that only processes which are present can have consequence, but in Buddhism we are taught to appreciate the effect of what is absent as well. Absences can be very consequential.

In the Satipatthana Sutta, to which we have referred before, we find that mindfulness includes not only 'When sensual desire is present in him, he is aware: sensual desire is present in me' but also 'When sensual desire is not present in him, he is aware: sensual desire is not present in me'; not only 'When anger is present in him, he is aware: anger is present in me' but also 'When anger is not present in him, he is aware: anger is not present in me' and so on, and further: 'When already arisen sensual desire (etc.) is abandoned, he is aware of it. When sensual desire (etc.) already abandoned will not arise again in the future, he is aware of it.' Therapy necessarily focuses on a person's troubles but its goal must be their extinction. There is actually, therefore, the danger that through the therapy process itself we come to hang on to what we are trying to let go of. Noticing that some things have been abandoned, however, can be immensely strengthening.

The feeling of having let go, however, can sometimes be difficult to appreciate. At first we may miss our delusions when they go. This has been said to me in so many words by some clients who have recovered from psychosis. They will say that the madness was not pleasant, but it was not dull either. Being caught up in the whirlwind of delusion was perhaps even exciting. When it subsides, the first phase of 'sanity' may not infrequently be a form of depression. Freedom from madness is not necessarily immediately appreciated. The same is true at all levels of delusion; otherwise, why do we cling to it so?

Nonetheless, the theory of vipaka alerts us to the fact that great joy in due course comes from becoming aware of what is absent, knowing a passion has become extinct, a karma has run its course, a provocation no longer has any hold upon us. These absences give us a taste of the peace of nirvana.

· 15 ·

Feeding

THE THEORY OF FOOD RELATION (Ahara paccaya)

The theory of ahara states that we keep our conditioning going by feeding it.

The theory of feeding follows on from the theory of karma. We act in ways that continue our own troubles. If we feel resentment or hate, all too often, rather than recognizing that it is like fire scorching our life, we feed it. We actually go out looking for more evidence of how hateful our enemies or oppressors are and so feed the fire. We do just the same with greed. Instead of seeing what it is doing to us, we indulge and encourage it. Zen does not see this kind of behaviour as 'sinful' so much as simply misguided. The root of all our troubles is ignorance. We do not really understand what we are doing to ourselves. If we did, we would wake up immediately.

The food theory suggests that the way we feed our conditioning is threefold. The three are called contact, will and consciousness. Contact means that we stay in contact with temptation. We allow ourselves to be drawn to it. In therapy, we may have to unscramble how it is that the client over and over again 'just finds themselves' in situations where the same feelings, conflicts and problems are going to arise. It can take quite an effort to realize that the will has actually been involved in this. We generally do not like to recognize that we have chosen to feed our greed, hate and delusion. However, recognizing the part our will plays can be the first step to freedom, since if we can choose one thing, we can choose another. It is better to see ourselves as villain than as victim. Accepting responsibility in this way, however, involves a shift of consciousness.

Consciousness is a matter of attitude, or, we could say, prejudice. We do not see things cleanly. Thus, for many years, English and American people were conditioned to regard Russians as the enemy. The political situation has changed and now we are conscious of Russian people in a different way. An important step in this process was the accident at Chernobyl, when a nuclear power station released its lethal contents into the atmosphere. This was a disaster. One consequence, however, was that, for the first time, westerners saw ordinary Russian citizens being interviewed on TV about their plight. We saw that Russians were ordinary people, just like us, with homes and children and jobs. They were no longer the evil menace. Our consciousness of them changed. The same sort of thing often happens in therapy groups. The task of the facilitator is to bring out the humanity of individuals in ways which enable the group members to become more fully conscious of one another. Whether this process happens at the level of small groups and families or between nations, it is the basic spirit of therapy, healing the rifts between people. While we feed our hate, we will never have peace.

ATTITUDE

In root relations theory we saw that basic ignorance, avidya, manifests as the three poisons, greed, hate and delusion. When avidya is in a state of stasis, it is delusion. When it moves hungrily toward something it becomes greed. When it shrinks away from something it becomes hate. This is at the basic level of sensuality. When these three poisons develop as a 'self' they manifest in new colours. When the basic delusion of self becomes expansive, it appears as pride. When it contracts it manifests as doubt. Thus we have:

Fig. 12. How self is derived from sensuality

	+ve	o	−ve
Self	Pride	Delusion	Doubt
Sensuality	Greed	Delusion	Hate

So we arrive at what are sometimes called the five dullnesses: greed, hate, delusion, pride and doubt. When these are raised to the intellectual level, instead of being dull, these kleshas become sharp, taking on the form of contentiousness, thus:

Fig. 13. How opinionatedness derive from the five dullnesses

Dull kleshas	Sharp kleshas (*drishti*)
Greed	Perverted views
Hate	Extremism
Delusion	Unreal views
Pride	Personality views
Doubt	Superstition

The chatter that goes on in our heads, and the conflicts that arise between people, thus arise from the same roots that we have already examined. If we group all the contentious opinions together, we now have a new list of six fundamental obscurations (*mula-klesha*): greed, hate, delusion, pride, doubt and opinionatedness. Opinionatedness, or attachment to views, is called *drishti*.

We can see from the analysis just presented that drishti is the tip of the iceberg of self. When the Buddha first presented his teaching as a 'Noble Eightfold Path' the first step was to do something about drishti. It is drishti, our opinionatedness, that we are always feeding. The other seven steps, right thought, right speech, right action, right livelihood, right effort, right mindfulness and right concentration, only really become possible insofar as we are able to work on this problem of narrow-mindedness.

This concern about drishti is a particular feature of Buddhism. The Buddha emphasized that we have to overcome our attachment to *all* views, even Buddhist ones, if we are to liberate our minds. In the so-called Snake Sutra (Pali: Alagaddupama Sutta; Skt.: Arittha Sutra) the Buddha rebukes a monk called Arittha for holding on to wrong opinions and goes on to give two powerful similes. The first is the simile of the raft: the teachings are simply a means, like a makeshift raft, to get one across the flood of delusion, not something to hold on to when one has reached the other side. However, as Nyanaponika Thera points out, the problem is generally not so much that people reach the other shore and refuse to put the raft down, as that they abuse the raft *before* they have used it: 'this famous Parable of the Raft will in most cases apply to those who, in the words of the Dhammapada (v. 85), "run up and down the river's bank" on this side of the stream, without daring or wishing to cross. We find them using the raft for a variety of purposes: they will adorn it and adore it, discuss it, compare it – indeed anything else than use it' (Nyanaponika 1974, pp. 5–6).

The other simile is the simile of the snake, in which he says that all teachings have to be grasped the right way, just as there is a special way to catch a snake with a forked stick. If one just gets hold of the snake by the tail, one may receive a fatal bite. Similarly, if one gets hold of the Buddhadharma as though it were an opinion with which to win arguments and boost one's ego, it will turn on you and give you a poisonous bite.

The Snake Sutra also deals with the subjects of self and sensuality. It was Arittha's opinion that sensual pleasures (*kama*) are no obstacle to spiritual progress. This is also a common view nowadays. However, it is our love of self-indulgence that feeds the root of our troubles. Zen Master Nhat Hanh, in his excellent commentary upon this sutra, says, 'In my opinion, Arittha's misunderstanding stems from his failure to see the difference between attachment to sense pleasures and the joy and happiness that arise from a peaceful mind. On many occasions, the Buddha taught that joy and happiness are nourishing to us, while indulging in sense pleasures can cause us suffering . . . the practice of the Dharma does not exclude the enjoyment of the fresh air, the setting sun, a glass of cool water, and so on . . . Once we recognize that all of these things are impermanent, we have no problem enjoying them . . . The Buddha often revealed himself as someone who was able to appreciate these kinds of simple joys . . . But the Buddha did speak of the five sense pleasures (money, sex, fame, overeating and sleeping too much) as obstacles to the practice' (Hanh 1993c, p. 22–23).

In fact, the Buddha repeatedly affirms that the happiness from letting go of self and sensuality far exceeds any happiness which can arise from their indulgence:

Whatever the happiness associated with sense desires in this world, whatever heavenly feelings they bring, it is not worth a sixteenth part of the happiness that accompanies the destruction of craving. (*Udana* v. 10.)

Self-indulgence feeds our conditioning. From sensuality arise the three poisons and from their development into a self-passion come pride and doubt. Upon these five arise all the conflicting opinions and contentious behaviours which create karma. In passing, we can note that there is quite a strong parallel between this Buddhist view of the dynamics of human life as based in the ego passion built upon sensuality, and the Freudian view of the primacy of ego instincts and libido (Freud 1914).

SELF

According to Buddhist psychology, self generates karma and karma constitutes the self. They exist in a circular relationship and, in the last analysis, neither is real. There is no entity corresponding to the idea we have of self. Self is simply the karmic constellation which is manifesting. As we make more karma, we reinforce the delusion of self. When we stop making new karma or extinguish old karma, the sense of self weakens.

That the weakening of self is taken to be a desirable end is generally seen as one of the most significant differences between Buddhist and western psychology. The latter is generally concerned with feeding the ego. Numerous attempts have been made to reconcile this divide between the theories (Epstein 1988) which is considerably confused by the fact that usage of the terms 'self' and 'ego' is far from consistent (Engler 1986, Brazier 1993).

From the Zen perspective, it appears that western psychology digs itself into a hole over this issue by putting together characteristics which, to a Buddhist, do not seem to belong together. Thus talking about 'strengthening the ego' can mean gaining in courage and it can also mean being more selfish. It can mean overcoming one's undesirable habits and it can mean 'thinking about myself for a change'. From the perspective being advanced in this book, the first of each of these pairs is part of giving up self while the second is part of giving in to it. In this respect, the Buddhist use of the term 'ego', for instance, is much closer to that of the non-professional public than is the western psychological application of the term. Most ordinary people, when they say some such thing as, 'That person is all ego,' are using the term in the Buddhist rather than the western psychology sense.

In this book, 'ego' and 'self' are used interchangeably. They refer to a constellation of concepts and images which a person holds deeply and tenaciously in mind as representing themselves. Even though a person is actually more like a river which flows continuously, we like to think of ourselves as fixed entities. We tend to believe that we only have one self or ego, but in practice, we have as many different concepts and images of ourselves as we have social contexts that we identify with. And even within one context we are not always consistent. Getting evidence of our own inconsistency can be disturbing.

Western psychology tends to the view that achieving a consistent self is important and valuable. This is the standpoint of many in the field of humanistic psychology. However, when we look at a text such as *A Process Conception of Psychotherapy* by Carl Rogers, one of the leading humanistic psychologists, what we find is the following:

> In trying to grasp and conceptualize the process of change ... what gradually emerged in my understanding ... was a continuum of a different sort than I had conceptualized before.
>
> Individuals move, I began to see, not from a fixity or homeostasis through change to a new fixity, though such a process is indeed possible. But much the more significant continuum is from fixity to changingness, from rigid structure to flow, from stasis to process. (Rogers 1967, p. 131.)

This conclusion is in line with Zen. The goal of therapy is not that a person establish a strong and predictable self. The goal is that the person become flowing, flexible, responsive and spontaneous: that they move from stasis to process.

In this context it is interesting to point out that in conventional psychological terminology, conditions such as depression, anxiety and obsession are all referred to as 'disorders'. It does not, however, take a lot of thought to realize that this is an abuse of the English language. The thoughts and behaviour of a person suffering from any of these distressing conditions are far more orderly than those of people who are living happy, varied, socially engaged lives. The depressed person and the anxious person both tend to think the same thing over and over again while the obsessional person does the same thing over and over. These are not states in which there is a deficiency of order. They are states in which there is a superfluity of it, hyperorder rather than disorder. What the depressed, anxious or obsessional person needs is to become more disordered rather than less.

These questions of terminology betray underlying prejudices. The psychological systems which invent terms like 'disorder' for conditions of this kind are essentially repressive. They carry the constant implication that whatever does not conform must be stifled. Zen is, in many respects, a more disciplined approach to therapy and spiritual growth than many, but its goal is the liberation of the human spirit. We must always be careful that we are not inadvertently fostering those trends which would reduce people to machines.

Another common confusion on this topic revolves around the idea of a 'damaged' self. It is not uncommon for therapists to talk about clients as 'damaged'. This is a dangerous practice based on another linguistic misconception. The self is the sense or picture a person has of themselves. Many clients do, indeed, themselves believe that they are damaged. We have to be careful, however, not to confuse a damaged picture with a picture of something damaged. That the client has a very much intact picture of himself as damaged is not at all the same thing as *being* damaged. After all, his picture of himself is intact and strongly held – too much so. The problem for such a person is not how best to repair his picture of himself, but how to break it.

As long as we feed the fire of self-passion, we will continue to have a distorted, and overly static, view of reality. Clarity will elude us and we will go on piling up adverse karma, all the while remaining blind to what we are doing. Feeding our faults is not the only option, however.

THE THEORY OF POTENTIALITIES (Indriya paccaya)

The indriya theory states that we have potentialities which can be developed. These include both the common faculties such as the senses, intelligence, life and sexuality, and also the less commonly realized potential for an enlightened life.

In the case of an ordinary person, the indriyas are generally listed as the six senses, masculinity, femininity and life itself, though longer lists are also found. These are our basic stock upon which we trade in life. In the course of an ordinary life, they may wax and wane somewhat. Sometimes we are more full of life than at other times. Sometimes we are more in touch with our masculinity, sometimes more in touch with our femininity. Some of us may develop the visual faculty to a high pitch of acuteness while others may depend more upon sound or touch. These are variables which have been written about a great deal in western psychology.

In the course of spiritual training, however, we realize new potentialities. In particular we acquire five indriyas which appear among the 'factors of enlightenment'. These are shown in figure 14.

Fig. 14. Indriyas: the five higher potentials	
English	Pali
Faith	Saddha
Energy	Viriya (Skt. Virya)
Mindfulness	Sati
Centredness	Samadhi
Wisdom	Panna (Skt. Prajna)

An ordinary person has potential which is based upon the features they were born with – the senses, sexuality and life. The spiritual person develops new faculties which become much more important to them. A spiritually advanced person becomes a rather different sort of being because they have developed these new faculties and so rely less upon the older ones. An ordinary person relies upon their senses, their charms and their basic life energy to get them through. A spiritual person relies upon their faith, energy, mindfulness, centredness and wisdom. They have become a very different sort of creature.

These higher potentials are the ones which we need to develop as therapists. They are also the ones which can help the client rise above the vicissitudes of ordinary life. Therapy, nowadays, is not just about helping people get back to normal. It is about helping people realize their fullest potential. Indriya theory suggests that our behaviour and way of being in the world are strongly conditioned by the faculties available to us. If we have developed the higher faculties we will naturally have a different way of being and this latter way will be naturally therapeutic and enlightening, both for ourselves and others. On the other hand, if we do not possess the higher faculties, it will not make much difference what therapeutic techniques we learn, they will not work in a desirable way because we have not got what matters.

Zen, as we saw at the beginning of this book, relies upon each person having buddha nature. This means that everyone possesses vast potential for enlightenment and constructive engagement in existence. A person can waste their life, or they can make a contribution which inspires. We should not just think about what our clients need. We should also think about what they offer: about the great potentiality of their life. Zen is about expanding our hearts. It goes beyond self-actualization. It rests upon a basic trust in human beings, and in all existence, to fulfil the inherent potentiality, not just of an individuated self, but of the whole: the group, the community, humanity, the biosphere, the cosmos.

At a simple level, we can readily see that if we feed our greed, hate, delusion, pride, doubt and opinionatedness, we will come to grief, and if we develop, instead, faith, energy, mindfulness, centredness and wisdom, we will grow into happier beings in a happier world. Actually finding a 'diet' for ourselves which feeds the higher potentials rather than the lower ones may mean substantial changes in outlook and lifestyle, however.

· 16 ·

Dhyana and Path

(Jhana paccaya and magga paccaya)

The dhyana theory states that it is possible to tame the mind. The marga theory states that everyone creates a path for themselves. For those who follow the way of Zen, taming the mind and following one's chosen path coincide.

The word dhyana (or jhana in Pali) is the Indian word which the Japanese later pronounced 'zen'. Zen is the approach to Buddhism which gives central importance to taming the mind. The analogy here is to taming a wild animal.

One of the best-known portrayals of Zen is the series of drawings called the Ox Herding Pictures drawn by Zen Master Kakuan about eight hundred years ago. Many people feel inspired by these pictures even while knowing little or nothing about Buddhism. Many versions of this text are readily available (e.g. Reps 1957, pp. 133–147; Sunim 1985, pp. 153–171). The series of ten pictures depicts the spiritual path.

The first picture shows a person looking for the ox, but at this stage the seeker is readily distracted and easily tires of the search. In the second picture footprints are sighted. In the third, the ox itself is seen, or, at least, a part of it. In the fourth picture, the ox is seized and a terrific struggle ensues. In picture five, the ox is tamed and becomes naturally gentle and obedient. In the next drawing, the person is able to ride the ox home. In picture seven person and bull rest, the struggle transcended. Picture eight is an empty circle. Picture nine is called 'reaching the source' and represents full acceptance of what is. The final picture shows the person in the world again, like a dead tree that has come back to life.

These famous pictures bring alive for us the struggle that we all go through on the path to enlightenment. Yet I think it would be a mistake to think that the sequence shown represents stages of an actual lifespan. We go through all ten pictures in every incident of life. The 'path' is not a set of sequential steps to be taken one after another. All the steps are in every step. Time and again we have to get out of our complacency and find the ox. At first the ox seems like our enemy, the force which is creating havoc in our life. Later we realize that it has become our friend, carrying us home. Later still we have no need to struggle, but find our direction in a life of natural compassion, love and understanding, giving whatever we have to give and smiling at whatever the world brings to us.

In the history of Tibetan Buddhism, one of the greatest saints is a yogin named Mila-repa. Mila was born in comfortable circumstances but his father died when he was young and he was cheated out of his inheritance by a wicked uncle. Mila grew up extremely bitter and his one aim in life was to get revenge upon his uncle. To this end he worked assiduously upon the study of black magic and eventually found a way to contrive his uncle's death and to bring great misfortunes upon his uncle's family. It was while he was in search of yet more terrible powers that he came across the Buddhist practitioner Marpa. Marpa took him on as a disciple and put him through a severe series of tests of character. Mila must have found his teacher an alarming and unpredictable personality, but somehow he knew that Marpa had what he needed even though he did not yet know what it was. Through the process of training, Mila developed new potentialities. As a result, he began to change the direction of his life. Eventually he became one of Tibet's greatest teachers and most virtuous exemplars. None of this would have been achieved if Marpa had given up on him because his goals in life were not positive ones, or because he was a murderer. Nor would much have been achieved if Marpa had just gone along with Mila's own original goals.

So in therapy, what is necessary is that we appreciate the direction which the client already has, the ox they have already got, and see what can be done. Mila had great determination. Marpa could see that he was powerful, like a young bull. The problem was how to tame him. Marpa's strategy was, at first, to frustrate Mila again and again, telling him that he could not have what he wanted until he had done this, that or the other. The tasks kept changing. Mila kept working to accomplish the tasks in order to get what he thought he wanted. As he performed the tasks, however, he acquired new faculties and, as he did so, as we saw from the indriya theory, his life ceased to be conditioned in the old way and new potentials opened up for him.

This is not an uncommon pattern. Enlightenment is not generally obtained by seeking it since the unenlightened person does not know where to aim. Enlightenment is a by-product of doing what reality gives us to do. The trainee comes to the Zen master and says: 'I spend all day weeding the garden, but what I really want is to be obtaining kensho experience.' The Zen master says: 'Where else do you expect to get your kensho experience than in such tasks as weeding the garden?' This is because, if we are trying to get something, we are acting from ego, whereas when we give something up, then we experience freedom. Gain is delusion. Loss is enlightenment. As we weed the garden outside, we also weed the garden of our mind.

Nonetheless, as we advance, we find that the power to direct our lives grows and does become a basis for practice. This takes the form, on the one hand, of the concentration involved in meditation and mindfulness, and, on the other, of the transforming power of living by vow. Mindfulness we have already examined. To live by vow is to set ourselves upon a one-way path, even though we do not know where it will take us.

THE BODHISATTVA VOW

In early Buddhism, the Pali term *bodhisatta* meant someone who is intent (*satta*) upon enlightenment (*bodhi*) (Narada 1973, p. 337). A bodhisatta is, therefore, a person who is on the way to becoming a buddha. The word bodhi, which is usually translated as wisdom, does not refer to a form of learning or knowledge, but to a way of being and experiencing. To have bodhi means to be in the flow of existence just as it is.

In the later branches of Buddhism which collected their texts in Sanskrit, and which in due course gave rise to Zen, the Pali term bodhisatta got transmuted into the Sanskrit *bodhisattva*. In this translation, however, some shift of meaning has occurred since *sattva* means being. A bodhisattva, then, is a wisdom being, as well as a wisdom seeker.

The bodhisattva has a wisdom mind (*bodhichitta*). This term too may be taken as a mind which is set on achieving wisdom – the mind that seeks the way – or as a mind which is already imbued with wisdom. This is a deliberate conflation of meanings since, from the Zen perspective, these two things coincide. 'Training and enlightenment are the same,' says Dogen Zenji, the founder of Soto Zen in Japan. The wisest thing is to be on the path. In another text, Dogen says, 'Travelling is hindered by arrival.' Bodhi is not a matter of having got somewhere but of being in process, in the flow. A person who has reached the point in Buddhist understanding beyond which progress becomes irreversible is called a 'stream enterer'.

Chitta is the conscious attentive part of the mind. In ordinary people the chitta is led about by all the different objects which come into view, both internal objects (memory and imagination) arising from the alaya storehouse, and external objects presented by the senses. In the bodhisattva, however, chitta is focused upon bodhi, wisdom, and this provides purposefulness. No matter what objects arise, the bodhisattva is able to see them in terms of bodhi. Thus, 'Even if the sun were to rise from the west, the Bodhisattva has only one way. His way is in each moment to express his nature and his sincerity' (Suzuki 1970, p. 54). This is really what, in Buddhism, is meant by living by vow.

Ordinary people, then, live by their karma whereas bodhisattvas live by their vow:

> Ordinary people live thinking only about their own personal, narrow circumstances connected with their desires. In contrast to that, a bodhisattva, though undeniably still an ordinary human being like everyone else, lives by vow. Because of that, the significance of his or her life is not the same. (Uchiyama 1993, p. 196.)

You have to expect to be trampled on by difficult circumstances, maybe even for many years, but don't lose your life force under all the trampling. Unless you have that vow, you *will* lose it. Only when you live by vow does everything you meet – wherever, whenever, whatever happens – reinforce your life as buddhadharma. As long as you have that vow to live out your life whatever you are, sooner or later spring will come. And when it does, you will have the strength to grow ... this is completely different from selfish ambition. (Uchiyama 1993, p. 178.)

The bodhisattva vow may be expressed in many ways. The form which has come down in the Zen tradition from Bodhidharma is as follows:

Innumerable are sentient beings: *we vow to save them all*.
Inexhaustible are deluded passions: *we vow to extinguish them all*.
Immeasurable are the Dharma teachings: *we vow to master them all*.
Infinite is the Buddha's way: *we vow to fulfil it completely*.

Here again, as when we were discussing the Precepts, we see that the aspiration required in Zen has nothing to do with what we think we can achieve with our little ordinary minds and bodies. The bodhisattva spirit is to go completely beyond our little mind and body and identify ourselves with the great mind and body, which is our identity with the universe itself.

There are other forms of the bodhisattva vow. The bodhisattva Samantabhadra vows not to enter enlightenment until the hells are empty. The bodhisattva Dharmakara made forty-eight vows and became Amida Buddha. These particular vows, however, are all expressions of one vow, of what is called the tathagata's primal vow. We have already seen that a tathagata is a person who lives in a completely non-neurotic way, fully in each moment. The tathagata's primal vow is the will to live just like that. So we may say that it is a vow in the sense that it is a direction which we give to our lives. We may say that it is to grasp our will and set ourselves upon the path. But it would be closer to the mark to say that the primal vow is a matter of surrendering. It is to surrender to the buddha in ourselves who is always calling to us.

> Buddha's infinite vow, the original way, is sitting Here-Now eating a meal and drinking tea; without being haunted by any dreams, or empty theories (Hogen 1993, pp. 46–47.)

To live by vow, then, is to live authentically, that is to say, to live from one's depths, whether in simple matters or in those we are apt to call heroic. In therapy, a person has a small sample of such a way of living. In the meeting with the therapist, implicitly or explicitly, there is an undertaking that, at least for the contact time, be it an hour a week or whatever, there will be a sincere attempt to be authentic, to look at everything and not censor, to be willing to face and explore whatever presents itself. It is a period of cultivating 'the mind that seeks the truth'. This is the basic rule, the basic vow, which carries one through all the difficult straits of the therapeutic path. Precisely the same principle holds in this respect for the therapist as for the client.

CONTRITION

The power to live by vow comes from contrition. This is a subject that one sees very little comment on in western books on Buddhism, and even less in psychology, yet it is of immense practical importance. Buddhism is the attempt to free oneself from the grip of basic delusion and self-passion. This requires great energy. This energy springs from a change of heart. The techniques of Zen are all designed to plunge the trainee into a radical reconsideration of his or her approach to life.

Such a root and branch reappraisal cannot be an emotionless affair. When we honestly review how our lives have been, without using walls of self-defence to ward off all that does not create a comfortable picture of ourselves, we are likely to be deeply distressed at how much time and energy we have wasted, how many opportunities to help others we have passed by, and how many times we have acted to bolster our own ego rather than assist others.

> Not to commit wrongs,
> To practise good,
> To help others and
> Purify the mind;
> This is the teaching of the buddhas.

Contrition is the act of facing ourselves and feeling deeply the pain of our own deluded state. This is, or should be, the work of therapy. There are many therapies which effectively collude in avoiding what the client knows in their own heart to be true. Such is not the way of Zen. It is the duty of the therapist to take a longer term view of the client's well-being. In the short run the client may have to go through much pain, and such pain often comes from facing what they have done, their responsibility in their own life. When the therapist can support the client through this difficult task without losing faith, much will be achieved.

We are unlikely to be able to do so, however, unless contrition is part of our own lives. Unless we have examined our own follies and cried our own tears for them, we will not have the confidence which will enable us to accompany the client through their dark valley. Yet the real light is only found in the darkest place. 'The silent voice of emptiness arises from the abyss of painful despair' (Hogen 1993, p. 47). There are many times in therapy when a client comes and confesses the most terrible things and, finding the therapist not in the least shocked, feels great relief. When a person feels contrition, shares it and is heard, they feel restored to wholeness.

A person who understands karma feels the effects of what they do. A Zen practitioner does not give up eating meat because there is a rule saying 'do not kill'. They give up eating meat because they are open to the suffering of the animal. We live in a world in which it is impossible not to be involved in the creation of suffering. To open our hearts in this way is to expose ourselves to the 'great grief'. This great grief, however, can displace all our little individual griefs and open us to a world of great love, great compassion and great joy.

Contrition is the beginning of Zen training and the heart of Zen therapy. Nothing is actually ever achieved in our personal lives without a change of heart. A person can practise as much meditation as they like, perform ceremonies, give to charity and so on, but if there is no contrition, there will be no real change. A change of heart comes by searching our lives and being willing to make changes in ourselves. It involves giving up the habit of self-defence. The task of the therapist is to create a space which is safe enough for the client to undertake such a process of self-examination.

The subject of guilt is central to much therapy. Many people are driven mad by their sense of their own guilt. It is important for us to distinguish, therefore, between real guilt and humiliation. Often enough a client will say that they feel guilty, but they have done nothing to deserve it. They feel guilty because others disapprove. This is a quite different case from the person who themselves genuinely repents of some action they have carried out.

Facing our guilt is one of the greatest tests of character we can expect in life. The ego likes to believe in its own purity and perfection. Yet, however hard we try, we still find that our passions take us unawares and almost before we know it we have hurt this person and cheated a little in that matter and forgotten that other thing which we know we really should have done.

Contrition shakes the ego's grip. In Zen, we say: 'All the harm done by my body, speech and mind is caused by greed, hate and delusion, which have no beginning. I now face and confess it all from the bottom of my heart.' This verse shows us that we must take responsibility for ourselves even though we seem to have very little real control. Generally, in life, a person is only supposed to be held responsible for the things over which they had control. However, in Zen, we have to assume responsibility by a voluntary act while knowing that the harm we have done was committed in blindness. Really, in Buddhism, there is no such thing as sin, only ignorance. From a Buddhist perspective, the villains of history are not evil, simply stupid. We ourselves have participated in the same stupor. The whole enterprise of Buddhist training is an attempt to wake ourselves up.

THE ZEN WAY

The path offered by Zen, therefore, is a life of continually, in each moment, liberating ourselves from ourselves by engagement with the needs of the reality around us. It is a bodhisattva path which puts the spiritual need of the world first as it manifests in each concrete situation. As such it is the path of therapy. Real therapeusis is more than a professional or technical role, it is a way of being which has inherent healing power. It is not simply the therapy of this or that client, but the mind which seeks the healing truth of each and every encounter.

The Zen approach is to see whatever is already happening as an opportunity for liberation. Thus Zen Master Dogen wrote: 'When one studies Buddhism one studies oneself; when one studies oneself one forgets oneself; when one forgets oneself one is enlightened by everything and this very enlightenment breaks the bonds of clinging to both body and mind not only for oneself but for all beings as well. If the enlightenment is true, it wipes out even clinging to enlightenment' (Kennett 1976, p. 172).

Zen therapy sees that the dilemma which brings a client to a therapist is some manifestation of the client's buddha nature calling the client to liberate themselves from conditioning. It is an opportunity. To take such an opportunity, however, requires considerable courage. This kind of courage can arise from the companionship which therapy provides. Therapist and client set out together. As we have seen, eventually the client will have to start taking steps on their own. This is like helping a child to walk. The aim is that the child walk freely and confidently on their own, but this process can be facilitated by the helping hand of the parent. Just so, in Buddhist training, we benefit from having a 'good friend' beside us.

CONCLUSION TO PART TWO

By way of conclusion to this part of the book, let me highlight some of the points made as we have reviewed the paccayas:

Root relations: The root of our troubles is basic ignorance, manifesting as greed, hate and delusion. The remedy is to rely upon original sanity, manifesting as compassion, love and understanding.

Object relation: Mind is conditioned by its object. Life can be improved by focusing upon wholesome objects and by transforming unwholesome ones.

Predominance: Ordinarily the mind is dominated by kleshas, but it can be liberated by the predominant influence of intention, attention, energy and enquiry.

Association: Each moment of mental activity is conditioned by the one before. The chain can be broken by mindfulness which returns us to direct perception of reality.

Interdependence: Since all aspects of samsara are interdependent, it is possible to sweep them all away in a single realization. Zen favours the 'sudden' approach.

Nissaya: Everything grows out of something. Body and mind are not separable. Zen practice is physical.

Support: The offer of support to others is both the natural expression of the therapist's way of being and the path to healing for the client.

Habit: Establishing wholesome and orderly habits of life provides a springboard for spontaneity and creativity, not a restriction of them.

Karma: Deliberate actions have consequences. Selfless actions have powerful consequences for the world, but do not create karma for the doer.

Vipaka: Exhausted karma provides a background of effortless calm which strengthens our Zen practice.

Food: Generally we feed our failings, but we do not have to do so. In particular we are inclined to feed our prejudices.

Indriya: Everybody has the faculties of body and senses, sexuality and life. The Zen path allows us to realize higher potentials which permit a more useful and blissful way of being.

Dhyana: It is possible to tame the mind and Zen provides the way to do so.

Marga: We all create a path for ourselves. The Zen path is to live by mindfulness and by vow, thus realizing our highest potential.

Part 3

Therapy as a Zen Way

· 17 ·

Compassion

CONFORMING TO THE TAO

Zen incorporates the Chinese concept of Tao. Tao (Japanese *do*) indicates both a living tradition and a way of being. Every art has its way. The universe itself has its way. The concept of Tao thus indicates both the discipline of a traditional craft and the spontaneity of nature. A craftsperson who works with natural materials conforms to the nature of those materials and to the traditions of the craft, and from this produces a masterpiece of beauty and originality. Also, the craftsperson gives their all to their work, yet also manages to make it look effortless. These are the characteristics of a person who follows a way.

One suggestion of this third part of the book is that therapy too can be a Zen way. The therapist must conform to the Tao as it manifests in the client. A therapist is made by a long apprenticeship which is character-building rather than merely technical. A skilled therapist gives total attention to their work, yet the effect is to allow it to flow naturally. The therapy way conforms to the Zen pattern.

Compassion (*karuna*) means to wish others free of suffering. In one sense, it is the passive dimension of spiritual training, where love is the active side. Compassion is the feminine, receptive aspect. It simply wishes the other to be free from whatever hinders them. In Zen, however, we aim for more than just sympathy for people in distress. The Buddhist idea of 'great' compassion (*maha-karuna*) implies something universal. Ordinary compassion is to feel sorry for someone. Great compassion means to be in unity with the needs of all beings, even the plants and inanimate phenomena of nature.

Mahakaruna, then, is more than empathy. In empathy, I retain my separate existence. I can empathize with the person drowning in the river while knowing that it is not me that is drowning. In mahakaruna, I *know* that it *is* me that is drowning in the river. This, perhaps, is the difference between Buddhism and humanism. The enlightenment experience of Zen is to know one's identity with everything.

Nor is mahakaruna the same as ordinary pity, though it may manifest in many separate acts of kindness. Ordinary compassion is partial. To kill the fleas which are irritating one's cat is an act of partial compassion. It contains compassion for the cat, but not for the fleas. Nor is great compassion the same as mundane compassion. Mundane compassion is kindness based upon a materialistic view. Thus to give someone a present with a mind that is conscious of a giver, a gift and a receiver of the gift is mundane compassion. At some level one is keeping score. There is still an element of trade and calculation involved. In great compassion one gives without any sense of giver, gift or receiver. One does not really think of it as a gift at all. One is just following the Tao, doing whatever the situation demands.

The self, or separate identity, is generally drawn from some collective identification. We identify ourselves by the groups we align with – our family, our work, our sports team, our sort of people. Mahakaruna is to expand this 'we-consciousness' to include the whole universe so that there are no longer any 'out groups' for us.

Then we see that each being has its own way which is an expression of the great way. The great way (Tao) is mysterious, but omnipresent. Compassion is to tune in to the way of the individual who is in front of us now. Great compassion is to flow with the Tao. When we can do this, it is as though our actions are mysteriously aided by an 'other power' (*oyasama*).

BODHISATTVAS

In Buddhist mythology there are many ideal beings given to us as models of wisdom. They are called *bodhisattvas*. These beings also personify 'other power'. The personification of oyasama gives other power a human face. It is important to understand, however, that, in the Buddhist conception, this does not imply divine intervention. Oyasama is, rather, a natural law of the universe which works without fail.

A bodhisattva is someone who is on the way to becoming a buddha. All of us become bodhisattvas as soon as we start to take our Zen work seriously and the work we do contributes to creating a world in which all good actions become more efficacious.

In the Far East, the most widely acknowledged story conveying the idea of other power is that of Dharmakara Bodhisattva, who was so compassionate that he felt all the sufferings of others as his own, and as a result of deep faith and diligent training, became a buddha himself, called Amida. According to the story, Amida still exists in 'the western paradise' ready to come to the aid of whoever has real faith in him. This is an archetypal story which conveys to us the message that compassionate and enlightened action will always be aided in ways that we cannot necessarily explain from a commonsense or materialist perspective.

Amida Buddha is said to have an assistant called Avalokita. Avalokita is the bodhisattva of compassion, 'the one who sees deeply'. He can appear in male or female form. When female she is called Quan-yin, 'one who sees the world's tears'. Quan-yin, then, is the spirit of great compassion in the world. She is closer to us. She responds to our suffering and helps us find the great compassion in ourselves.

The bodhisattva, then, is a therapist for the world. Quan-yin never turns away from suffering, but can only really help someone who turns toward her, be it ever so little. In the same way, we as therapists need to detect the part of the client that turns toward a more enlightened, that is compassionate, life. Quan-yin has boundless concern for all beings, and is like a good mother to everyone. Zen mind is also, therefore, called 'parental mind' (roshin).

Recently, in a dharma group, a friend who serves as a volunteer hospice worker raised the question: What does compassion feel like? Working with dying people he wondered if he was becoming too involved or too detached. The Buddhist texts suggest that the bodhisattva views all beings as if they were one's only child. However, for most people, if one's only child were dying, one would be in terrible turmoil. The parental mind of the bodhisattva has the same depth of care that we have for our children, but is big enough to encompass all beings.

We are bodhisattvas, but, as yet, we are only apprentices. We are trying to move ourselves into this world of great compassion and unbounded goodwill. At the moment we are probably far from it, but if we make it our pole star, the point we navigate by, always having it in mind when we make our choices in life, little by little, we will come closer to it. As we do, we will become better therapists for the world. In this endeavour, the stories of Dharmakara and Avalokita can sustain us.

SELF AND OTHER

Compassion overcomes ego since it means to value others. Many people think that therapy means helping people to value themselves, but this is not the Zen way. According to both Buddhism and Taoism, valuing self is counter-productive. Satisfaction comes from selflessness (*muga*), that is, from conforming to the Tao rather than to selfish whims. In Taoism, as in Christianity, they say that the one who puts themselves last, comes first; the Tibetan Buddhist lama Thubten Zopa writes:

> You are just one person. Even if you are reborn in the hells, you are just one person – nothing much to get depressed about. Even if you achieve liberation from samsara, you are just one person – nothing much to get excited about. All of the numberless sentient beings – those who are called 'others' – are just like you in wanting happiness and not wanting suffering. Their wishes are exactly the same as yours and they are numberless. Each one is as important and as precious as you think you are; and these others, each of whom is so important and so precious, are numberless. (Zopa 1994, p. 115–6.)

All the suffering we experience comes from our involvement in defending our self. If we let it go, we simultaneously let go of mental suffering. In particular, compassion is the remedy for aversion. When we looked at the 'three root kleshas' we saw that they are greed, hate and delusion. In aversion or hatred I wish another person harm. In compassion, I wish them freedom from harm. Cultivating compassion dispels hatred.

Compassion is to understand the other person's subjective world without stealing anything. Stealing means taking over. In compassion, I become the other; I do not force them to become me. In compassion one sees through the eyes of the other, and feels with their heart, without any private agenda. Great compassion is achieved by identifying oneself with the whole cosmos. We become at one with every being. This means having no separate position that one is trying to defend.

Compassion is to speak and act upon an accurate intuition of another person's world as seen, felt and understood from the inside. It is to know the person's suffering as one's own without losing freedom or wisdom in the process. Compassion is distinct from ordinary identification, which is what occurs when our ego gets involved, looking for something for itself. Thus one may have compassion with both parties to a dispute whereas one could only agree with one side or the other. Indeed, compassion requires objectivity about ourselves (Figurski 1987, p. 200). Compassion involves unconditional acceptance and is intrinsically therapeutic. As Carl Rogers, the founder of person-centred psychotherapy, wrote: 'To be with another in this way means that for the time being, you lay aside your own views and values in order to enter another's world without prejudice. In some sense it means to lay aside your self' (Rogers 1980, p. 143).

We are all naturally caring and we can learn to be more so. For instance, we can learn to listen. We can stop and notice things. We can think about the other person's perspective. We all actually have much greater capacity to understand others than we suspect. When we hear others a powerful transforming process can be released in people's hearts. Our world is torn apart by hatreds and compassion is the only solution. Rogers, for instance, commenting upon his work with groups of black and white people, points out that many of the responses made by white people are quite inadequate to the depth of feeling being expressed:

> Rage needs to be *heard*. This does not mean that it simply needs to be listened to. It needs to be accepted, taken within, and understood empathically. While the diatribes and accusations appear to be deliberate attempts to hurt the whites – an act of catharsis to dissolve centuries of abuse, oppression, and injustice – the truth about rage is that it only dissolves when it is really heard and understood, without reservations. (Rogers 1978, p. 133.)

COMPASSION HEALS

It is not only, however, that people need to be recipients of compassionate action. They also need to find the same spirit in themselves. The best compassion is that which supports compassion in the other. Oppression in society is pernicious because it overtaxes oppressed people's basic will to act from their hearts, punishing them even when they do their best. When we despair of acting from our hearts, our lives become distorted and we fall sick, physically or emotionally. It is very hard to live in an oppressive society without becoming demoralized.

Nonetheless, it is still the compassion which the client finds within which really heals, shifting their centre of gravity out of themselves and engaging them more healthily in their world. The task of therapy is not simply to develop compassion for the client, but to foster the spirit of compassion *in* the client. Buddhist therapy is not so much concerned with feeling sorry for people as with helping them develop the best in themselves.

Compassion grows from the basic skills of mindfulness. The client generally already has plenty of positive qualities inside them. They are not using them because they have become self-preoccupied. Western therapies tend to concentrate upon unravelling the stories of the traumas which have led to this self-preoccupation. Zen focuses mostly upon doing something about it. Therapy may, therefore, start with redirecting the client's attention outward. This can be simply by cultivating observation. When we are self-preoccupied we quite literally do not see most of what is around us. Therapy does not have to reinforce obsessional inward questing. The client can simply be asked to observe things around them. In due course, they can be encouraged to start noticing what the situations around them need. The plants need watering. A room needs to be tidied. Clothes need mending. These are all acts of compassion, even though the 'recipient' is not necessarily an animate being. The more the client opens their eyes to their surroundings, the less trapped in aversive feelings they will be. The more they can give themselves to constructive activity, the less dominance ephemeral feelings will have.

People derive their sense of purpose from their capacity for compassion. Joe is a client in his seventies. All his life he has been a heavy user of alcohol. He neglects to feed himself, preferring to spend what money he has on drink. His living conditions in his small terraced house are rather squalid. Now he suffers from memory loss which has been medically diagnosed as being a consequence of alcoholism and malnutrition. As far as most of the welfare and medical services were concerned he was a hopeless case. The best that had been achieved to date was to stave off his admission to institutional care by providing some domestic help funded by the welfare services. However, Joe has a dog and the therapist noticed that the dog was rather better fed than Joe himself. The dog, however, has not been in good health recently. Perhaps the logical, materialist solution would be to get rid of the dog that eats all Joe's food and that Joe can hardly look after properly. The therapist decided on the opposite approach, however. Joe cares about the dog. This is the most positive thing in his life. This is the remaining element of compassion which gives Joe's existence meaning. If the dog goes, there is nothing else Joe can put compassion into. His family rejected him and have not been seen for years. The therapist made little attempt to change Joe directly, but built up an alliance with him around the task of caring for the dog. This involved trips to the veterinary clinic and giving Joe responsibility for the dog's medication, diet and exercise. All attention focused on the needs of the dog. On the second trip to the veterinary clinic, the therapist noticed that Joe had taken considerably more care with his appearance. Little by little improvements began to occur in the way Joe kept house. Joe did not stop drinking, but he did start eating. Enough was achieved to ensure that he would be able to remain out of hospital and institutional care when this fate had initially seemed imminent. People will do things out of compassion that they would not do for self.

When people believe that they have nothing to give that anyone would appreciate, they become suicide risks. Elderly people nowadays are particularly at risk of feeling useless, but this sense is common to many people of all ages in our overly complex and, in many respects, callous society. From a Buddhist perspective, it is the power to give which is what really matters, rather than the power to get. Allison told the therapist, at the end of a session, that she was going to commit suicide. The therapist was immediately filled with strong feelings and said that he would not allow her to do any such thing: that, if necessary, he would not let her leave his office. She protested that it was none of his business whether she killed herself or not. He retorted that it now felt like it was very much his business – how could he live with himself if he let her go and she were dead the next day? Eventually she promised not to kill herself before seeing him again and left. Later she told him that this encounter had made a great impression on her because she realized that her being alive made a difference to someone else. She stayed alive that week because she did not want to inflict hurt upon him. In due course she found more reasons.

In psychodrama role reversal is used to allow the protagonist to experience the world through the eyes of another. Role reversal is, in effect, a western way of operationalizing the ancient Buddhist teaching of 'exchanging self and other' (Gyatso 1986, pp. 264–282). Xerka Moreno, one of the world's leading psychodramatists, has commented that in her experience, the use of role reversal is one of the most important, if not *the* most important technique in psychotherapy. Certainly this is the Buddhist view. When we are skilled in reversing roles with others, we can understand the multifaceted wonder of this world.

In psychodrama, role reversal is acted out. The client changes places with a person playing the part of a significant other and acts out that other person's part in life. Thus, through role reversal, I might play the part of my mother, my child, my friend, my rival or whoever. Through role reversal people frequently arrive at cathartic insights which irreversibly shift their perception of life. Role reversal is, in particular, a technique used to encourage reconciliation and forgiveness.

Exchanging self and other can also be achieved through dialogue and imagination without dramatic enactment. When a client talks deeply about a loved one, struggling to appreciate the difficulties which that person is experiencing, enhanced compassion for the other is achieved. This often melts hardened attitudes. In place of suspicion or hurt, appreciation and caring take over. The 'problem', seen from a new angle, suddenly becomes simply a human situation. Developing compassion for the significant people in our lives is an essential step toward maturity and happiness (Figurski 1987, p. 197). The solution to psychological problems is the achievement of a bigger heart capable of appreciating a wider spectrum of viewpoints and rising above particular frustrations.

Compassion is not just a matter of having feelings for people. Sometimes we invest our caring in our pets, like Joe did, or in our gardens, or in artistic or work activities. All employment which contributes to some positive end, relieving suffering, feeding, clothing, housing or helping people in practical or psychological ways, is compassion. Creating something beautiful is a kind of compassion too, since it involves putting one's energy, caring and attention outside oneself and into improving the world. The creation of beauty is thus therapeutic.

For some years, Caroline Beech and I have been offering workshops called 'Healing the Creative Spirit'. At these events, participants practise tranquil meditation to achieve a degree of inner peace. Then, equipped with the heightened sensitivity this brings, they allow their intuition to draw them to particular arts media or natural objects, and work with them. Often the workshops are done at our retreat centre in France and much of the work is done outdoors. In a variety of exercises we come into contact with stones and wood, paint and clay, sounds and movements. In each case, however, the aim is not to express what is in us, so much as to bring out what is already present in the natural forms. This kind of work is not really self-expression so much as the attempt to empathize with the object and make its deep character tangible. We have found that much more is achieved by feeling with and conforming to the material than by trying to impose one's own idea, feeling or plan upon it.

Failure to achieve compassion is the root of the sharpest forms of mental suffering. Compassion is the antidote to hatred and aversion. Role reversal is the path to the healing of hurt relationships. In this world in which we find so many fragmented lives and broken communities, the need for compassion has never been so great. The modern materialistic selfish world needs the touch of Quan-yin more than ever.

CONCLUSION

Compassion is the antidote to aversion. It overcomes the bitter root of hate which causes so much trouble in our lives. We can cultivate it. We are all capable of thinking about the needs of others in a kind way, wishing them free from their suffering and acting upon such wishes. We can begin this process by focusing our attention upon a small number of people close to us. As therapists we can do so with our clients. Any act of compassion sows a good seed which can then grow in our consciousness and begin the work of transforming our life.

Compassion is natural and is the basis of our remaining alive from the very first bond of mother and child. Therapy is about planting and maturing good seeds in the mind. Compassion restores meaning to life, mutuality to relationships and reality to our world.

Compassion may begin as a set of observational, empathic and caring skills – thoughtfulness, giving time and attention, listening, helping and generous action – which we can all improve with good effects upon both our professional work and our private lives. As it grows it becomes, inexorably, a challenge to us to overcome the obstacles (*kleshas*) to life within ourselves and to flow with the boundless Tao in which we lose our attachment to separateness. The world needs kindness.

· 18 ·

Love

Just as Avalokita symbolizes great compassion, Samantabhadra, the bodhisattva of patience and action, symbolizes great love. Love is an art of knowing when to be patient and when to act. Here, even more than with compassion, however, it seems necessary to draw the distinction between great love and ordinary love. Ordinary love is the love we have for the things and people which are important to ourselves. Great love is non-possessive and unconditional. People who have this kind of love can heal the wounds of the world because they do not discriminate in favour of one group and against another. They are genuinely non-blaming.

Love heals greed, as compassion heals hate. In greed, I want to get things for myself, to incorporate everything into me and my orbit. In love, I want to give to others, to respect things just as they are, unconditionally. In the comparison with humanistic psychology which runs through much of this book, just as compassion is close to empathy, love is close to the quality of positive regard.

Again, these qualities are not just for the therapist. If the client is gripped by attachment, then they need to find the love in themselves. In western therapies, we tend to think simply of the client's need to be loved. The real shift occurs, however, when the client rediscovers their own capacity (*indriya*). This may happen through receiving the unconditional respect of the therapist which models the quality the client needs, but this might not be enough: necessary but not sufficient. The client might just feel inadequate. Or, the client might be so much in the grip of a fixed idea that they cannot see what the therapist offers. The therapist must also recognize occasions when the client is grounded in their own love faculty and acknowledge them. Recognition accesses the client's truth.

A client apologizes for being late. She explains that she had stopped by to take something to a friend and when she arrived found that the friend's window had just been broken. She stayed to help mend the window. As a result, she was late for her appointment. The client then said, 'I am no good at looking after myself – I shouldn't have offered to help her.'

Therapist: 'You looked after your friend: how can you look after yourself better than by looking after a friend?'

Client: 'No, I can't let myself get away with it that easily. I want to be angry with myself about it.'

Therapist: 'OK, I'll listen.'

Client: 'Well, I could have left home earlier in the first place.'

Therapist: 'Yes, you could. What you did was good, but that would have been even better.'

In this sequence we see the therapist highlighting the client's kind action and refusing to accept the client's initial proposal that she should not have helped the friend. The therapist does not get unduly caught up in a debate about whether the client is of good character or not, but indicates, both by what is said and by a smile, that the client's kindness to her friend is appreciated and that the therapist does not feel angry.

This client had learnt from involvement in other kinds of therapy that looking after her own interests was more important than caring for her friend. This is a crazy idea which is quite common. With this belief, the client feels perpetually guilty, but not in a constructive way. The whole idea is pernicious. Having accepted that it is right to be selfish she now feels guilty when she does something kind as well as when she does something cruel. Consequently, there is nothing she can do which does not make her feel worse. This makes work for therapists, but it does not help people.

The fact that, to some, the central tenet of therapy seems to be that one should learn to be more selfish, is very sad. Again and again I hear people who have been in other therapy say: 'I know that I should be thinking of my own needs more;' or: 'I find that I still sometimes think of others when I should be thinking of myself;' or: 'I used to put others first, but I have learned from therapy that that is not the thing to do.' They feel guilty that they are not being selfish enough, and they also still feel guilty when they really are selfish, because this is natural and appropriate.

Nobody is made happier by cultivating a selfish world. If selfishness is the message of therapy, then we are deeply misunderstanding human nature. Some may need to learn how to care for others more wisely or less compulsively and to do so in ways which are generous rather than martyrish, but the idea that we will be healthier if we will just stop caring for others is a recipe for personal and collective disaster. Madness, in fact. There is a serious danger of therapy becoming the handmaiden of consumerism, unrealistically trying to get people to be selfish and blocking their natural feelings of shame about it.

The way to increase people's confidence is not by turning them into more selfish individualists, but by helping them find dignity in the qualities of love and compassion which they already have. This idea is unacceptable to many therapists because they associate it with a political view about the place of women in society. They want women to become as selfish as they believe men already are, in order to achieve a kind of equality. There are, however, much better ways to improve society than reducing everything to the lowest common denominator. As therapist, our task is to find the best in people, not the worst.

This means that the therapist has to be like a mirror which reflects both the deep and the shallow part of the person. The method called 'mirroring' in which the therapist adopts behaviour similar to that of the client in order to give the client opportunity to consciously choose their own lifeway, is an established part of Zen method which is relatively little discussed in the west, not least because of the potential for abuse. Nonetheless, a skilled Zen practitioner who has got their own ego out of the way knows how to reflect the client's characteristics to them, not just verbally, but by actions which are often unexpected, sometimes even shocking. This kind of mirroring is not something that can be contrived as a kind of trick. It depends upon the therapist having their own desires firmly under control and being completely willing to let go of 'playing the therapist', acting entirely from their deep sense of the Truth in the client's life.

When therapy begins, the client, quite rightly, is likely to test the therapist in a variety of ways to find out if the latter is really trustworthy, non-judgemental and able to avoid having their own selfish desires cloud the therapy process. Later, once the client has established trust in the therapist, the testing may occur the other way round. If the client is going to grow, there are bound to arise a series of tests in the relationship as well as in the client's life, which they will have to surmount. These situations may have been fostered by the therapist or may arise quite naturally. They help to ripen the client's koan, which will, in one form or another, be to do with the question of how to be a more uninhibitedly loving person in this world of hurts and sorrows.

MAITREYA

A therapist first must care about the client. This is the bottom line. Therapy is about cherishing others. It simply would not work if the therapist spent the time with the client being primarily concerned about his or her own needs. The Buddhist word for love is *maitri*. Maitri is loving kindness, impartial friendliness. A therapist is a spiritual friend to the client: a friend to the Truth, or Tao, in them. According to Buddhist belief, the next Buddha in this world will be called Maitreya, 'the loving one'. To make the next Buddha appear we have to find the spirit of loving kindness in ourselves.

To do therapy, it is essential to be able to love without resentment. If there is a voice inside the therapist demanding, 'What about me?', the therapeutic endeavour is hardly likely to be successful. If one believes that by attending to others one is losing something, therapy of any depth will not happen. One cannot be unconditional while believing that there is only a finite amount of love to go round.

The unconditional spirit means acting without regard to getting something in return. The emergence of therapy as a profession owes much to the fact that recently, everything, even love, has become a commodity to be bought and sold. Even though we live in conformity to this society our work has to be in a different spirit, the spirit of Maitreya. Therapy as a formal institution, in which a client pays a therapist for an hour of the latter's time, all belongs to Caesar. It is simply one of the conventions of our age. In other ages, tribal people might have brought gifts to the village shaman who would then make a journey to the spirit world for them. The gift, as it happens, enables the shaman to continue being available to others for this purpose. It also endows the client with a certain dignity.

Within this conventional framework, the sacred work must be created beginning with the therapist's surrender of self-concern. Zen begins with the emptying of the therapist. The best therapy is completely empty (*shunya*). Empty of what? Empty of ego. Shunyata (emptiness) means the therapist is wholly there for the client, the other. As therapy proceeds the client also becomes shunya. Then they can examine their life without ego getting in the way. The client's ego is getting in the way of their life. The therapist's ego gets in the way of the therapy. To love is to surrender the ego. Therapy, at best, is an experience of shunyata.

When the client's ego grip is too strong, they fear to let the process flow, say only what they think the therapist wants to hear and want guarantees and specifications about the outcome before launching into the work. The very effort to retain so much control, however, defeats the object, like trying to swim while still holding the side of the pool.

The techniques of therapy may be as variegated as our imaginations, resources and courage permit. They all serve to induce shunyata, so that spontaneous love will have a chance. Love is to be open to real understanding. It is not just a sentiment. Without depth of understanding, love does not happen. And deep understanding requires space. When we give someone space, we find that they have good intentions and a human heart just like everyone else. Fundamentally there is nothing wrong with the client. The more times we really see this, the more confidence we develop that even the most unprepossessing individual has treasure hidden somewhere upon their person. If we can just create the right conditions, they will be induced to take it out and show it to us.

TENDERNESS

Shunyata is innocent. A child picks up an unfamiliar object and turns it over in his hand. He looks from this side and from that. We can do the same. Pick up a stone. Turn it over in your hand. Become familiar with it. Notice its colour, its contours, its crevices. As you do so, the stone becomes real for you. It becomes something. Close your eyes. Continue to explore the stone. Feel its weight in your hand. Feel its temperature and texture. The stone is beginning to become a friend. You may notice other mental factors beginning to come into play: possess- iveness, memories, gentle or aggressive feelings, aesthetic judge- ments pass through one's mind. If you allow these to get a grip, direct experience of the stone will be lost and you will, willy nilly, be thinking about other stones, other times, other exercises . . . whatever. Try, however, to keep your attention here with this stone. It is also possible for your imagination to come into play without losing direct contact. The stone fleetingly becomes an implement or something decorative. The surface of the stone becomes a landscape, a miniature world. To the innocent mind, the stone may be anything at all. And yet, not quite anything, since it does have particular qualities which present themselves and make a real impression upon us. The stone is always other: wonderful and mysterious. As such it can be a friend and not simply an extension of myself.

Thus tenderness grows. We start to care about the stone. Just like a child, we invest caring in the object. From a materialistic viewpoint this is absurd. The rock has no monetary value and minimal utility. But is this not precisely the nature of caring? We do not care in order to get something back. We do not have tender feelings for something in order to be able to sell or use it. We simply appreciate the thing itself. In some ways a stone is particularly easy to care for since it asks nothing in return. Now I am tempted to ask: Is the stone a therapist? Is the best therapist a stone? In a way, yes (cf. Kopp 1985). And many people do indeed find this simple exercise of holding a stone in their hand comforting. We go for a walk on the beach. Along the way we pause and pick up a small rock. Perhaps we have been attracted by its colour or shape, by something distinctive or just by its ordinariness. The stone becomes a friend, perhaps for a minute or perhaps for many years. The stone does not mind. The stone does not require us to sign a contract nor pay a fee. The stone has no agenda to change us. And yet, we find the stone a comfort, something solid in contrast to the unreliable impulses we experience within ourselves.

The client describes the phenomena of his life. The therapist and client cherish them together, like so many stones turned over in the hand. It is the quality of caring which either endows them with precious qualities or converts them to dross. What is generally presented are scenes; significant memories. Sometimes the client talks in abstract terms or simply about feelings, but generally this kind of speech is being triggered by some specific personal material. The therapist needs to get into the client's world and so, perhaps, begins in a descriptive way. Describing scenes given to me by the client, I begin to appreciate their finer textures. The therapist does not jump to conclusions – avoids bias in how they listen. As the client and I become more familiar with the phenomena presented we can begin to make friends with them. I lose my self in attention to the client's world, and so does the client.

Of course, speech is not the only nor even necessarily the best medium in which the phenomena of lives can be represented. The client may find it more useful to draw, paint, act, mould clay or make 'sculpts' with objects to hand. This last can be particularly powerful. Using a variety of objects such as might be found in one's pocket or handbag to represent the most salient features one may construct a representation of a family, a work situation or a whole life world.

My client takes four cushions and uses them to make a boundary for a square, like a small fortress. She stands and looks at it for a moment. She then replaces the cushions with wooden stools, commenting that their hardness more suitably conveys what she is trying to represent. 'I'm inside there,' she says.

Casting round the room she picks two other cushions, dark, smooth and comfortable, and places them half overlapping each other, about four feet away from the stockade of stools. She is not yet settled, however. She picks up a drum and drumstick from the corner and places them with the cushions. 'That's my family,' she says. I clarify that she means the household of her parents who live in another part of the country, which she affirms. She places another drum to represent one of her children and indicates a space for another child whom she does not wish to represent by any object. At each step of this process she stops and regards the whole sculpt. The picture unfolds before us. She goes on adding more objects – a clock, soft toys, a set of Russian dolls, a pot plant – to represent different characters, not excepting the family cat. My role is to remain attentive, to provide space and, occasionally, to comment on distinctive features of the objects chosen, to reflect and empathize with any interpretations she offers, but not to be searching for them. The process of perception itself drives forward the necessary work and my part is more one of self-restraint and gentle appreciation. I am not here to fix anything. I am to appreciate another person's world and to intensify their experience of it. Eventually she feels the layout is complete. Again she takes stock. Silence. At last I ask if there is any way she would like to change the sculpt. 'I would like to make the walls softer,' she says, and replaces two of the stools with cushions again. She then moves them outward a little, so as not to be too confining. 'I think that might be possible.' She reviews her work. 'I feel tired,' she says.

Zen works on the principle of emptying rather than filling. Love is to give a person space in which to follow intuition and put burdens down. When we reach emptiness we feel tired, yet lighter. In the case just described, the client is using a tangible medium to tease out her picture of her own world. Such work relies upon her willingness to follow her intuition. The therapist's task is to protect the space, rather than to extract from it solutions, advice or snippets of wisdom. Such things are, at best, reminders. The real learning is by experience (*taiken*). We do the work for the experience of tenderness in doing it.

There is a common fallacy that one 'does a piece of work' in order to deal with a particular 'issue'. This is the mechanistic fallacy creeping back in. We do a sculpt or a psychodrama or a verbal session or a painting, not to banish an issue, but to train ourselves to trust spontaneous creativity. The issue is simply the raw material. The work is art not logic. By the ritual of the work we transform the issue into raw material for creative living.

A person comes to a therapist looking for a fresh view. The therapist has an open mind. Clients present matters in which they have been immersed for a long time. The therapist sees them fresh. In Zen, however, the aim is not that the client be able to collect the therapist's fresh view and add it to the views they already have. To do so would destroy its freshness. The aim is to induce the client into freshness of their own. Therapy must free the client from pre-established views (*drishti*). Being unconditional means being there and it also means leaving the client alone.

A new client comes into my consulting room. She smiles at me. I smile in return. I notice, however, that my smile feels tense and unnatural. I stop smiling. She bursts into tears. She then begins to unfold the tragic facts which she has been hiding from everyone. This thirty-second non-verbal interaction with a stranger illustrates in a simple way how our lives are dominated by conventional responses and how powerful even a small break with them can be. If, as convention prescribes, I had continued to smile politely, it would have taken longer to get to the point and established an ethos of artificiality. Therapy has to begin with something which jolts the person out of the conventional attitude. One might think that the space will be safer if I smile and sometimes this might be true. But it is far more important that I be genuine. Therapy is not to get rid of discomfort, but to experience truth, which means that the therapist must be beyond needing to be popular.

TRAINING OURSELVES

Love is patient. It also involves action and skill. The competent therapist will benefit from knowing how to do sculpting, art therapy, psychodrama, encounter groups, behavioural programmes, transactional analysis, reframing, hypnosis, meditation and so on. The therapist needs imagination and inner freedom (*muga*) to create skilful means to suit each situation, weaving all and any method into the work. To achieve such versatility we have to do something about ourselves, for it is we who get in our own way.

A trainee therapist tells how an elderly male client brought pornographic material to a therapy session. 'I thought afterwards: Is he getting sexual stimulation from trying to shock me in this way?'

Supervisor: 'How does that make you feel?'

Trainee: 'Used. It's repulsive.'

Supervisor: 'So what sort of regard should we have for this client?'

Suddenly, the trainee's demeanour changes. She realizes that her commitment to *unconditional* positive regard means something. At this point she lets go of her self-defence.

Trainee: 'Thank you. This session has been really useful.'

It is absurd to think that people can become therapists just by following a college course or accumulating a certain number of hours of experience. This guarantees nothing. Indeed, some may be worse for their training since it carries many pitfalls. Two which are widespread are, firstly, that we may harden our hearts and start to think diagnostically about clients in ways which distance us from their humanity. This is the path of professional detachment. On this path we can become so boundaried that we are never really touched by the client's life. Or, alternatively, we may go down the path of becoming more and more preoccupied with 'our own needs' to the point where listening to the client is hardly possible. Much that passes for personal growth simply encourages us to be more self-indulgent and less concerned. There is no evidence that such 'growth' enhances anybody's ability to be a therapist. It is in fact diametrically the opposite to what is required.

During many years of being a trainer, I have been struck by the number of times that people who seemed marginal candidates turn out to do best. Similarly, we cannot know in advance what transformations a client will achieve. Zen Master Kusan Sunim tells us that 'it is not always the most virtuous or intelligent person who makes the swiftest progress. Sometimes the opposite is true. There are many cases of troublesome and ill-behaved people who, upon turning their attention inward to the practice of meditation, have quickly experienced a break-through' (Kusan Sunim 1985, p. 62). All the great Zen teachers of the past had their besetting faults. It was by doing something about them that they became teachers.

We, therefore, need humility. There are very few foibles found in my clients that I cannot also see the seeds of in myself. The kind of personal growth which we need is not ever increasing assertiveness in the interests of getting *my* needs met, but the kind of emptiness which Zen asks for: the constant attempt to put self aside in order to learn from the flow of events.

SUMMARY

In Zen we learn to listen deeply, observe carefully, and notice appreciatively. To train ourselves to do so means more than simply applying techniques for fifty minutes at a time. Rather we are challenged to do something about our lives as a whole: to find a 'way of being' not just an ideology. Therapy is an encounter in which experience of the fullest aliveness is possible. Therapy happens heart to heart and unfolds according to its own inner process which is not predictable. The better we can be at letting go of self-preoccupation, the more successful we will be in creating good conditions for it. There is no novelty in my conclusion that the fundamental healing principles are love and understanding. Our task is to eliminate the barriers to them within ourselves.

· 19 ·

Wisdom

THE BEGINNING OF ZEN

The Buddha established a place of retreat called Vulture Peak. It was here that he gave many of his most important teachings in the later part of his life. It is recorded that one day the god Brahma came to Vulture Peak and, giving the Buddha a golden flower, asked him to deliver a teaching as though he were on the point of laying down his life. The Buddha got up on to the teaching seat and lifted up a flower. The audience did not understand what was going on. Kashyapa, however, understood and smiled. The Buddha then said: 'I have the Dharma-gate of the Treasure-house of the Dharma-eye, and I now hand it to great Kashyapa: guard it well.'

This piece of interaction was the beginning of the transmission of Zen. Zen is enacted in dialogue. The dialogue may be between one buddha and another or it may be between a person and a blade of grass or it may even be between inanimate things. There is so much in this short dialogue that it would take forever to explain it completely. And even then, it would not have been explained, since understanding is not to be found in explanation but in experiencing for oneself (*taiken*). The Buddha always said that his dharma was *ehipasiko*, that is, something for each wise person to sample for themselves.

Nonetheless, there are some things we can say about this dialogue. This story is presented in part because it is full of trip wires and each time we fall over one of them we learn something about ourselves. First, Brahma came to the Vulture Peak. If we believe that Brahma is the god who creates the whole world, why would he come to ask for teaching from a mortal? If we do not believe in world-creating gods like Brahma, what is the Buddha doing talking to one of them? All this, however, is just chop logic. Zen is to chop our way out of such chopping.

Brahma asked Buddha to teach as though he were about to lay down his life. This is much easier to understand, but very hard to do. True wisdom is to lay down one's life every time. To really live in the here and now is to lay down one's life in each action. This is real faith. Faith has nothing to do with believing in Brahma or not believing in Brahma. Faith is about laying down one's life. Everyone is willing to lay down their life for something. When we find out what we are willing to lay down our life for, then we know what our religion is. The enlightenment of Buddha is to be converted to this Way: willingness to lay down one's life for the Truth all the time.

This is actually an everyday matter. What is our life? Is it the continuation of our story about ourselves? Is it the satisfaction of our desires and plans? Is it what has happened to the bearer of our name over the years which have now disappeared? None of these is really our life. There is a well-known story of two monks coming to a stream where a geisha girl is trying to cross without wetting her silk gown. The senior monk picks up the young woman in his arms, carries her across the stream and puts her down on the far bank. They exchange a few kind words. The two monks then go on their way. Some time later, the junior monk bursts out with: 'Whatever did you think you were doing with that woman? Carrying a woman in your arms is completely forbidden for a monk, as you well know!' The senior monk is surprised. Then he says: 'Are you still carrying the woman? I put her down at the stream.' Being a monk is a story. When he picked up the woman, he was no longer a monk. The monk died. Carrying the woman is another story. When he put her down, that story died too. But neither story died for the younger monk and so he was left with pain and confusion as the two stories battled it out. In psychotherapy, our clients come to us as victims of many stories that battle it out inside them and will not die.

A client comes to me and says, I am a good family man with a loyal wife and a fine child that I care about very much and I am also a philanderer who cannot say no to any of the several other women who want my affections. I do not know which is the real me. I seem to be a good husband, but I cannot be because I cheat on my wife. This client is being lived by his stories about himself. Several more stories emerge in the course of our discussion. His story about himself as an enterprising and innovative worker presents further conflicts with the two stories already described. This is the common plight. We think we are a single unified ego, but experience reveals us to be the victim of many different seductive stories. The idea of being a unified ego, of having a true self, is itself simply another story. The challenge in therapy, the key to the Dharma-gate, is to be found in Brahma's request. Can we say a true word as though on the point of laying down our life?

Buddha ascended to the teaching seat. When our buddha-nature ascends to the teaching seat we should be willing to listen. The wisdom we need is not to be found in attachment to doctrines. It is found when we allow the Buddha to ascend to the teaching seat. When the Buddha is on the teaching seat, the stories we have about who we are die. There is just the necessity to perform a true action now.

On this occasion, the Buddha's teaching was of the utmost simplicity. It usually is. He raised a flower with his hand. There is no magic in it being a flower. This is not symbolism. It happened to be a flower. The audience were all waiting for the Buddha to give them something, but they did not see what he gave. Later, Ananda asked Kashyapa, 'What did the Buddha give you?' Kashyapa said to Ananda, 'Cut down the flagpole by the gate and leave it lying.' In English we have a saying: 'Nailing your colours to the mast'. When we nail our colours, our flag, to the mast, we are saying what we are willing to fight and die for. Kashyapa tells Ananda to die now, before the fight starts. This is the best way. The Buddha died straight away. He did not give the audience anything. He did not fight them waving a doctrine or an identity. He had already cut his flagpole down. Whatever he held up, it would have been radiant for Kashyapa since Kashyapa had opened the source of radiance in his own mind.

In therapy, the therapist must die all the time. Really the therapist does not give the client any particular thing. But the client may notice that the therapist keeps dying. Each time the therapist dies, a part of the client's prison dies with him. Again and again the client comes back with a new flagpole and the therapist helps him cut it down.

The Buddha said, 'I have the Dharma-gate of the Treasure-house of the Dharma-eye.' When a person dies, they pass on their property to their heirs. What property does the Buddha have? He does not have any land or titles to pass on. What he does have is the gateway to the treasure-house. What is the treasure-house? The treasure-house is the same storehouse, the same alaya consciousness, as contains all the karma of ordinary people. The alaya storehouse which contains all our karmic conditioning becomes the storehouse of spiritual treasures, the source of radiance, when it is seen with the dharma-eye. A buddha has the eye which sees even the lifting of a flower as a perfect moment. Who is the Buddha's heir? The Buddha's heir is anybody who can awaken this dharma-eye. In the assembly on Vulture Peak it was Kashyapa. But we are always in the assembly on Vulture Peak and Kashyapa is always here in us. We are no different from Kashyapa, if we will just see the Buddha and die with him in this moment.

PRAJNA PARAMITA

A Buddhist word for wisdom is *prajna*. Etymologically this word is quite close to our own word 'diagnosis'. Prajna refers to the ability to see into the heart of the matter, not as a result of erudition, but as a consequence of having given up all that obscures clear perception. The obscurations we have already discussed. They are called *kleshas*. Clear perception we have also discussed. It is called *vidya* and is the opposite of delusion (*avidya*). Another term we have also considered is the word *paramita*. Paramita means perfect or boundless. Prajna paramita is the term for seeing into the heart of things without any constraint or conditioning getting in the way. The Buddha gave a series of teachings upon prajna paramita and these are used extensively in the Zen approach.

The most commonly used prajna paramita text nowadays is

the Heart Sutra. This is a very short series of statements which deny all the things which one might cling to as a basis for constructing the kind of story which might provide a Buddhist identity for oneself. The text is set out in figure 15.

Fig. 15.   *The Heart Sutra*

Avalokita Bodhisattva,when practising deep prajna paramita, realizes the five skandhas are all empty and thus goes beyond every suffering. Shariputra, form is no different from emptiness, emptiness no different from form. Form is the emptiness, emptiness the form. Feelings, perceptions, mental confections and consciousness are also like this. Shariputra, all real things are manifestations of emptiness: not born, not disappearing, not defiled, not pure, not gaining anything, not losing anything. Therefore, in the heart of emptiness there are no forms, no feelings, perceptions, mental confections, consciousnesses; no eye, ear, nose, tongue, body, mind; no colour, sound, smell, taste, touch, objects; no eye-world and so on to no consciousness-world; no ignorance and no getting rid of ignorance; and so on until there is no old age and death and no getting rid of old age and death; no cause of suffering, nor nirvana nor path; no wisdom, and no attainment. Letting go of attainment, bodhisattvas rely on boundless wisdom. Mind has no obstacle. When there is no obstacle, there is no fear. To go beyond all troublesome views is to do nirvana. All buddhas, past, present and future, depend on prajna paramita. So profit from complete understanding – utmost, perfect enlightenment. By this, know that prajna paramita is the great unexplainable true word, the great true word that is radiant, unequalled, incomparable; able to erase all suffering; truth without blemish. So declare true words of boundless wisdom and those true words will say: *Gate gate paragate parasamgate bodhi svaha* (Enlightenment is to go beyond, utterly beyond, svaha).

When the Heart Sutra says 'not born, not disappearing, not defiled, not pure, not gaining anything, not losing anything' it is demolishing the components out of which our stories are constructed. We think that we live a life which is born somewhere and will die somewhere else, which, along the way, does some good and some bad, makes some profits and some losses. This kind of story is the stuff out of which we create an identity for ourselves. Much therapy is commonly concerned with helping a person refine their story, helping to make it fit better the evidence of their real life. Real Zen, however, brings the realization that however good a story we concoct it will never be the real truth. The Heart Sutra is telling us that all stories of this kind are just 'cover stories'. They are never satisfactory in anything more than a very makeshift fashion. All of us go through life under false pretences. Only when we become bodhisattvas, like Avalokita, actually practising boundless wisdom, do we see that all the component parts of our life as we identify it, the *skandhas*, are empty. Only then can we find real freedom and boundless wisdom.

Not only are all our worldly stories about ourselves meaningless in the last analysis, but it is also worse than useless to start thinking that we can escape from their clutches by constructing a spiritual identity for ourselves. The Sutra, therefore, goes on to pull the rug out from all the elements of Buddhism itself which people quite commonly use to construct a spiritual ego story. Even clinging to nirvana and the path is taken away from us. In an earlier chapter, we saw that the idea of a path is the final form of self-conditioning. Nirvana, the Sutra says, is not something we can have, it is only something we can do. And we can only do it when we leave all our troublesome opinions aside. Only then do we practise real understanding.

The Sutra ends with a mantra. A mantra is a true word. It is also a guardian of the mind. The challenge in any Zen dialogue is to speak a true word which will protect the mind from delusion. This is not a rarefied abstraction. There are many situations in life when we are called upon to speak up for the truth, even though we are surrounded by common human madness. How often do we pass the test? In therapy too, the client will often simply repeat all the nonsense that others have fed into them and the therapist may have to say: 'Yes, that is what others have said to you ... And what do you say? What is the truth, really?' To find our own truth we cannot rely upon our history as anything more than a springboard. When we say a true word, we have jumped off. Then we have gone over the edge, gone completely beyond. Then we are in the ocean of real truth, learning to swim.

FOUR WISDOMS

In Zen, prajna encompasses compassion and love. Karuna and maitri are part of wisdom. Zen Master Dogen (in *Shushogi*) says that there are four wisdoms: generosity, loving words, goodwill and identifying ourselves with others.

'Generosity' means giving without expecting anything in return. The scale of the gift is not the point. What matters is the boundless mind of giving. All work is an act of generosity if done in this spirit.

'Loving words' means to speak tenderly, full of compassionate respect, regarding others as one would one's own children. To hear loving words spoken brightens the heart. An even greater effect results from discovering that good words have been said about you in your absence. Loving words have a revolutionary impact upon the minds of others.

'Goodwill' means to think of ways to benefit others. Nowadays it is common to scoff at the idea that pure altruism can exist. People say that nobody does anything that is not selfish in the last analysis. This is to misunderstand the situation. Since we are all part of one another, whatever we do for others will benefit us anyway. We do not need to calculate what our benefit will be. We can just act and forget.

'Identification', in the sense in which Dogen is speaking, means not to distinguish between self and others, but simply to be full of great compassion.

BEING OUR BEAST

In Buddhist iconography, the bodhisattva of wisdom is Manjushri. Manjushri is commonly depicted sitting in completely tranquil meditation on top of a ferocious beast. Thus, the wisdom we are talking about here is one which remains composed even in the most dire situations. However, there is more to this symbolism than at first meets the eye. We are not here just looking at a depiction of a good person keeping their animal nature in constant check. The beast and Mānjushri together symbolize the wisdom we are looking for.

When a person has prajna, they also have vidya. They see the world just as it is and they appear to others just as they are. They do not have a hidden shadow side. The beast is on view too. This is also called being 'just so' (*tathata*). It is a person not trying to appear to be anything other than what they are. It is the opposite of dissemblance. It is closely related to honesty, authenticity, transparency, immediacy, and spontaneity; or, in the language of humanistic psychology, congruence, yet its meaning does not precisely coincide with any of these. Principally, prajna refers to the mind which can transcend every situation, rising above conditioning and restoring harmony. It allows us to live in the universe as our true home and allows the universe to live in us as one of its true beings. To be as wise as Manjushri means simply to live the reality of our life.

A conditioned life jangles. It is out of kilter with itself, inharmonious. We may speak here particularly of harmony between body, speech and mind. By body we mean behaviour: all the movements and sensations which constitute our experience of our physical being. Mind refers to our sentiments, beliefs, emotions, thoughts and imagery. Sometimes we make similar distinction by talking about a person's 'outer' and 'inner' lives.

In practice, the lines between body, speech and mind cannot be drawn with precision. Nonetheless, the distinction is meaningful so long as we do not start to think that it is absolute. The more harmonious we are, the less easy it becomes to distinguish one from the other.

A person who smiles (body) while saying (speech) that they feel miserable (mind), appears inharmonious. Much psychotherapy, personal growth and spiritual work revolves around the attempt to achieve self-harmony, to eliminate incongruence. Disharmony is one of the most used signposts in psychotherapy. When the client manifests signs of disharmony, that is where the therapist is likely to focus attention.

While what has just been said is not untrue, there is a more revealing way to think about it. To say that therapy is about eliminating incongruence, or that Zen is about eliminating delusion, gives an over-simple idea of the process. If this were it, then Manjushri would just kill the beast, like St George did. Buddhism, however, is not that kind of approach. The human being is infinitely more complex than this simple prescription suggests. It is actually the beast that leads us to the Truth; or, we may say, it is the alaya storehouse of karmic troubles which turns out, in the end, to be the treasure-house. When we focus upon some element of apparent disharmony in ourselves or in another person, therefore, we find ourselves entering into an appreciation of human depth (cf. Neumann 1969).

We could say, therefore, that therapy, rather than being a matter of helping a person get rid of disharmony, is actually more a process of coming to appreciate the full complexity of the person, by learning from it. Disharmony is really just superficial. When my client covers his misery with a smile there is an appearance of disharmony. Beyond this apparent self-contradiction, however, we find everything which makes this person a character rather than simply a façade. His smile, for instance, is harmonious, perhaps, with his desire not to put me ill at ease and it may well be this sensitivity to the needs of others which, in juxtaposition to adverse circumstances common in the world, accounts for his misery. Thus, in this hypothetical instance, we quickly see that there is no inconsistency between his misery and his smile after all. Both derive from a single aspect of his character which I had failed to appreciate immediately. There is a deeper wisdom.

Apparent disharmony between different aspects of a character gives us a bearing, as it were, upon the parts which we cannot immediately perceive. The most deeply hidden part is the buddha nature. When the hidden part is perceived, what had been taken to be delusion no longer seems so. Thus by attending to what we see as disharmony we discover the secret parts of the person and as we attend to this secret reality, we have the experience of the clouds of delusion disappearing. They do not disappear because one of the aspects of surface appearance has been removed or changed. They disappear because we begin to see a bigger panorama.

All psychotherapy is concerned with understanding what is

going on when people are 'not themselves'. This much-used colloquialism is recognizable as meaningful to nearly all of us even though logic tells us it does not make sense. How can one not be oneself? Clearly, 'self' can cover a great range of perceptions which a person has of themselves, a great range of different things which, nonetheless, we have learnt to consider as one thing, namely our self.

I do not wish at this point to return to deep analysis of the concept of 'self', but merely to note that it is not a unitary entity. Self is what one identifies with and so it is not necessarily fixed, even from moment to moment. We have many ego stories like the many clouds which float across the sky. While we long for clear weather, the clouds are an obstacle to our happiness. When we learn to appreciate the whole sky, the clouds are seen simply as its adornment.

To refer back to the example given earlier, if I were to confront my client with a statement such as: 'I hear that you feel miserable, yet I observe that you are smiling,' it is quite likely that this person would not be able to offer any immediately satisfactory explanation and might well say: 'Yes, I'm silly like that sometimes,' or make some equally unrevealing apology. And yet, even this apology does again reveal the person, because it is also congruent with the same sensitivity we referred to earlier. People can apologize, dissimulate, lie and even deceive themselves, but they can never depart from the realm of truth. It is by examining our lies that we discover the truth, and someone who can see the truth sees beyond the disharmony of appearances.

When one is harmonious, one's outward manifestation in behaviour, facial expression, speech and so on is all of a piece with one's inner sentiments, beliefs and thoughts as they arise. However, what is consistent and what is inconsistent is more a function of the depth of perception of the observer than a description of the actual state of the person in question.

The deep wisdom of each person is thus not necessarily readily accessible. Manjushri lives in the hearts of all, but it takes a wise person to perceive this. Prajna is the ability to see the deep harmony of each person and each world we encounter, to see the sky and appreciate its clouds. A deluded person experiences a world divided into enlightened and unenlightened, good and bad, congruent and incongruent beings. An enlightened person experiences a world in which all are enlightened. A deluded person is attracted, repulsed or confused by everything. An enlightened person is enlightened by everything. A good therapist is one who is not ready to discard any part of the client, but sees how all is a manifestation of the hidden truth.

· 20 ·

Secret Way

A SECRET WAY

Let us make a small digression into the question of secrecy and consider whether it has any positive value. Nearly all theorists of psychotherapy seem to advocate openness and honesty in all things. There have, however, been some who have taken the view that this is a culture-specific attitude which may work less well in proportion as one becomes more distant from the United States of America!

A famous exponent of the Japanese No Theatre, Zeami, said: 'What is concealed is the flower. What is not concealed cannot be the flower. To know this distinction is the flower, and among all flowers this flower is the most important' (Doi 1986, p. 110). Doi comments upon this statement that 'For Zeami, secrets did not exist because what they made secret was important. It was the fact of making something secret itself that was important' (Doi 1986, p. 111).

Not only in Japan: in former times the acquisition of a skill, trade, profession or spiritual discipline typically involved being admitted to the 'mysteries'. These mysteries were guarded as a precious treasure. The importance of secrets as a repository of power pervaded most aspects of society. The power of women lay in their handing down of mysteries, just as did the power of societies of men. It was only in the 'modern' age that people came to believe that everything should be exposed and mystery be banished from our lives. Are we the richer for this?

This exposure of everything to scrutiny was begun by the early Protestants who wanted no priests between them and their god. Then came positivism, rationalism, progress and

223

modernism, giving birth to many advances in science and technology, but also a Pandora's box of problems. Now we live longer, eat better (some of us), kill each other more efficiently, have more complicated lives, sustain bigger cities (and smaller forests), but are not noticeably happier than we were. Science has not unravelled the mystery of the human heart.

Sometimes we find in a bookshop a volume which purports to reveal in a few chapters the secrets of some esoteric society or tradition. We know, of course, that no book is really capable of such a thing. The 'mystery' of a carpenter, for instance, does not reside in the instructions in a DIY manual, but is lodged, rather, in the harmony of his body and mind when interacting with a piece of timber. Such a thing is not at all easy to convey in words, but it may inspire wonderment if we can become aware of its presence. In the east, this mysterious quality is called Tao. Zen appreciates the Tao and attempts to restore our sense of wonder before it. It does not try over-hastily to explain everything away. Better return to emptiness. No explanation is, in any case, ever adequate to experience.

Therapy can also be considered a Way, a development of character. Just as a master carpenter would work with the grain of timber, so the follower of the therapy Way responds deeply to the grain of the client's life. The client embodies the mystery. Our task is to appreciate and not destroy it. The mystery of mysteries is the buddhata, the most precious treasure. Only a buddha has the key to the storehouse of this treasure.

The client, of course, does not necessarily know that they have precious treasure upon them. She may believe that she suffers from her secret self and think that the sooner she gets rid of it the better. The experienced therapist, however, is by no means so enthusiastic to expose and dispose of everything too quickly. To do so is rather unseemly and shows disrespect.

The client brings us a precious gift, carefully wrapped. To simply rip off the paper as quickly as possible to get at the contents would evidence only shallowness. In Japan, there is a sophisticated art in wrapping presents so that it is by no means obvious how they are to be undone. Their secret is to be revealed only slowly and with care. When we tear off the paper with undue haste we betray the fact that we are more interested in the contents than in the meaning of the gift: we display greed rather than love.

CONGRUENCE AND SECRETS

In one sense, vidya is about not having secrets: the enlightened person has nothing to hide. In a more important sense, however, it is about being true to one's secrets: the secret essence laid up in our hearts to which it is impossible to do full justice, save through our manner of being itself.

We might say that love is what occurs when we become open to the secret life of another person. Therapy involves an attempt to appreciate these 'secrets'; and because words are so often inadequate we can use all the great variety of artistic, dramatic and expressive media which people have developed for this purpose. However, the aim is not to expose the secrets, but to experience their depth.

The first rule of therapy is confidentiality: secrecy. Therapy is in the tradition of the mysteries in creating a special place in which to do its magic work. In this crucible we create compassion, love and understanding. The wisdom of the therapist springs from her capacity to be true to the secret reality. This faithfulness enables the client to rediscover and cherish his own mystery again. Love is signified by doing this secret work together. The client's hidden wounds are also the key to his heart. The 'confession of a secret is the same in essence as a confession of love' (Doi 1986, p. 133).

THE MIND HAS ITS OWN WAY

Having said a little about secrecy, let us now return to our exploration of harmony. We have seen that Zen, rather than bringing everything to consciousness, accepts that the mind has its own Way. Allowing it without being trapped by it, rather than resisting it, is the Zen approach. Let us look at some western views of incongruence and see how Zen contrasts with them.

a) Dissimulation and the unconscious

Disharmony between a person's acts and their inner state may be rationalized by reference to unconscious motivation. Why would a person not reveal some aspect of self? One answer might be to deliberately hide something while another might be that the person is simply not aware of what they are not disclosing.

If one is going for a job interview, one might not wish to reveal how nervous one feels. One might choose to dissimulate by dressing smartly, wearing a smile and talking in a louder voice. Dissimulation is not unconscious because the person knows their own inner state.

Then there are situations of lowered awareness. If we are not offered the job and are asked how we feel about it, we might answer straight away that we feel disappointed. Later we realize that we only said 'disappointed' because that is what people expect you to say, whereas really we felt relieved not to have to take on a job that was too difficult.

Then there are situations in which some aspect of our being is completely out of reach of consciousness until revealed by a detailed analysis of our whole situation. These are the sort of occasions catalogued by Freud in which we make 'mistakes' like choosing a wrong word or phrase which nonetheless reveals an unconscious wish, or where we managed to forget an appointment with someone who had stood us up on a previous occasion, or where we quite inadvertently leave some item behind when leaving a place to which we would like to return, thus giving ourselves an innocent motive to carry out our desire.

Avidya can thus be related to the psychoanalytic concept of the unconscious. Avidya is behaviour motivated by unconscious desires. Vidya, from this perspective, is the (exceedingly rare) condition of being free from repressed motives.

The attempt to bring everything to consciousness, however, is vain and unnecessary. The enlightenment offered by Zen allows us to use the radiance of the alaya-vijnana (the unconscious), rather than to empty it. The depths of the person are mysterious, radiant and inexhaustible.

From these depths love, compassion and wisdom arise quite

naturally. Often it is more important for the client to learn to use this boundless energy than to remain locked into an interminable analysis predicated upon the assumption that 'there is something wrong with me'. Love needs protection. The therapist who seeks over-hastily to lay bare the client's soul may do more damage than good, but the one who is patient and gentle while remaining grounded in appreciation of inner mysteries may be able to help even the most wounded client to a renewed appreciation of life.

b) Conditions of worth

A second explanation of incongruence is Rogers' theory of 'conditions of worth' (Thorne 1992, p. 32). This part of Rogers' theory is not original on his part and may seem common sense. The general idea is that a child is shaped by its need to receive love. It is said that instead of providing unconditional acceptance, parents trade upon children's needs in order to get them to behave acceptably, or to meet the narcissistic needs of the parents. The parents place conditions upon their affirmation of the child's worth, saying, in effect: I will affirm that you are a good child so long as you behave in an acceptable manner. The child thus learns to disguise some of its needs, to dissimulate, and thus becomes incongruent. The theory of conditions of worth is part of a general tendency in modern western psychology to blame parents for everything.

The theory is open to criticism, however. It seems somehow unsatisfactory to assert that the process by which all children are necessarily socialized goes against their basic nature in a fundamental way. I have argued elsewhere (Brazier 1993) that rather than being shaped by its need to receive affection, it is just as possible that the child is formed by its own efforts to express love. Pleasing behaviour in a child is not a betrayal of true nature for the ulterior motive of obtaining approval. In general, people enjoy pleasing others and this enjoyment neither seems to be a false sentiment nor need it be mediated by some secondary consequence such as approval seeking. Indeed, it is only when it is so false or mediated that we are inclined to call it incongruent. Being rewarded by the person we have pleased may actually detract from the pure joy of seeing their pleasure.

We learn to be incongruent, primarily, in order to protect our inner capacity for love. When the circumstances are inauspicious, the best part of ourselves goes into hibernation, like the princess in Sleeping Beauty. When we encounter a client in this state, the therapist may have to find his way through a forbidding thicket and over decaying battlements before he is able to provide the kiss of life. The Sleeping Beauty story is a depiction of the common koan.

The theory of conditions of worth, therefore, seems to be based upon a somewhat pessimistic view of human nature as essentially self-seeking which, in many respects, seems out of keeping with the general tone of Rogers' theory and certainly does not fit the Zen view. Clinical experience suggests that when one gets to the core of the client's personality one does not generally find a grasping nature, but rather a capacity for love. When one gets to understand more and more people ever more deeply, one repeatedly has the experience of finding that even self-defeating or destructive behaviours have actually been the acting out of deep (hidden, secret) motives which one can recognize as positive, and, in this, I am sure Rogers would concur.

c) Search for personal consistency

Humans alternate between 'simply being', when one is lost in one's engagement with the world, and 'reflective being', when one stops this flow in order to take stock. When our stock-taking shows that what is revealed by our contact with the environment is in harmony with what we inwardly believe and value, we feel confirmed. When our experience (body) and beliefs (mind) disaffirm one another we feel disturbed.

In some circumstances such disturbance is pleasurable, in others distressing (Apter 1989). If our experience is always confirming, life becomes boring. If it is repeatedly disconfirming we begin to lose our sanity, we become confused and distrustful. In order to reduce the danger of insanity we screen out a great deal of the information which would otherwise be available to our senses. Freud suggested that our sense organs function not so much to gather sensory data as to protect us from overload. We only accept a partial experience. The struggle to achieve integration, inner consistency, elimination of incongruence, is thus a normal part of our everyday psychology and can never be complete. Zen does not attempt to complete it, but to return us to our original nature before such complications set in. Actually, some degree of inner harmony returns naturally when we give ourselves to something beyond self. Complete harmony (*ku*) comes with complete self-surrender (*muga*).

d) Alternative stories

Another idea is that incongruence comes from the stories we tell ourselves about ourselves. Each project we take up in life gives us a role in a story. Since we have many projects, the stories are not always consistent, nor the roles compatible with each other. This can be conducive to richness of life or lead to inner conflict as we struggle to evolve an over-arching story within which each of our projects can find an acceptable place as sub-plots.

The stories or 'scripts' which we live may have a variety of origins. Often they can be traced to the fact that our ancestors continue to live in us. Although ancestor worship has gone out of fashion, we still often do live out patterns of behaviour which speak of an unconscious identification with figures from our family history. Thus, one part of my client may be living out a story which has as its prototype her great great grandmother who, as family legend has it, was a bit of a libertine. Another part of the same client may be trying to live up to the example of an aunt who was always kind to her and who expected good behaviour. These two parts of my client may have difficulties with each other.

Now the idea of congruence becomes more elusive. How can a person be true to two conflicting plots simultaneously? Often, of course, what our client exhibits is ambivalence, and this may well be truly congruent. It is by attending to the client's ambivalence that the therapist gets to hear more than one story and so starts to appreciate the real depth of the person who turns out to be not so much 'in-dividual' as, if I may coin a term, richly dividuated.

Of course, if one pursues this line of logic one comes to a point at which one can say that a person is always necessarily congruent in the sense that whatever they do must correspond with some aspect of their 'life story', with one sub-plot or another. Zen, however, is not seeking the construction of an over-arching story. It seeks, rather, a pre-story identity: the face we had before we or anyone else ever conceived of us. If we can return to the root in this way, then we can appreciate all the stories without being enslaved by any of them. The therapist who can do this is free to play whatever part is needed. The client who can do it will no longer be trapped in neurotic worry.

A PERSON IS LIKE A LANDSCAPE

A physical landscape has a history. Here frost has sculpted a slope of scree. Further down a grassy bank of runkled turf has been created where rain has made the surface slip. Further down still water has gathered into a stream and a change in the water table has led this stream to incise itself between banks which now look like miniature cliffs. Yet in this natural landscape we can also experience the spirit of eternity.

A person too has a history and a varied personal landscape produced by exposure to adventitious circumstances. This scenery of our life is not the buddha nature, yet none of it is apart from the buddha nature either. Its history can be deciphered, but it can also impart the spirit of eternity.

One can regard a landscape in different frames of mind. If it is familiar, one probably takes a good deal for granted. This is the everyday mind of people lost in the conventional attitude. Or one might take a more scientific interest, trying to see through the surface forms (diagnosis) to identify the forces (analysis) which have been at work: glaciation here, fluvial erosion there and so on. This is the approach of the analyst. Or we might be like the poet, noticing each feature for its special 'character' or spirit and allowing each to work its own particular magic upon us until the whole phenomenon becomes infused with charm and its own special coherence, somehow coming alive. This last is more akin to Zen.

These three approaches are equally available in our dealings with people: the everyday (conventional), the scientific (reductionist), and the Zen (intuitive). In Zen therapy, the client's story, or koan, is worked over repeatedly, until a breakthrough occurs in the person's identity. It is worked away at with great energy by the client who for a long time can neither put it down nor go beyond it, until many tributary tales have flowed into it, until it has here and there broken its banks and found more conducive channels, until its flooding has rendered the lowlands of life fertile again, until it has found its way to the ocean of common humanity where all our separate stories find their common outlet and merge together in the shining sea.

TRUE WORD GROUPS

A Way has traditional forms, but it is also a living force. When the two Ways of Zen and therapy are cross-fertilized new forms emerge. We have made considerable use of the Tea Ceremony tradition, in which a simple act – drinking tea together – becomes the basis for sharing and reconciliation. From this have also developed groups which retain the deepening effects of Zen ritual while incorporating many of the features of western sensitivity groups. Here we create a ceremonial space in which tender secrets can be acknowledged.

Jane gets up from her seat quietly. She walks slowly to the centre of the circle, bows to the vase of flowers there, picks it up and returns to her place. She puts the vase down in front of her cushion and sits down. Everyone waits for her to speak. The ritual adds seriousness to the occasion. She searches for words, choosing them carefully. Then she speaks. She speaks directly to another member of the group, Harry. She says how she had noticed a small act of kindness he had performed for someone a few days before. She recounts how this observation touched her, although she herself was not involved, and she thanks him for it. When she has finished, she gets up and carefully replaces the vase in the centre of the circle. She returns to her seat. The bell sounds. Everyone bows, to thank Jane for her words. There is an interval of silence. Then Carl gets up from his seat and, in the same ritual way, takes the vase to his place. Carl speaks to Anita, telling her how an action of hers has set off an angry turmoil in him, how he is observing its effect and wondering what its true origins in him are: why he reacted so strongly. Carl has worked hard to express what he has to say without turning it into an accusation. He is sincere in saying that the incident has become a focus for his personal meditation. When he has finished he returns the vase to the centre. He returns to his seat. The bell rings and all bow. There is much strength of feeling in the room as each individual works hard to say what is true. Another group member speaks, using the same ritual procedure. Maria says how, while listening to Carl, it had occurred to her that she had herself, on another occasion recently, acted in a similar way to his description of Anita, and how listening to him had made her realize that what she had done could have upset someone. The group proceeds for about three-quarters of an hour.

Groups of this kind are opportunities to practise 'speaking a true word'. They are an opportunity to train ourselves in love, compassion and wisdom. Whatever a person says in the group is received as a gift. Nobody is obliged to reply, nor to defend themselves. It is a prerequisite for participation in a 'true word group' that members have at least reached the stage of realizing that 'where there is hurt there is self'; that is, that when we feel mental pain as a consequence of someone else's action, this is an opportunity to study our own conditioning. Such groups are simple procedures. They marry western ideas drawn from encounter groups with Zen mondo (dialogue).

A bit later on, Anita speaks. She says how she was affected by Carl's comments: the feelings she noticed arise within her as he spoke. 'I am glad you told me. As you did so, although I felt rebuked, I also felt real love from you. You were sharing your pain, but also caring for me. I just want to say that I am sorry I hurt you and I will think hard about my own part in what happened.' Towards the end of the group, Peter, who is a new-comer to this kind of work, says how he feels 'overwhelmed by the amount of love there seems to be in this room today'.

People sometimes think that Zen is a matter of becoming emotionless and uptight. This is far from the case. Zen is the original spirit of Buddhism. By its rituals we rediscover and share the secret love hidden within us.

· 21 ·

Loss as Teacher

Reading his discourses, one senses the Buddha's compassion and his ability to converse with all kinds of people. One also recognizes an ironic humour. His enlightenment revealed to him the hollowness of most of our worldly pursuits. He saw how we invest so much time and energy in things which, by their very nature, cannot ever yield the satisfaction we hope for.

'*Sabbe sankhara anicca,*' he said. 'All confections are impermanent.' The term 'sankhara' is variously translated by different scholars, but the word 'confection' is the nearest to a direct equivalent in the English language. It is a slightly disparaging term, and I think this probably conveys the Buddha's sense quite well. Sankhara includes all our creations and contrivances, physical, social, psychological or spiritual: our projects, our pet ideas, our complexes, our bodies, our complicated lives.

Everything put together comes apart sooner or later. By making this statement a central pillar of his teaching, the Buddha faced our perennial habit of denial, and invited us to smile with him at the common human follies we all engage in again and again.

Nowadays, his words have even greater force than then. Gain is delusion, loss is enlightenment. This idea cuts away the whole basis of the rat race. The Zen view is that grief is a consequence of the unrealistic way we habitually perceive our world; a way which, notwithstanding its practical advantages and fleeting comforts, denies reality and stores up grief. From this perspective, therefore, grief, far from being a disease or abnormality, is, in fact, the experience of a moment of truth which penetrates

to the core of our being as few other events do. Grief is a
spiritual opportunity, a time when the world becomes vividly,
unavoidably and painfully real.

We are conditioned to think that more is better and loss is
disaster, but it is our attachment to many things which encum-
bers our lives. Loss frees us. The final loss, death, strips us of
everything. If we cling to the mind of attachment, death will be
the ultimate nightmare.

One summer's day when I was a young man, I was on holiday
in Cornwall. It was a hot summer. We went walking and, at
the end of the day, a swim in the sea seemed a good way to
cool off. We went to the nearest cove. In Cornwall the shore is
very pretty with many deep water inlets and sand beaches. I am
not a very good swimmer, but I thought I could swim across
the mouth of the cove which did not look very wide. About
half-way across I realized my mistake. It was further than I
thought and, after a day walking, I was tired. The sea was very
cold. My muscles no longer had any strength in them. I realized
that I could neither get to the other side, nor swim back. I felt
desperate, shouted, struggled to stay afloat, but knew I was
losing the battle. It seemed very unlikely anyone from the shore
would have noticed what was happening to me, nor did it seem
possible that they could reach me even if they did. In my inept
struggling with the waves I had, by now, swallowed a considerable quantity of salt water and could no longer keep my head
above the surface. Suddenly, it dawned upon me with complete
clarity: 'Now I am dying.' I was past the threshold. I knew with
certainty that this was it. At this point, everything inside me
changed. All the effort I had been making to survive ceased. I
felt totally calm. It was as if I felt all my possessions and connec-
tions and attachments fall off me, like a cloak slipping to the
floor. It was as though a voice said to me: 'The only thing you
have to do now is die well.' I felt unbelievably relieved. Things
seemed very bright, as though there were a white light everywhere. I no longer had to struggle, simply stay with the process
as it went on.

In fact, however, I was not allowed to go. I had been seen
from the shore and, as it happened, there was a man skilled in
life saving there who swam out and pulled me to the jetty. I

spent most of the following night vomiting up sea water. Looking back, I feel very fortunate to have had this brush with death. It has left a firm knowledge in me that dying is OK. In fact, while I still have all the common responses of struggling for survival in many situations, there is also another part of me that can hardly wait to get back to that point, to experience the next step, as one might say. I experience this knowing part of me as almost tangible, like a sphere a little bigger than a pearl, a little smaller than a marble, close to my heart. Even in the blackest times in life, it never completely fades from my consciousness.

People who really accept that they are dying are serene. Yet death is the ultimate discounting of all our self-building activity. The enlightenment experience of Zen is like dying before we die. It is called *kensho*: seeing into the nature of things. It is a time of spiritual nakedness. There have been many debates within Buddhism about whether enlightenment is a product of our own efforts or whether it is something granted to us by the 'other power'. But kensho occurs when self-power and other power merge: when we choose the light that death reveals. After near-death experiences, many people find new harmony in life.

The dying person who accepts death's coming may achieve serenity even when all around them are still in panic. Not uncommonly the dying person protects their relatives from the truth. They can see that those around them are not yet ready. Even though it is conventional to feel sorry for the dying person, sometimes the patient is in better psychological shape than the well. Mostly people conduct life as though death is not going to happen and may even refuse to let it be spoken of. When it happens to somebody else, they would rather not know. This is a common mentality. The function of therapy may often be simply to hear what nobody else is willing to listen to: to dissolve the taboo. To do so the therapist needs to be rooted in a deep 'inner' security, based upon acceptance rather than denial.

It seems important, at this point, to enter a word of caution against judgementalism. The fact that people avoid the subject of loss, grief and death, and deny many aspects of reality, is not really to be wondered at. Grief is terribly painful. It is only human that people defend themselves against it. The client who is struggling with such feelings may be very ambivalent about going into them. The relatives may be quite understandably cautious of talking about the subject. The therapist too may feel rattled from time to time. It may be as much a part of the therapist's role to understand deeply, patiently and compassionately why people are not facing the subject as it is to help them to do so.

Nonetheless, it is central to the Zen outlook that the common sense approach to gain and loss is topsy turvy. Insight and enlightenment do not come from accumulation, but from simplification; not from getting but from giving up. I met a woman from Thailand. She lived in America. I noticed that on her washing line there were a number of blouses all in the same attractive flower pattern as the one she was wearing. My commenting on this led her to tell me her story. She had emigrated from her own country at a young age. She had studied and gained a professional job, did well materially and saved. With her money she bought a business. The business prospered. She bought a second business. Soon she was very 'successful'. However, her health deteriorated. She developed a variety of stress symptoms. Had she been a westerner she would probably have gone to see a therapist or doctor. She was, however, Thai. Although she had not thought of herself as religious, she now thought, 'Since I am Thai, I had better go and see a Buddhist monk and find out what I need to do to get well again.' The monk said: 'Simplify your life.' So she did: just like that. She disposed of her businesses, arranging things so that her dependent relatives would be provided for, and undertook a radical simplification of her existence, even to the extent of dressing the same every day. When I met her she had a very light and joyful presence and I felt, 'This is a happy person.'

CHANGE AND CONTINUITY

'All confections are impermanent.' The road to happiness involves freeing ourselves from attachments to things which will inevitably let us down. Everything changes. Sticks on the fire burn and disappear. Although they disappear, they have not ceased to exist. They are now ash, smoke and heat. I put the ash on the garden. After a few days it has gone. Yet, again, the ash has not really ceased. It is now part of the soil. Should I lament the sticks or celebrate the enriching of the garden? Perhaps, one day, a tree will grow in this soil and the ash will have become sticks once again. Or, more likely, it will follow some other path. All will depend upon the conditions which prevail. I cannot know where the ashes of my life will be blown.

In this universe nothing is ever lost, but everything changes. Loss is really transformation. Things seem to disappear, like the sticks in the fire, but 'sticks' is actually just a concept in our minds for a particular stage in the evolution of earth becoming plant becoming branches becoming firewood becoming ash becoming earth. It is for this reason that virtually all funerary rites in different cultures include references to renewal and growth (Bloch & Parry 1982). We designate a particular stage in this on-going process 'sticks' for our own convenience. Because of this there arises the illusion of a world full of 'things' when what really confronts us is a world of processes – flow. 'Loss' brings us back to this reality.

Healing is available in the natural world around us. People who are grieving often gain solace from walking in the country. Zen has made gentle walking meditation into a profoundly regenerative exercise. We walk slowly, harmonizing our steps with our breath. We do not allow our attention to become dissipated in our surroundings, but, nonetheless, a sense of communion with the natural world grows in a subliminal way. Occasionally, we may stop and gaze at a flower or hug a tree or just touch the earth, but, for the most part, we just walk gently, each footfall making real contact with the earth. This simple practice is wonderful. In groups, pairs or alone, we can make walking meditation a regular part of our day. Generally, when we do walking meditation, we are not going anywhere. We walk simply for the sake of walking and of being in touch with life, step by step. Every so often, a member of the group may ring the mindfulness bell and we pause long enough to return to stillness inside. Once this practice is established as part of our life, we will begin to catch ourselves at other times hurrying unnecessarily, and we will stop a moment and then continue more slowly, enjoying each step and really being here, rather than just rushing on toward the future.

Walking meditation enables a person to regain connection with the elements. Even though the human world may sometimes seem barren, the wind and the flowers, the rivers and the clouds, still speak to us, and can teach us everything. Sometimes grief counselling should be conducted while walking slowly together in the open air. Sometimes we should just stop and look at flowers or touch a leaf.

When we walk in the countryside we admire the trees. They are covered in green leaves which offer a distinctive outline. The tree seems solid enough and it has a distinctive overall shape, characteristic of the particular kind of tree, yet modified by its particular circumstances. If we take the same walk a number of times the tree becomes familiar to us. We recognize it. It becomes one of the comfortingly familiar features of our world.

If we stop and look more closely, of course, we immediately see that the outline of the tree is not actually at all how we generally envisage it. Looking closer, we see that most of what makes up the 'boundary' of what seems like a 'solid mass' from a distance is actually empty space, gaps between leaves. And even those leaves are moving with the breeze. The notion of solidity is an illusion.

There is continuous change going on within the leaves and branches themselves. Our senses are not equipped to see this directly, but we know it is so. Sap moves. Cells grow and decay. There is constant movement of substances which themselves are being repeatedly transformed. We might say that new bits of tree are constantly being born and other bits are dying but even this implies discrete events whereas, in reality, there is a seamless process. The tree is a continuous flow of change. The actual material substances that make up the tree at any one time were, for the most part, not part of the tree in the past and will leave it again soon. We think of the tree as a material object, but the material of which it is composed is just passing through.

This continuous change is not, however, what we tend to perceive. We tend, rather, to experience the tree as a solid, enduring feature of the landscape. When we come for our walk in the autumn, we say: 'Oh look, the leaves have all turned brown.' But we did not see them turning. The change seems to us a sudden one. Leaves fall to the ground. We are impressed by the actual moment when a stalk finally breaks and the leaf begins its descent, though even this is something we rarely actually witness. The moments immediately before, however, were just as much a part of the process of dying. It would always be arbitrary to say at what point a particular leaf actually did die. Its death was inherent in its original coming into being, in all its growth and change throughout the summer. Nor does death end the transformation. The leaf is now returning to the earth to feed other plants.

So change is happening all the time. This is true not just of the tree but of everything: ourselves, mountains, the planet. It is true of all those who live with us. They are all changing, which is to say 'dying', all the time. If you are reading this in a room with other people, pause a moment and reflect upon the fact that the person near you is now dying. We do not know when this process of dying will become manifest as what we call a corpse, but we do know that it is under way. We do not usually perceive people or things this way, of course. We only perceive their death at a particular point when the conditions which support vital functions cease to operate, or when we are told that this will soon happen. Then we grieve.

In fact, we do not really grieve the loss of an individual person or object so much as the loss of the whole world of things which existed for us when they were in it, a world our mind constructed. It is our frame of reference, our illusion, which has been ruptured. Psychological adjustment, if all goes well, moves us toward acceptance of a 'new' world from which the lost one is absent. Spiritual insight, however, shows us the transient nature of all worlds. Presence and absence are, in practice, largely constructions. The point at which a person 'dies' for another is only loosely related to the time of clinical death. Many clients do not actually say goodbye to the deceased until many years later. Some, on the other hand, have mentally written the person off long before they actually die.

Grief may not actually be something to 'get over'. Grief may actually be a door which opens on to a reality which can hardly otherwise be reached. Rather than being a disruptive interlude after which normal service can be resumed, mourning may also move us toward a completely different way of viewing life. 'You never get over it,' a client said to me: 'you become a different person.'

A healthy encounter with loss may make us more accepting of the world and less intolerant. An unhealthy one may make us more rigid, more determined to hang on to whatever constancies seem to remain. This latter state is 'unhealthy' because it renders us even more vulnerable in the future. It is commonly the case that each loss a person experiences exacerbates the pain of other losses. Grief becomes cumulative. This does not have to be so, however. The manner of the therapist's contact with the client may sometimes be enough to make the difference between these two different kinds of outcome.

Looking back upon an important loss, one client recently wrote:

Death and what does it mean to me? I never knew and never had cause to wonder until Adam died, other than never being afraid of death myself. On the day Adam died it would be easy to say it was the worst day of my life, but I actually did not feel a great deal: I was too shocked. It was as if all my worst nightmares were happening in front of me: I couldn't take it in. I was watching from another place. I felt very separated from people as if what had happened had separated me from normal life. People's reactions to me were generally of horror and inability to talk to me. I didn't know then that I was about to experience the worst pain I had ever known and even now I can remember how bad it was. I never told anyone. Close friends found it embarrassing, I think, and a lot of people had the attitude that I should 'keep busy', that 'time would heal', and 'I was young enough to start again'. I found it very strange how clearly I could understand what it meant when someone you love dies, and how much people who should perhaps have had more sense were talking rubbish. I realized quite early that I had a choice: I could either accept Adam's death and so endure the pain, or I could attempt to run away from it and spend the rest of my life doing just that and probably end up quite ill and taking drugs.

I never did tell anyone involved what was happening. However, what I did not appreciate at the time was just how long I would be enduring the agony and pain. It was two years before I felt any better and since then it has been a long slow process of learning to live with Adam's death and learning what death means to me. The positive side of this story is one that I find difficult to talk about, almost as if there should not be one: would people be shocked if I said as much? I think a lot of people would find it harder to accept than me being ill. By accepting Adam's death, or at least always trying to, I found I somehow had the strength to do it and it became a point of growth. I was given insights into life that I would otherwise not have had: that life is eternal and that we never cease to exist. This is not something I had ever thought of, despite my Catholic upbringing. But at Adam's funeral I was acutely aware that not only was Adam not there but that he was somewhere else. Not something many people will listen to. Rather they would call me crazy.

The therapy of grief, then, can occur at a global level and a specific level. The global level has to do with appreciating the insight which loss thrusts upon us: re-examination of how we set ourselves up to suffer by failing to appreciate our situation in a deep enough way. The specific level is concerned with how we do or do not heal particular wounds, and with the vicissitudes which the process of grief may take. Western psychology has, for the most part, concerned itself with the latter, eastern psychology with the former. The two levels cannot, however, be readily separated since the way we respond to a particular loss will be substantially determined by our outlook on life as a whole, and our wisdom in regard to life will be formed according to the depth with which we experience particular losses. Sufferings can make or break us.

Grief is our collision with reality. One client of mine, for whom an important bereavement had been a pivotal point of her life, said that immediately after the loss 'I was nose to nose with reality and because I was, I was able to see the reality of other situations too.' The time of loss is an enlightenment. At such a time we are forced, against all our habitual tendencies to the contrary, to perceive reality in a more naked fashion. This can often lead people to a spiritual rebirth and the role of the therapist can be that of midwife. Then, one *knows* reality with a clarity which otherwise eludes us. At such times, the language of poetry and spirituality may be the only language which seems anywhere near adequate.

After such a rebirth, we are less afflicted by our own specific personal griefs. This is both because the points of loss no longer seem so discrete and acute and also because one has opened up to the condition of the whole world. Death and loss no longer affront us. This ability to perceive all beings coming into and going out of existence continuously was one of the attributes acquired by the Buddha as part and parcel of his enlightenment. On the other hand what comes with this is a more generalized grief, a 'great grief'; aware of the universality of suffering, we deeply understand the words of the poet John Donne who bid us not send to know for whom the bell tolls since, in *every* case, it tolls for us.

· 22 ·

Letting Go

When Jean arrived for her first therapy session she looked composed, but sat on the edge of her chair. She was smartly dressed and had come straight from work. She ran her own business. Jean told me that she was depressed, sleeping badly, unable to concentrate and mishandling relationships with her staff at work.

Her brother Tony had died two months earlier suddenly from a heart attack. The day he died, his wife, Sarah, had phoned Jean to say Tony had gone into hospital with chest pains. Jean was concerned, but had a busy day at work, so did not visit him. She intended to go the following day, but that night Sarah phoned again. Tony had died. Jean rushed round straight away to be with Sarah and the three children. She involved herself exhaustively in helping with arrangements for the funeral. At one point Sarah had asked Jean if she thought the children should go.

As she told me this, Jean's face, which until now had been remarkably unemotional, became reddened. ' "Of course they should!" I told her. "Children should always be allowed to go to funerals!" ' I commented on the sudden force in Jean's voice. Tears came into her eyes. 'I really believe children should be involved when there's been a death,' she said.

I asked if this had personal meaning for her. Jean seemed about to burst into sobs, but then regained her controlled look. She talked of other things, but soon was telling me how, when she was twelve, her father died of a heart attack. Tony, then aged eight, and their younger sister, Ann, were at home. Jean had been staying with her grandmother. Then, unexpectedly, Tony and Ann arrived at the grandmother's house to stay for a couple of weeks. Jean learned of her father's death from them.

When she asked her grandmother what was happening, she was just told not to worry.

When the three children returned home, things were much changed. Her father's death was not mentioned and she was given no indication of what had become of him. Later, as an adult, she would discover that he had been cremated, but she never did find out what had become of his ashes. Her mother was very downcast and did not recover. She became unable to cope with even the simplest things and often took to her bed, telling Jean that she was ill. Jean, a capable girl, willingly took on many of the jobs her mother had done previously. She would feed the two younger children and make sure that they were clean and tidy for school. She cleaned and shopped for the family, as well as doing her own school work. This pattern continued throughout her teens.

Everyone remarked on how cheerful and able she was, but Jean was not always happy. She would worry about her mother's health and wonder if her mother too was going to die. These thoughts never lasted for long, however, because Jean always had so much to do.

When she was sixteen, Jean's grandmother died. Jean wondered if she could go to the funeral, but her mother, who was herself inconsolably upset, told her she must look after the younger ones, because, in any case, funerals were not places for young people. Jean accepted this, but began to have worries about her own death. Looking back, Jean realized that her mother must have been mentally ill for many years after her father's death, but at the time she was constantly afraid that her mother's retreats to bed were a sign of serious physical disease. In fact her mother did die ten years later from cancer, after several years of illness. Jean, by then married, returned home daily to nurse her.

Jean recounted her story with little overt emotion. I noticed a few tears in her eyes at some points in the story, but they vanished as quickly as they appeared. Sometimes I would repeat a particularly poignant phrase back to her and she would cry briefly, as if hearing it for the first time: moments when I was almost unbearably touched by the depth of feeling, but she always regained control to carry on.

The second week Jean looked less composed. She had been quite ambivalent about returning and had been feeling more upset during the week, finding herself crying uncontrollably on two occasions. She complained that for the first time in her life she had not been able to override her pain. We spent most of the session talking about her fear of being overwhelmed by feelings. Growing up she had taught herself not to give way to emotion and this strategy had served her well for many years.

In subsequent sessions, Jean talked about the events around the time of her father's death and the difficult years that followed. She returned to the same events many times, but each time seemed to allow herself to experience more feelings.

After several months the therapy seemed to reach its culmination in which Jean psychodramatically enacted a scene in which she said goodbye to her father and mother. A continuing theme throughout the therapy had been the lack of any place which she could associate with her father. I asked her where she would like to place him and she suggested a garden. We spent some time in building together a mental image of the garden within the therapy room, laying out flower beds, lawns and trees. Jean saw a beautiful silver birch beside the window and decided that its shade would provide a spot where her parents could be happy together. We imagined her laying the bodies in the soft earth.

'Are there things which you want to say to your parents before we say goodbye?' I asked.

'I just hope they can rest now . . . and I want them to know that I love them both,' said Jean.

'Can you say that to them?'

'I want you to be happy now . . . to be at peace . . . and I love you, Daddy . . . I love you, Mum . . .'

Jean's eyes filled with tears. She looked at me.

'Are you ready to say goodbye?' I asked.

'Yes . . . I think so.' Jean bent over and touched the ground where we had placed her father. 'Goodbye, Daddy . . .' Then, touching the ground next to this, 'Goodbye, Mum.'

She stood up, her face full of emotion. 'They can lie at peace now,' she said, moving away, back to her chair at the other side of the room.

'And you can leave them together, knowing that,' I said.

Jean had two further sessions after the one in which she said goodbye to her parents. Although she was still very emotional, there seemed something more settled in her manner. She talked about her husband and children and her plans for developing her business.

I wondered if the therapy was nearing its end and asked Jean if she felt this. Jean said she had been thinking about finishing. I was wondering how Jean would feel about leaving. The therapy had been an important time for her and we had been through a lot together. It seemed important to make this ending a positive experience. I shared some of these thoughts with Jean.

Jean smiled. 'Yes, you're right. I would have just slipped away without saying anything, but that would have just been repeating the same pattern. I hate saying goodbye, but I've got to learn to do it.'

She talked about how her feelings had changed over the time we had been meeting. When the end of the session came, she told me that she would not make another appointment for the present. She then reached out and took my hand.

'I want to thank you . . . I want to say goodbye . . .' She held my hand warmly. 'I don't know if I'll be back sometime, but it is goodbye for now and that feels important to say.'

COMMENTARY

The Client's Strength and Wisdom

We all have inner wisdom and compassion: our basic sanity. Therapy relies on this. Jean had coped well with great obstacles. Even as a child she saw the needs of those around her and set to work to try to keep the family together. She had much to contend with: a mentally ill mother, no father and two dependent siblings. Nonetheless, she did well at school, became qualified, set up a career, married, had a family of her own and even, when the right time arrived, had the courage to seek out a therapist.

The Client's Koan

Jean knew about transience, yet resisted what she knew. It is as if she had learned half the lesson. She had learned that things do fall apart and that it *is* possible to get on and achieve things even when the world is falling down around you. She had not learned that it is all right to let things go, that it is possible to swim with the current rather than expending all one's energy struggling against it.

Her energy went into creating the appearances of adjustment and stability. These, however, belied what she knew about how unstable the world can be. She knew that her father had died, but he had not really died in her experience. She had not been there and nobody spoke of the matter. She knew her mother was ill and that, in one sense, she had lost her too, but it was not the kind of illness that could readily be understood. At age twelve, she knew that everything had changed, but all her efforts were devoted to keeping things as they had been. In the process she had learned to grasp her will, to care for others, and to do well in the terms which the world recognizes. But, in an important sense, the losses remained unreal.

Precipitation of the Healing Crisis

Jean had not really grieved. There are two layers to grieving: a personal and a universal lesson to digest. Jean had made a successful adjustment, in a practical way, to living in a world from which those she had lost were absent. She had not, however, touched the deeper level at which one knows that it is all right to let go. She still had work to do and, at some level, there was the wisdom in her to know this. To get to grips with this layer of her spiritual work required a healing crisis: a trigger. Life will always oblige sooner or later. In Jean's case, Tony died.

She told the story of Tony's dying and her involvement. Her insistence that children should always be allowed to go to funerals stood out for the emotion with which it was uttered. As Jean looked at her brother's children, without making a conscious link to her own experience, she recognized their need. This was, of course, from her own experience. She was able to do for others what she could not do for herself.

Some therapists would be inclined to see this as a failing on Jean's part, but I see it simply as part of her natural inherent compassion. Even though she herself had been prevented from doing what would have been best at the time, she did not hesitate to ensure that others were not similarly deprived.

She knew what the children needed, but she had, at first, no recollection of how she knew. We have experience. We learn from it. We keep the learning and forget the experience. Nonetheless, the learning is, in one sense, a memory trace, and through the therapist's observation, the source often comes to light.

Jean became aware that the difficulties she was having over her brother's death were related to the incompleteness of her experiences of losing her parents. The task of therapy was to help her let go. When we know something from experience we cannot go back. When the knowledge is not fully digested, however, rigidities arise in our character.

Struggle

The koan is something to work on. One Zen analogy says that it is like being a fish with an iron ball stuck in one's jaws. The fish can neither swallow it nor spit it out. The death of a parent early in one's life is undeniable evidence of the transitory nature of everything we rely upon. However, for Jean to start to face this, and the chaos it seems to her to unleash, is terrifying. Yet there is no other way to re-establish contact with reality; not only that of the past, but, also, that of her present. The road to truth lies through the pain of grief.

As Jean begins to tell her story, she experiences many new feelings, including intense fear of chaos. This fear comes as a shock to her. She dives into therapy, expecting that this is another activity which she can sail through in her capable way. Working with a client who is denying so much is a difficult balance for the therapist to keep. Many capable and efficient people approach therapy expecting to be able to 'deal with all this' in a few sessions and 'get it over with'.

The therapist may be seen initially as a potential ally in the battle against being overwhelmed by the truth that the client knows, but does not want to know. Therapy is an opportunity for a person to, at last, 'say a word of truth', but this is not what they initially want. The client is caught between their inner wisdom which has brought them into therapy and the conditioned habit of seeking peace through escape.

There is a real danger that the client may revert to the old pattern and simply try to push the feelings back. However, feelings, like cats, are often hard to get back into the bag! A client might even leave therapy, afraid of what may yet surface. We are all vulnerable to the fear of going mad.

The therapist tries to follow the leadings of the client's inner wisdom, but, since this is not the client's only voice, some discrimination is called for. The therapist listens very carefully, hearing also what is not being said, and picking up the significance of tone and facial expression which so often give away truths very different from the surface presentation. Generally actions speak louder than words.

Often the client thus reveals to the therapist things which she would rather deny. Her look may reveal distress about things she has trained herself to ignore. She says things in a matter-of-fact way, which, if repeated back, shock or distress her. The therapist will be aware of distressing areas of the client's world long before the client is able or willing to recognize their pain. If the therapist reflects back everything immediately, the client may feel overwhelmed and may stop the therapy. If the therapist colludes or picks up too little the client will stay caught in denial. Balance is needed. A therapist may well say to the client: 'We are doing important work here, but we do not need to rush. I can see that you have so many experiences that you want to look at. I'm wondering how we can best look at them without you feeling completely overwhelmed.'

Structure

The therapist may suggest ways of working that help contain the client's anxiety. Work with art materials can be useful in this respect, as can relaxation and meditation methods. We may also suggest things the client can do in between sessions, such as keeping a journal or talking with a friend or walking meditation, as it is often after the sessions that the full force of feelings become clear. The work is almost invariably assisted by the client developing skills in self-observation. Simple mindfulness exercises can be taught to help the client continue the work in their own way in their own time.

Therapy can provide a structure of support. When her father died Jean lacked this. She was not at home. She was not told anything about what was going on and was left to learn what she could from her younger brother and sister. She had no concrete event or time to which she could pin her anxiety and distress. Her father simply ceased to be there. There was no physical place with which she could associate him: no grave, no memorial. He had just disappeared. Excluded from the funerals in both his and her grandmother's case she found it hard to experience the reality of their deaths.

Her mother's death was also complicated. Where, with her father, it was difficult to believe he had actually died, with her mother, it was as though she died years before her decease. Consequently there was a lot that had never been said between them. Jean had already partially grieved for her mother, fearing she was dying for many years. This left her with a vague guilt, as though her thoughts had somehow contributed to her death. She felt guilty that when her mother actually died she experienced relief. Ambivalence clouded her view of her mother's decline and death and their effect on her. She returned to her earlier strategy of distracting herself.

Her brother's death, though traumatic, provided a first opportunity to repair. In this instance she could take an active part in events. This allowed her to start looking again at her past and its meaning. Her well of unexpressed emotions began to overflow. She began to feel real grief and this made her start to feel more real. She knew, although she did not know why she knew, how important it was that the children were not left out. Although she had no consciousness of the connection with her own past, her grief put her in touch with this inner knowledge.

However, Tony's death had its own difficulties. She felt guilty that she had not gone to see him on the day he died. She came to realize there had been an element of denial: afraid she could not cope, she had not wanted him to be ill or dying and had had some sense that if she pretended there was nothing to worry about, she could magically stop it from happening.

A Place for Grief

When someone close has died we need somewhere to lay them to rest and think of them. If there is a grave, then it is possible to gain great comfort from visiting it. The grave-side is a place of natural meditation. Buddhist temples generally contain relics of the Buddha or another saint. Modern people try to keep death at a distance, but Zen practice involves staying close to it.

We return to the person's presence, show our love, draw strength and then return to ordinary life. Where a death has occurred but its physicality is not experienced, as when a person is lost at sea, the bereaved person can be left unable to take even the first step in the grieving process: unable to recognize the event as real unless a memorial place is created.

So we need to experience the reality of the loss in a way that is psychologically concrete, and we need to be able to mentally locate the dead person outside ourselves; a place we can visit, but which we can also leave. Clients commonly need to create such a location if it does not already exist. This might be a monument or shrine, either in a public place or in their own home or garden. Such ritual externalization of the dead person often happens spontaneously and is natural. In Zen practice, it is common to create a memorial at which to remember one's ancestors going back several generations.

The Need for Ritual

The resolution of the therapy came in the enactment of a ritual. Ritual plays an important part in our successful negotiation of life transitions. Funerals are an important landmark in the grieving process, giving public recognition to grief. They acknowledge what otherwise may remain unspeakable. The skilful use of ritual is, and has from time immemorial been, a pre-eminent way of helping the inner person to emerge and grow.

Jean needed to find a way to let go. She had carried both her parents unburied for many years in her mind. Part of her need, no doubt, was to reunite them. Her teens had been dominated by her mother's distress at their separation. Jean had carried this sadness within her. Finding a way to bring her parents together allowed Jean to stop holding her mother's grief alongside her own.

First create a special space. Jean chose an imaginary place in which she could leave her parents, acting the scene out in a physical way. Although in Jean's case the place was not one to which she would be able to return in reality, this acting out of the scene was sufficient to give her a lasting mental image of her parents in a place outside herself: she could return in her imagination. Everything was done slowly and respectfully, creating the right atmosphere for a deep experience.

It was important that the scene should be as real as possible to Jean and that she should herself have a sense of actually being present with her parents. For this reason I encouraged her to address her parents directly rather than talking *about* what she might say to them. It was also important that she had the opportunity to say whatever she needed to them before she said goodbye. It was also important that Jean actually addressed each parent separately and used the names by which she called them in her mind. At the end of the scene, Jean moves away and sits down. She has really experienced letting go.

It is not uncommon for clients to repeat such significant scenes several times. Sometimes the scene may be an imagined one, other times it may be a repetition of a death-bed or funeral scene. It is crucial that the client is given the opportunity to say what feels right and to let go at her own pace. The therapist needs to be aware of whether the client actually seems to have said goodbye and moved away or whether this has just been a 'going through the motions'. If the latter is the case, the client is probably not yet ready.

Ending Therapy

The ending of therapy is significant, and in grief work particularly so. Ending can provide an opportunity to experience loss in a more conscious way. It is important that the end is properly acknowledged. When Jean said goodbye at the end of the last session her warmth and her recognition of the importance of the time we had spent together came over to me. I felt that this time she had not hidden her feelings. We had created a new pattern, broken the conditioning.

I experienced Jean as a person who was growing and changing fast. Although the sessions were often extremely painful, there was a newly emerging quality in Jean's presence. She had energy and warmth that became quite special. By the time the therapy ended, I felt that Jean was someone whom I had really known. Her relationships with others also changed positively. She would talk of her increasing feelings of involvement with her husband and children. Her circle of friends was changing as she found she no longer felt comfortable with those with whom she had spent time before. She wanted something more than her old friends were prepared for.

Recognizing and facing grief brought Jean to an engagement with life which she had not experienced before. It is impossible to know how she might have been had her father and brother not died, but it seemed that by coming to terms with their deaths she grew as a person and came to live with a new intensity.

· 23 ·

Coming Home

HARMONY THROUGH COMMUNITY

This final chapter touches upon the broad picture of the relation between psychotherapy, on the one hand, and community, society and the environment on the other. Psychotherapies are rooted in and draw their power from a life view or Way. The Zen Way is ecological, communitarian and universalist in ways that transcend individualism. Each of us must understand the truth for ourselves, and the key to doing so is surrender to the power greater than self (*oyasama*). Each searches for the buddha nature within, and discovers it is nobody's personal property. Buddhists sit in silent meditation, and find even this seemingly solitary activity amazingly deepened when done together in groups. Zen places the personal moral dilemma at the centre of the therapeutic work, and, by having each of us struggle with such koans, builds harmonious and aware communities. The bodhisattva, the ideal hero of Zen, realizes that a salvation for self alone is meaningless: that the essence of satisfaction is to live for others.

The term ecology comes from the Greek words *oikos* meaning house or home and *logos* meaning study or knowledge. Ecology is the study of our home in the external sense. It is about how all sentient beings can make a home together, benefiting one another. Therapy, on the other hand, is about helping a person return to a state which they inwardly recognize as home. It is about the 'home' within us: harmonization of the psyche. Zen is concerned with both of these, that is, with harmonizing outer and inner. As we have seen repeatedly through this book, from the Zen perspective, it is not possible to create a comfortable niche for ourselves, isolated from others. Peace of mind includes harmony with the world and it is by such outward harmony that we can understand the light within.

The blue planet is one of the smaller ones in this solar system. It orbits a fairly average star which occupies a fairly middling position within a fairly average galaxy. The blue planet is one tiny organism in a cosmos so vast that we cannot even imagine it. Living matter and the inanimate substances with which it interdepends, through nutrition, respiration and so on, constitute a very thin film over its surface of rock. This film is called the biosphere. Within this fragile biosphere, people have lived for only the tiniest fraction of the time of the earth's existence. When we think in these terms, our position seems vulnerable in the extreme. We are foolish not to care for one another – and Zen suggests that some of the most valuable psychological work is to make the 'we' in this sentence grow and grow until, ultimately, no beings are left out.

The common modern world view is that most things are more or less all right and that progress will eventually sort out the remaining problems. The Buddhist view is that, on the one hand, such complacency is ill founded. Our planet is sick. Our society is oppressive and poor in spirit. Our communities disintegrate. Our families fragment. War is ever more prevalent. Species become extinct at an unprecedented rate. Ecological disaster looms. Dukkha is everywhere and the mass of people seek distraction or oblivion rather than any real solution. On the other hand, the world is infinitely beautiful. Every conscious moment is a miracle. The buddha nature is an inexhaustible spring of compassion, love and wisdom. Every person carries light within them and there is 'other power' waiting to assist every good action.

Oppression, cruelty, dishonesty, intoxication, violence, pollution and war are not inevitable. People do destructive things without realizing what they are doing. The common idea that destructive things are all done by 'bad people' – a species unlike ourselves – is nonsense. We are all of one nature – just, we do not realize what that nature is: we do not see what we have got.

The task of therapy is to reconnect people to their own depths, to one another and to the world. In the Buddha's day, the monks would collect tatters of cast-off cloth and sew the pieces together to make robes. The robe made by such patchwork is considered a most precious symbol of the Buddhist life. Our work as therapists of the human heart is similarly to put together what had been regarded as rubbish and reveal its potential as something radiant. The real robe is not made of cotton nor silk, of course. Some people are born with it and others acquire it by changing their understanding of life. We too can do so and have something to offer others. Otherwise, it is like the blind leading the blind.

It is a basic Buddhist principle that inner and outer peace reflect each other. We cannot find a private salvation cut off from the life of the planet any more than a limb could be healthy cut off from a body, however many artificial support systems were in place to keep it functioning. Nor will the planet itself return to health and wholeness until we find harmony within and amongst ourselves. The human being is increasingly becoming a creature living within its own artificial support system, cut off from its natural roots. We could be mother earth's hand of compassion, but we are in danger of becoming her executioner. When the Buddha was enlightened, he reached down and touched the earth. We too must become enlightened and reach out to the earth once again.

A SENSE OF COMMUNITY

In modern mythology, the almost unquestioned assumption is progress. According to Buddhist mythology, however, a gradual process of degeneration is under way which will continue unless we wake ourselves up. The progress we do have is in terms of technology and numbers. It is much harder to claim that there has been progress in our spiritual evolution. This is because what we have gained in technological power, we have lost in the destruction of tradition and displacement of communities by mass society. We need, therefore, to recreate what Buddhists call *sangha*: harmonious community. This is not just politics, it is essential for mental health.

History has generally been the story of how society has regulated and destroyed communities. Our modern ideals are framed in terms of the open society, democracy and justice. There have always, however, been those who have regretted the passing of community and have looked for a more caring, smaller scale approach to life, people like the Buddhist economist Dr Schumacher (1973), whose ironically titled book *Small is Beautiful: A study of economics as if people mattered* is well known. Buddhists seek to create, or recreate, community.

Community in modern society, however, is now restricted, in many cases, to within families; even the family has been pared down to its irreducibly minimum size and rendered unstable. The natural development of liberal society would seem to be to get rid of families altogether and just have individuals, but this does not work. While adults can, at a cost, cope with the 'rationality' of society, children cannot. In contemporary society, however, we do see an unprecedented degree of family breakdown, and this makes work for therapists.

The psychological cost of replacing community with society is stress. In a community we are surrounded most of the time by friends, kith and kin, people we know. In society we are surrounded by strangers. Like any other animal, the human being is alarmed by strangers. In order for our open societies to work at all, everybody has to cope with and disguise an unnaturally high level of stress.

Because community is impoverished in modern society we have therapy instead. In the country where this process has gone furthest, the USA, there is more therapy than anywhere else. The therapy relationship provides one of the very few places outside the family where a real sense of personal organic relating can take place, where a person can be accepted as they are. Even this, however, is under threat.

Therapy as part of a movement toward community is a threat to mass society. Society, therefore, tries to subvert therapy to its own ends by regulating, professionalizing and recruiting it. Professionalization is a method of putting a tight wall around therapy and the human potentials movement in order that their revolutionary impact, a tiny glimpse of which became apparent in the 1960s and '70s, is stifled. Already the profession is beginning to be given social policing functions.

The question nonetheless remains whether and in what ways

therapy might provide a route back to a more extensive concept or practice of community. This would be real preventive mental health. The people who are least likely to break down psychologically are those who have a living faith and a community they trust and contribute to. The practice of therapeutic community, however, is something which has also been virtually regulated out of existence, though it remains what many clients need. Thus, we need to reassert the therapeutic potential of community and the communitarian affiliations of therapy. In the institutes of those who want therapy to become a lucrative career alongside other para-medical experts, this will fall on deaf ears.

Every therapy encounter, however, does something to heal the torn fabric of human community. The therapist comes to know the client not just in an arm's-length way. Whatever people may think about the importance of contracts and boundaries, the therapy relationship means more than a commercial bargain. Both parties are touched. Some therapy is very brief, some longer, but in as much as it changes us, a karmic connection has been put in place between two people which will benefit the world in some way in time to come.

SANGHA BUILDING

One of the most important parts of Zen, and all Buddhism, is the creation of sangha. A sangha is a group of people who support each other's Zen work. The idea is to recreate real community. The importance of creating links of this kind is particularly great in the alienating conditions of modern society. Unless we can do so, people have nothing to believe in (Hanh 1992, p. 101). Building community is preventive mental health. Therapy depends upon relationship. Let me quote some famous contemporary Buddhist teachers.

Thich Nhat Hanh: 'Interpersonal relationships are the key for success in the practice. Without an intimate, deep relationship with at least one person, transformation is unlikely. With the support of one person, you have stability and support, and later you can reach out to a third person, and eventually be a brother or sister to everyone in the sangha. You demonstrate your willingness and capacity to live in peace and harmony with everyone in the sangha. It is my deep desire that communities of practice in the west be organized in this way, as families, in a friendly, warm atmosphere, so that people can succeed in their practice' (1992, p. 107). 'Each of us needs a sangha. If we don't have a good sangha yet, we should spend our time and energy building one. If you are a psychotherapist, a doctor, a social worker, a peace worker, or if you are working for the environment, you need a sangha. Without a sangha, you will not have enough support and you will burn out very soon' (p. 112).

Chogyam Trungpa: 'We must create a structure which allows real communication . . . There has to be real communication. And someone has to start. If no one begins nothing will happen. And having started and developed and been able to contact one person then one is able to communicate to a third person, and then a fourth gradually develops and so on . . . Like in London it's not so much the colours, the chairs, the walls of the underground which depress us but the faces, the people moving like ants, people moving in and out, in and out, each with their own depression. Let us begin to create a body of people moving about and carrying their own light' (Trungpa 1969, p. 26).

Uchiyama Roshi quotes his own teacher as having given this useful analogy: 'Sawaki Roshi often said that a monastery is like a charcoal fire in a hibachi. If you put in just one little coal, it will go out right away. But if you gather many small coals, each glowing just a little bit, then the fire will flare up. In the same way, every one of us should contribute a little bodhi-mind and thus enable our sangha to thrive' (Uchiyama 1993, p. 183).

Zen, then, is not a matter of separated individualism, but of unity together. True aloneness does not cut off relationships: it enriches them by making us responsible within them. The Buddhist word for true aloneness is *bhaddekaratta* which literally means 'the best kind (*bhadd*) of delight (*ratta*) in singleness (*eka*)'. To make a good community we each have to try to practise this bhaddekaratta. We each, on our own, have to resolve to put as much in as possible. Our contribution is not conditional. We do not make sangha communities by negotiation based upon selfish concern. We do not say, 'I won't clean up that mess because I did not make it.' We act in a unilaterally generous way. That is the bodhisattva path. A true community is, perhaps paradoxically, created by people who are capable of being alone, for they can give freely.

In the time of the Buddha, to be a 'lone-dweller' was something held in high regard. Hermits were greatly respected. When the Buddha talks about a person being a 'lone-dweller', however, he means one who is not accompanied everywhere they go by selfish concerns. Thus the Buddha says: 'A bhikkhu who lives this way, even if he is dwelling in a village along with bhikkhus, bhikkunis, upasakas, upasikas, royalty, officials, and teachers and followers of other paths, is still a "lone-dweller". Why? Because his "second" is selfish craving and that is abandoned by him. That is why he is called "lone-dweller"' (Migajala Sutta, Samyutta Nikaya 4).

The Buddha was, in fact, rather unusual in the degree of stress he laid upon the importance of community. Sangha is one of the three refuges of the Buddhist and so is established at the very heart of this spiritual path. This is why the Buddha-dharma has survived for twenty-five centuries. Zen's aim to transcend worldly conditions generates a community-building energy which seeks a complete transformation of human society. On a 'bottom up' basis, there is, inherent in the Buddhist approach, the impetus for a complete reformulation of civilization (Ling 1976). After all, 'A sangha is also a community of resistance, resisting the speed, violence, and unwholesome ways of living that are prevalent in our society' (Hanh 1992, p. 114).

Good company and community building are therapeutic. Modelling upon and responding to others are the way that we all as children learn most of our skills and attitudes. Western therapies have not recently given enough attention to community, perhaps because it makes therapy more all-encompassing, and less simply a job. John Heaton in the *Journal of the Society for Existential Analysis* recently talked about 'philosophical therapy', pointing to the dialogues of Socrates, Pyrrho, the Cynics, Stoics, Sceptics, Crates and Galen, and going on to say, 'Philosophical therapy arises out of the philosopher's life; thus the Greeks and Romans were very interested in how the philosopher lived his life and how he died. For the mark of a philosopher was that he was not a slave to pleasure and pain and he had overcome irrational fears of death. It would have struck them as absurd to go to someone for therapy who was ambitious, greedy, or envious; for these are diseases of the soul and if the therapist is not cured of them how could he hope to cure others?' (Heaton 1990, p. 5).

A group is a very powerful medium for helping people. Whether a sangha is temporary or lasting, growth comes from sharing. To be part of such a group is a powerful experience. Real community is therapeutic. A person who lives Zen is in community even when alone, and alone even in the midst of others.

PART OF ONE ANOTHER

Zen is an ecological state of mind. It is consciousness of inter-connectedness leading to an ethic of non-harm. Living in harmony flows naturally from having a sense of our place in the greater order of things. Therapy is to re-establish such a sense by the practice of compassion, love and understanding and contact with what is natural.

I remember a client who would come to me each week with an unending catalogue of personal disasters about which, it seemed, she could do next to nothing. Nonetheless, through the window of the room where we met there streamed sunshine. Sometimes I would draw her attention to it and we would enjoy a few moments of silence together. It was springtime. 'When I go away from here,' she said to me once, 'nothing has changed in my situation at home, but somehow I feel I have been turned around, so that I do not see it in the same way.' I really had nothing to offer this woman except the sunshine, but through our being together she healed herself.

When we open up to something greater than ourselves we are inclined to use the word spiritual. Some people like this word. Others do not. In Zen, it does not really matter what we call it. Modern people have become detached from it, however, in proportion as we have become detached from nature.

The idea that therapy can be a spiritual path is not the usual one. Generally, therapy is seen as a job or a quasi-medical activity. Nonetheless, there is, in the world of therapy, a good deal of interest in the spiritual dimension, hence this book. The word 'profession' originally referred to what a person believed (i.e. professed), but now means that for which one is paid. This reflects the modern decay of values. To suggest that therapy is a path toward spiritual wholeness is against the grain of recent times. There are some signs, however, that things may be beginning to swing back, as the damage done by a purely utilitarian approach makes itself more and more apparent.

Where were you last year?

Breathe deep,
Breathe deep.

The air fills my lungs and then?
My blood receives
This grace by which
I live a few moments more,
My every cell replenished.
With every breath
A part of me departs
And something new
Is put in place.

The rice I ate yesterday,
Where is it now?
In my muscle, in my bone.
The juice we shared,
Where has it gone?
In our arms and legs and all.

Last month
The rice waved in the sunshine
In other lands:
In the low flood plains
Of the Mississippi
Or Irrawaddy;
And the fruit hung

On trees in Cyprus
Sicily or Spain.

And before that?
Before that their substance
Was in the soil,
Was in the air,
Was in the seas.
Was in the seas
Waiting to be gathered up
Waiting to soar up into the highest reaches of the sky,
Waiting to become rain.

You and I
Are mostly water.
Last year
Most of each of us
Was in the ocean.
We circulated together
In the Atlantic,
Or the Pacific perhaps,
For we are mostly water.

And that water was lifted
By sunshine heat,
By the impact of photons
Cascading down,
Beating upon the ocean's face.

And every photon
Comes from the sun,
From the belly of the star;
You and I were stars last year.
We chased each other
In the turbulent heart of the sun.

So who was it that lived in your house last year?
And where will you be next week?
Who is your true friend and who your foe?
And who will you be next year?

Breathe deep,
Breathe deep.

This air is me.
This air is you.
This air we share.
I give my substance to you and
You yours to me.

With each breath I am linked
In a single orbit
With the great forests.
My out breath is their food,
Theirs fills my lungs.
Last year
I was a tree
And the tree was me.

Each day
We gather up substance
And continue the task
Of endlessly
Remaking ourselves
From one another.

Each day
We discard a portion
And continue the cycle
Of endlessly
Returning ourselves
To others.

Day by day we change
And become one another,
The substance of the universe,
Stardust and all,
Passing through us each
And we through it.

Where were you last year?
Breathe deep,
Breathe deep.

The challenge for us is to realize our unity with all life, and even with the inanimate world around us. The seas with their currents, the atmosphere and the continents of the earth are all in motion, stirring with their own kinds of life. Our malaise as a civilized people comes in large measure from our ability to distance ourselves from nature and from one another. A real therapy is one with a vision, not only of the individual person, but also of how the whole planet is to be healed.

Glossary

Abhidharma (S) collection of Buddhist texts on the analysis of mind.

adhipati (P) predominance, the third paccaya.

ahara paccaya (P) food relation; the fifteenth paccaya.

alaya (S) storehouse consciousness; the repository in the mind of all past karma.

amara (P) the deathless.

Amida (J) the Buddha of Infinite Light, a personification of oyasama.

Amitabha (S) Amida.

anantara (P) association, the fourth paccaya.

anatma (S) no-self; selflessness.

anicca (P) impermanent.

anjali (S) the position of the hands in prayer.

annyamannya (P) reciprocal dependence; the seventh paccaya.

arammana (P) object relations, the second paccaya.

arhat (S) saint; one who has defeated delusion.

asevanna (P) habit; the twelfth paccaya.

atma (S) soul.

avidya (S) basic ignorance, the activity of the deluded mind.

bhaddekaratta (P) ideal solitariness.

bhikkhu (P) Buddhist monk.

bhikkhuni (P) Buddhist nun.

bodhi (P,S) enlightenment; wisdom.

bodhichitta (S) mind that seeks enlightenment.

Bodhidharma Zen teacher who took the teaching from India to China.

bodhisatta (P) a person who is close to and on the way toward enlightenment.

bodhisattva (S) a being on the path of awakening.

Brahma (S) supreme god in Indian mythology.

buddha (S,P) an awakened
one.

buddhata (S) buddha nature;
the inherent harmony of
self and other.

chandra (S) intention.

citta/chitta (S) attention; the
conscious mind.

dana (P,S) generosity; giving.

Dharma (S) the teachings of
the Buddha.

Dharmakara (S) the
bodhisattva who became
Amida Buddha.

dhyana (S) meditation;
purposefulness of mind;
zen.

do (J) Tao; Way.

dosa (P) hate

drishti (S) views;
opinionatedness.

dukkha (P,S) suffering;
bitterness; bad states of
mind; ill-being.

ehipasiko (P) to be tried out
by each for him/herself.

eka (P) one; single.

ekagata (P) aloneness; going
singly.

Fugen (J) Samantabhadra.

gathas (S) an inspirational
verse.

hara (S) lower abdomen;
tanden.

hetu (P) root; cause.

Indra (S) creator god of
Indian mythology.

indriya (P) faculty; potential.

jhana (P) dhyana.

jnana (S) primordial
awareness; gnosis;
non-dualistic
consciousness.

kalyanamitra (S) spiritual
friend, a term for a teacher
or experienced Buddhist
practitioner who can help
us.

kama (P) sensual pleasure.

karma (S) action; the law of
moral effect.

karuna (S) compassion.

kensho (J) seeing into the
nature of things;
enlightenment experience.

kleshas (S) mental
contaminants,
obscurations, or obstacles.

koan (J) test; story
highlighting a spiritual
obstacle.

ku (J) emptiness; purity.

lobha (P) greed

lokavid (S) seer of worlds; an
epithet of the Buddha.

magga (P) marga.

maitri (S) loving kindness.

Maitreya (S) the loving one;
the Buddha to come.

mahakaruna (S) great, i.e.
unconditional, compassion.

manas (S) mind, especially the
part of the psyche which
regulates mental processes.

Mara (S) the snatcher of
life; the devil in Indian
myth.

marga (S) path.

mensetsu (J) naikan interview.

metta (P) see: *maitri*.

Miroku (J) Maitreya.

moha (P) delusion

mudra (S) gesture; posture, especially of the hands.

muga (J) no-self; anatma.

mula-klesha (S) fundamental obstacles to mental clarity.

naikan (J) seeing into our own responsibility; the work of naikan therapy.

naikansha (J) a client/student of naikan therapy.

nirvana (P,S) the world as experienced by the enlightened mind; the extinction of ego-passion.

nissaya (P) dependence; the eighth paccaya.

oyasama (J) 'other power'; the principle that the universe assists the good.

paccaya (P) condition; relation; dependency.

pacchajata (P) on-going dependence; the eleventh paccaya.

paramita (S) transcendent quality; perfection; something unconditional.

Pattana (P) Book of Origination; 7th book of the Abhidharma.

piti (P) absorption.

prajna (S) wisdom.

purejata (P) pre-condition; the tenth paccaya.

ratta (P) delight.

roshin (J) parental mind.

rupa (P) form.

sabbe (P) all.

saddha (P) faith.

sahajati (P) co-origination; the sixth paccaya.

samadhi (S) single-pointedness of mind; tranquil absorption.

Samantabhadra (S) the bodhisattva of patience and action, the 'all good one' who excels in making offerings.

samanantara (P) orderly association; the fifth paccaya.

samjna (S) recognition; perception.

samsara (P,S) the world as experienced by the deluded mind; delusion itself; going round in circles.

samskara (S) confection; mental formation.

samyak sambuddha (S) completely enlightened one.

sangha (S) group or community.

sankhara (P) samskara.

sati (P) stopping; mindfulness.

satori (J) kensho.

satta (P) intent.

sattva (S) a being.

sensei (J) teacher.

Shakyamuni the historical buddha.

shamatha (P,S) serenity meditation.

shikan (J) just; nothing but.

shikantaza (J) just sitting.

shingon (J) tantra.

shunya (S) empty (of ego); unconditioned.

shunyata (S) emptiness; the unconditional; spontaneous creativity.

sila (P) ethics; moral discipline.

skandha (S) heap; aggregate; component of the person.

sugata (S) one whose life is blissful.

sukha (S) sweet.

sutra (S) words of the Buddha and his immediate disciples; texts recording these.

taiken (J) experiential learning.

tanden (J) lower abdomen; hara.

tantra (S) continuity (between samsara and nirvana); the practice of transforming ordinary appearance into the path.

tathagata (S) one who is just so, natural; an epithet of the Buddha.

tathagata-garbha (S) buddha-embryo; the buddha nature growing within each of us, waiting to be born into the world through our enlightened actions.

tathata (S) thusness; the quality of according with reality.

upanissaya (P) strong dependence; the ninth paccaya.

upasaka (S) Buddhist layman.

upasika (S) Buddhist laywoman.

upeksha (S) equanimity.

vedana (P,S) feeling (positive, negative or neutral).

vidya (S) clear perception; the activity of the enlightened mind.

vidya-carana samapana (S) one who has mastered spiritual practice through clear seeing; an epithet of the Buddha.

vijnana (S) dualistic consciousness.

vimamsa (S) enquiry.

vinaya (P,S) Buddhist code of monastic discipline.

vipaka (P) extinguished karma; the fourteenth paccaya.

virya (S) energy; enthusiasm.

zazen (J) sitting zen.

J = Japanese
P = Pali
S = Sanskrit

Bibliography

Apter, M. J. (1989) *Reversal Theory*. London: Routledge.

Barrett, W. (1961) *Irrational Man: A study in existential philosophy*. London: Heinemann.

Beech, C. J. (1994) Private communication.

Bettelheim, B. (1992) *Recollections and Reflections*. London: Penguin.

Binswanger, L. (1975) (trans. and ed. Needleman, J.) *Being-in-the-World*. London: Souvenir.

Bloch, M., and Parry, J. (1982) *Death and the Regeneration of Life*. Cambridge: Cambridge University Press.

Boss, M. (1982) (trans. Lefebre, L.B.) *Psychoanalysis and Daseinanalysis*. New York: Da Capo Press.

Brazier, D. J. (1992) *Mitwelt*. Newcastle upon Tyne: Eigenwelt Amida.

Brazier, D. J. (1993) 'The Necessary Condition is Love', in *Beyond Carl Rogers*. London: Constable.

Brooke, R. (1991) *Jung and Phenomenology*. London: Routledge.

Brooks, C. V. W. (1982) *Sensory Awareness: The rediscovery of experiencing*. Santa Barbara, CA: Ross-Erikson.

Cox, M., and Theilgaard, A. (1987) *Mutative Metaphors in Psychotherapy*. London: Tavistock.

Chung, C. Y. (1968) 'Differences of the Ego as Demanded in Psychotherapy in the East and West', *Korean Journal of Neuropsychiatry* 7, 2, October 1968.

Chung, C. Y. (1990) 'Psychotherapist and Expansion of Awareness', *Psychotherapy and Psychosomatics*, 53, pp. 28–32.

Cornell, A.W. (1993) 'Teaching Focusing with Five Steps and

Four Skills', in D. J. Brazier (ed.), *Beyond Carl Rogers*. London: Constable.

Doi, T. (1986) *The Anatomy of Self: The individual versus society*. Tokyo: Kodansha.

Engler, J. (1986) 'Therapeutic aims in psychotherapy and meditation', in K. Wilber and D.P. Brown (eds.), *Transformations of Consciousness*. Boston: New Science Library.

Epstein, M. (1988) 'The deconstruction of the self: ego and "egolessness" in Buddhist insight meditation', *Journal of Transpersonal Psychology* 20, 1, pp. 61–69.

Figurski, T. J. (1987) 'Self-awareness and other-awareness: The use of perspective in everyday life', in K. Yardley and T. Honess (eds.), *Self and Identity*. Chichester: John Wiley & Sons.

Fox, W. (1990) *Toward a Transpersonal Ecology*. London: Shambhala.

Frankl, V. E. (1967) *Psychotherapy and Existentialism*. New York: Square Press.

Freud, S. (1901) *The Psychopathology of Everyday Life*. London: Penguin (1975).

Freud, S. (1914) 'On Narcissism', in *On Metapsychology*. London: Penguin (1984).

Gendlin, E. T. (1962) *Experiencing and the Creation of Meaning*. Glencoe, Il: Free Press.

Gendlin, E. T. (1981) *Focusing*. New York: Bantam.

Gyatso, K. (1986) *Meaningful to Behold*. London: Tharpa.

Gyatso, K. (1990) *Essence of Good Fortune*. Tharpa, London.

Hanh, N. (1990) *Present Moment Wonderful Moment*. Berkeley: Parallax.

Hanh, N. (1992) *Touching Peace*. Berkeley: Parallax.

Hanh, N. (1993a) *For a Future to be Possible: Commentaries on the Five Wonderful Precepts*. Berkeley: Parallax.

Hanh, N. (1993b) *The Blooming of a Lotus*. Boston: Beacon.

Hanh, N. (1993c) *Thundering Silence: Sutra on knowing the better way to catch a snake*. Berkeley: Parallax.

Hayashi, S., Kuno, T., Morotomi, Y., Osawa, M., Shimizu, M., and Suetake, Y. (1994) *A Re-evaluation of Client-centered Therapy through the Work of F. Tomoda and its Cultural Implications in Japan*. Paper presented at the 3rd International Conference on Client-Centred and Experiential Psychotherapy, Gmunden, Austria, September 1994.

Heaton, J. M. (1990) 'What is Existential Analysis?', *Journal of the Society for Existential Analysis, 1,* pp. 2–5.

Hogen, Y. (1993) *On the Open Way.* Liskeard, Cornwall: Jiko Oasis Books.

Holmes, P. (1992) *The Inner World Outside: Object relations theory and psychodrama.* London: Routledge.

Husserl, E. (1925) (trans. Scanlon, J.) *Phenomenological Psychology.* Hague: Martinus Nijhoff, 1977.

Husserl, E. (1929) *The Paris Lectures.* Hague: Martinus Nijhoff.

Husserl, E. (1931a) *Ideas: General introduction to pure phenomenology.* New York: Macmillan.

Husserl, E. (1931b) (trans. Cairns, D.) *Cartesian Meditations.* Hague: Martinus Nijhoff.

Husserl, E. (1983) (trans. Kersten, F.) *Ideas Pertaining to a Pure Phenomenology and to a Phenomenological Philosophy.* Hague: Martinus Nijhoff.

James, W. (1890) *The Principles of Psychology,* Volume 1. New York: Dover (1950).

Jung, C. G. (1907) 'The Psychology of Dementia Praecox', in *The Psychogenesis of Mental Disease.* London: Routledge (1991).

Jung, C. G. (1978) *Psychology and the East.* London: RKP.

Kalu (1987) *The Gem Ornament of Manifold Oral Instructions.* New York: Snow Lion.

Kennett, J. (1976) *Zen is Eternal Life.* Emeryville, CA: Dharma Publishing.

Kohut, H. (1971) *The Analysis of the Self.* London: Hogarth Press.

Kohut, H. (1977) *The Restoration of the Self.* New York: International Universities Press.

Kopp, S. (1985) *Even a Stone can be a Teacher.* Los Angeles: Tarcher.

Kornfield, J., Dass, R., and Miyuki, M. (1983) 'Psychological Adjustment is not Liberation', in J. Welwood (1985) *Awakening the Heart: East west approaches to psychotherapy and the healing relationship.* London: Shambhala.

Laing, R. D. (1961) *Self and Others.* London: Penguin.

Leidloff (1986) *The Continuum Concept*. London: Penguin.

Ling, T. (1976) *The Buddha*. London: Penguin.

Macy, J. (1991) *World as Lover, World as Self*. Berkeley: Parallax Press.

Marineau, R. F. (1989) *Jacob Levy Moreno 1889–1974: Father of psychodrama, sociometry and group psychotherapy*. London: Routledge.

May, R. (1983) *The Discovery of Being*. New York: Norton.

Merleau-Ponty, M. (1964b) 'The Film and the New Psychology', in H. L. and P. A. Dreyfus (trans.), *Sense and Non-Sense*. Chicago: Northwestern University Press.

Mikulas, W. (1990) 'Mindfulness, self-control and personal growth', in M. G. T. Kwee (ed.), *Psychotherapy, Meditation and Health*. Proceedings of the 1st International Conference on Psychotherapy, Meditation and Health. London: East-West Publications.

Moacanin, R. (1986) *Jung's Psychology and Tibetan Buddhism*. London: Wisdom.

Moreno, J. L. (1985) *Psychodrama*, Volume 1. Ambler, Pennsylvania: Beacon House.

Narada (1973) *The Buddha and his Teachings*. Singapore: Singapore Buddhist Meditation Centre.

Neumann, E. (1969) *Depth Psychology and a New Ethic*. London: Hodder and Stoughton.

Nyanaponika (1974) *The Snake Simile*. Kandy, Sri Lanka: Buddhist Publication Society: Wheel Publication number 48/49.

O'Hara, M. (1989) 'When I use the term Humanistic Psychology . . .', *Journal of Humanistic Psychology*, 29, pp. 263–273.

Okuda, Y. (translator) (1989) *The Discourse on the Inexhaustible Lamp of the Zen School*, by Zen Master Torei Enji. London: Zen Centre.

Perls, F. (1969) *Gestalt Therapy Verbatim*. Berkeley: Real People Press.

Price, A. F., and Wong, M. L. (1969) *The Diamond Sutra and the Sutra of Hui Neng*. Boston: Shambhala.

Punnaji (1978) 'Buddhism and Psychotherapy', *Buddhist Quarterly* 10, 2–3, pp. 44–52.

Purton, C. (1994) *The Deep Structure of the Core Conditions: A Buddhist perspective*. Paper presented to the 3rd International Conference on Client-Centred and Experiential Psychotherapy, Gmunden, Austria, September 1994.

Reps, P. (1957) *Zen Flesh Zen Bones*. London: Penguin.

Reynolds, D. (1989) *Flowing Bridges, Quiet Waters: Japanese Psychotherapies, Morita and Naikan*. New York: State University Press.

Rhee, D. (1990) 'The Tao, Psychoanalysis and Existential Thought', *Psychotherapy and Psychosomatics, 53*, 1–4, pp. 21–27.

Rogers, C. R. (1942) *Counseling and Psychotherapy: New concepts in practice*. Boston: Houghton Mifflin.

Rogers, C. R. (1951) *Client Centred Therapy*. London: Constable.

Rogers, C.R. (1967) *On Becoming a Person*. London: Constable.

Rogers, C. R. (1978) *On Personal Power*. London: Constable.

Rogers, C. R. (1980) *A Way of Being*. Boston: Houghton Mifflin.

Schneider, D. (1993) *Street Zen*. London: Shambhala.

Schumacher, E. F. (1973) *Small is Beautiful: A study of economics as if people mattered*. London: Sphere/Penguin.

Sekida, K. (1975) *Zen Training: Methods and philosophy*. New York: Weatherhill.

Seligman, M. E. (1975) *Helplessness: On depression, development and death*. San Francisco: W.H. Freeman.

Solomon, R. C. (1988) *Continental Philosophy since 1750*. Oxford: Oxford University Press.

Spiegelman, M. J., and Miyuki, M. (1987) *Buddhism and Jungian Psychology*. Phoenix, Arizona: Falcon.

Spinelli, E. (1989) *The Interpreted World*. London: Sage.

Stevens, A. (1990) *On Jung*. London: Routledge.

Sunim, K. (1985) *The Way of Korean Zen*. New York: Weatherhill.

Suzuki, D. T. (1949) *An Introduction to Zen Buddhism*. London: Rider.

Suzuki, D. T. (1950) *Essays in Zen Buddhism: Second series*. London: Rider.

Suzuki, D. T. (1969) *The Zen Doctrine of No Mind*. London: Rider (1986).

Suzuki, D. T., (1972) *Living by Zen*. London: Rider (1982).

Suzuki, S. (1970) *Zen Mind Beginners Mind*. New York: Weatherhill.

Tanahashi, K. (1985) *Moon in a Dewdrop: Writings of Zen Master Dogen*. San Francisco: North Point Press.

Thien-an (1975) *Zen Philosophy Zen Practice*. Berkeley: Dharma Publishing.

Thorne, B. (1992) *Carl Rogers*. London: Sage.

Trungpa, C. (1969) 'The New Age', *International Times* 63 (29 August–11 September 1969), p. 26.

Uchiyama, K. (1993) *Opening the Hand of Thought*. London: Arkana/Penguin.

Watts, A.W. (1957) *The Way of Zen*. London: Penguin.

Wilber, K. (1985) *No Boundary: Eastern and western approaches to personal growth*. London: Shambhala.

Zopa, T. (1994) *The Door to Satisfaction*. Boston: Wisdom.

Index

Note: Page numbers in *italics* indicate an entry in the glossary